Collins

Cambridge Lower Secondary

Maths

STAGE 7: TEACHER'S GUIDE

Michele Conway, Sarah Sharratt, Deborah McCarthy, Caroline Fawcus, Alastair Duncombe
Series Editors: Michele Conway and Sarah Sharratt

Collins

William Collins' dream of knowledge for all began with the publication of his first book in 1819.

A self-educated mill worker, he not only enriched millions of lives, but also founded a flourishing publishing house. Today, staying true to this spirit, Collins books are packed with inspiration, innovation and practical expertise. They place you at the centre of a world of possibility and give you exactly what you need to explore it.

Collins. Freedom to teach.

Published by Collins
An imprint of HarperCollins*Publishers*
The News Building
1 London Bridge Street
London
SE1 9GF

Browse the complete Collins catalogue at
www.collins.co.uk

© HarperCollins*Publishers* Limited 2018

10 9 8 7 6 5 4 3 2

ISBN 978-0-00-821351-0

MIX
Paper from
responsible sources
FSC
www.fsc.org **FSC™ C007454**

This book is produced from independently certified FSC paper to ensure responsible forest management.

For more information visit: **www.harpercollins.co.uk/green**

British Library Cataloguing in Publication Data.
A catalogue record for this publication is available from the British Library.

Authors: Michele Conway, Sarah Sharratt, Deborah McCarthy, Caroline Fawcus and Alastair Duncombe
Series editors: Michele Conway and Sarah Sharratt
Contributors: Matt Nixon and Gill Hewlett
Publisher: Celia Wigley
Commissioning editor: Karen Jamieson
In-house project editors: Amanda Redstone/Isabelle Sinclair
Managing editor: Wendy Alderton
Project manager: Maheswari Pon Saravanan at Jouve
Copyeditor: Alison Bewsher
Proofreader: Jan Schubert
Answer checker: Steven Matchett
Cover designer: Gordon MacGilp
Cover illustrator: Maria Herbert-Liew
Typesetter: Jouve India Private Limited
Production controller: Tina Paul
Printed and bound by: CPI Group UK

Acknowledgements

The publishers gratefully acknowledge the permission granted to reproduce the copyright material in this book. Every effort has been made to trace copyright holders and to obtain their permission for the use of copyright material. The publishers will gladly receive any information enabling them to rectify any error or omission at the first opportunity.

p. 143 © Collins Bartholomew Ltd; p. 238 LilKar/Shutterstock.

All exam-style questions and sample answers have been written by the authors.

Contents

Introduction

This highly supportive Teacher's Guide provides step-by-step, detailed notes and a wealth of ideas on how to use the *Collins Cambridge Lower Secondary Maths* course effectively with students. Problem-solving tasks are clearly signposted, as well as opportunities for adaptation and extension so that lessons can be adapted to suit the needs of individual students.

For every chapter:
Useful list of learning objectives clearly displayed

Prior knowledge assumptions listed, so students can be encouraged to build on what they already know

Starter ideas given, to help get the lesson going and get students thinking about the topic

Key terms identified for quick reference

Guidance given on the 'hook', so that students can start to familiarise with the main concepts of the chapter, through enjoyable and engaging games and activities

Discussion ideas suggested, so that students can build confidence when talking about mathematical concepts

Common misconceptions identified, to help avoid pitfalls

Fix and *stretch* ideas given, for developing conceptual understanding

Suggestions for end-of-chapter quizzes and activities, to enhance mental maths skills

Technology recommendations, to support students with online work

Ideas for investigation and research tasks, to extend learning

---

Recognise squares of whole numbers to at least 20 × 20 and the corresponding square roots; use the notation 7^2 and $\sqrt{49}$

* FIX: Ask students to draw squares of the different dimensions and calculate the areas to discover square numbers for themselves.

STRETCH: Students can investigate the difference between the square of a number, x, and the product of the two numbers either side. For example, what is the difference between 6^2 and 5×7, 8^2 and 7×9, 13^2 and 12×14? Can they describe their findings? Avoid using algebraic notation with students at this stage.

End of chapter mental maths exercise

1 Write all the factors of 45	6 What is the lowest common multiple of 10 and 8?
2 What is the square root of 64?	7 Write a square number that is 1 more than a prime number.
3 How many factors does the number 28 have?	8 676 is a multiple of 13. Write down the next biggest multiple of 13.
4 Write the even factors of the number.	
5 What factors do 20 and 30 have in common?	

Technology recommendations

* How can you calculate a square root using a calculator? Ask all students to demonstrate that they can find and use the $\sqrt{\ }$ key. Students can investigate what happens if they attempt to take the square root of a number that is not a square number, for example, $\sqrt{70}$. Ask students to explain their findings. They should notice:
  * The solution is not a whole number.
  * The decimal number fills their calculator display.
* Use a spreadsheet to calculate common multiples quickly.

Investigation/research tasks

1. **Rulers** (photocopiable resource)   *Problem solving*

Give students a 30 cm strip of paper, which they will use to make a ruler. Start by giving the students a smaller 5 cm strip of paper. How can they use the 5 cm strip to start marking the scale on the 30 cm ruler? Elicit from students that they can mark the multiples of 5. For example:

Now provide the 7 cm strip of paper so that students can mark the multiples of 7.

Challenge students to use both two strips of paper to mark the rest of scale on the ruler. For example, as 20 cm has been marked, they can use the 7 cm ruler to mark 27 cm.

When students have completed it, ask them to repeat the activity using the 8 cm and 9 cm strip. Is it possible to mark every centimetre? Why not?

TIP: They can use the other side of the 30 cm ruler.

Students should discover that they are only able to mark the multiples of 3.

92 • Unit 2A: Number and calculation   © HarperCollinsPublishers 2018

In addition to the many useful features identified in the reduced pages shown, the following supporting materials can be found, free-to-download, at **www.Collins.co.uk/CCLSM**.

For students to access:

- 34 x consolidation exercises (one per chapter), for embedding concepts covered in each chapter
- 9 x review units (one per unit), so students can check their progress at the end of a block of work

For teachers to access:

- 34 x end-of-chapter tests, to monitor and assess students' progress
- 50+ photocopiable resources to accompany Teacher's Guide activities, to support teaching of core mathematical concepts
- Answer keys for all exercises (Student's Book, Workbook and the above listed, free, online exercises and tests)

More information on how and when to use these materials can also be found online at the above address.

Place value and rounding

Learning objectives

Learning objectives covered in this chapter: 7Np1, 7Np2 and 7Np3
- Interpret decimal notation and place value.
- Multiply and divide whole numbers and decimals by 10, 100 or 1000.
- Order decimals including measurements, changing these to the same units.
- Round whole numbers to the nearest 10, 100 or 1000 and decimals, including measurements, to the nearest whole number or one decimal place.

Key terms
- digit
- place value grid
- state
- ordering
- round; rounding; rounded; to the nearest ...
- whole number
- decimal
- decimal place
- multiply
- divide

Prior knowledge assumptions
- Students know what each digit represents in whole numbers up to 1 million.
- Students know what each digit represents in decimals of up to 2 decimal places.
- Students can multiply and divide whole numbers by 10, 100 and 1000 where the answer is a whole number.
- Students can round numbers to the nearest 10, 100 or 1000.
- Students know the relationships between simple units of measurement, for example, centimetres and metres.

Guidance on the hook

Purpose: this hook encourages students to consider the place value of different digits in decimals with up to 2 decimal places, and to reason about how to maximise or minimise the value of such a number.

Use of the hook: Start by rolling a dice yourself and asking students to position the resulting numbers in any position on the grid, repeating until it is full. You should find that different students have produced different final numbers.

Ask if anyone thinks they have the biggest number and, if so, how they know that no one else can have a bigger number.

Then ask if anyone thinks they have the smallest number and, if so, how they know that no one else can have a smaller number.

Then ask students to explore the activity with their own dice in pairs. They should begin to think about the best strategy to make the largest (or smallest) possible number each time.

Bring the whole class back together for a discussion of their strategies.

BEWARE: Some students may perceive that numbers with more high-value digits are greater than those with fewer high-value digits, without realising that the first digit matters the most when deciding the size of the number and so on.

Adaptation: You could use an 8-sided dice or pack of number cards to change the possible digits being produced (and alter whether or not they can be repeated).

Extension: You could give students two empty grids to fill up at the same time (thus rolling 8 numbers) and ask them to position numbers to produce the largest and smallest possible pair of numbers.

Starter ideas

Mental maths starter

Write this number in numerals: Forty-three thousand and sixteen	Write this number in numerals: Eight thousand, two hundred and ninety	Write this number in numerals: Ten thousand and four	Write this number in numerals: Fourteen thousand, nine hundred and seven
Calculate 47 × 100	Calculate 290 × 10	Calculate 402 × 100	Calculate 450 × 10
Calculate 5000 ÷ 10	Calculate 4000 ÷ 100	Calculate 8900 ÷ 10	Calculate 8760 ÷ 10
Write the number that is one more than 8979	Write the number that is one less than 4100	Write the number that is one more than 12 699	Write the number that is one less than 11 000
Round 875 to the nearest 100	Round 878 to the nearest 10	Round 48 to the nearest 100	Round 192 to the nearest 10

Start point check: Where did it come from?

Give each student a mini-whiteboard and ask them to try to answer these questions with a <u>unique answer</u>.

After each question, get students to hold up their boards and discuss the range of answers provided. Then seek out any unique answers, awarding these students with one point each.

1. Write a number that has 4 tens.
2. Write a number that has 4 tens and 9 thousands.
3. Write a number that has 3 tenths and 7 hundredths.
4. Write a number that has 3 tens and 7 hundreds.
5. Write a number that lies between 389 and 393.
6. Write a number that lies between 24 and 25.
7. A whole number has been rounded to 140 to the nearest 10. What could it be?
8. A whole number has been rounded to 3000 to the nearest 1000. What could it be?

After all the questions, see which students have the most points.

Ask the students which of the questions were easiest to obtain a unique answer on and why this might be.

Human number line

You will need a space where students can stand in a line and the remaining students can view what they are holding.

Give each student a number (on a piece of card or on a mini-whiteboard) and ask them to stand in order.

For example, use a subset of the decimal cards shown in the photocopiable resources. For example, 12.9, 13, 12.6, 12.96 and 13.9.

Then give some additional students numbers and ask them to go to stand in the correct place between the students already in the line. For example, add in the numbers 12.69 and 12.962.

Discuss how each student can find their position with the whole class.

Continue with additional numbers as required.

Note: You could also introduce the idea of scale by marking the end points of the number line and asking students to estimate where they should stand. (For example, for the numbers above you could mark the ends of the number line at 10 and 15 or at 12 and 14.)

Discussion ideas

Probing questions	Teacher prompts
Convince me/a friend that 0.378 < 0.39.	You could encourage students to use place value equipment to represent these numbers to show why one is larger than the other. They may wish to exchange a hundredth for ten thousandths, for example.
What's the same and what's different? 200 thousandths, 0.2, 20 hundredths, 2 tenths, 1 tenth and 10 hundredths	Again, you could get students to use place value equipment to represent these numbers to discover those that are equivalent. Then, challenge them to come up with a list of 5 numbers that are equivalent!
True or False? When you divide a number by 1000, you get a decimal answer.	Encourage students to try out different numbers first and then to give a structured answer that explains that numbers that end in 3 or more zeroes will give a whole number when divided by 1000, but all other numbers with give a decimal.
Convince me/a friend that 17 567 is closer to 18 000 than 17 000.	You may wish to encourage students to use a number line to represent the numbers – suggest that they include the halfway value of 17 500 to help them.
Alice says, "The population of Romania is 22 million to the nearest million, and the population of Sri Lanka is 21.9 million to the nearest hundred thousand so Romania must have a higher population than Sri Lanka." Do you agree with Alice?	Encourage students to explain that Romania's population can be anything from 21 500 000 to 22 499 999, and Sri Lanka's population can be anything from 21 850 000 to 21 949 999 and hence it is possible for Sri Lanka to have a higher population than Romania.

Common errors/misconceptions

Misconception	Strategies to address
Misreading or misrepresenting numbers with 0s in, for example, 47 008	Ensure you include examples where some digits are 0.
Reducing multiplying by 10 to simply 'adding a 0' and hence making errors when multiplying a decimal by 10	Start by showing students that this rule cannot work. For example, can 4.5 ×10 – 4.50? Why not? Instead of using such a rule, encourage students to represent numbers with place value equipment to see why the tens become hundreds, ones become tens, tenths become ones etc. when you multiply by 10.

Misconception	Strategies to address
Dividing by 10 by simply 'removing a 0' and hence making errors when there is no 0 to remove	Start by showing students that this rule cannot work. For example, how do you remove a 0 when calculating 73 ÷ 10? Instead of using such a rule, encourage students to represent numbers with place value equipment to see why the hundreds become tens, tens become ones, ones become tenths etc. when you divide by 10.
Making errors when crossing from a whole number to a decimal or vice versa For example, students may calculate 2.3 × 100 and wrongly obtain 2300, 2 300 or even 23.0.	Start by checking whether the answer seems reasonable using estimation. For example, how do we know that 2.3 × 100 cannot be 2300? (What is 2 × 100 and so what kind of answer are we expecting?) Try using the place value grid will help to eliminate these errors.
Finding it difficult to identify the near multiples of 10, 100, 1000 etc. when rounding	This error suggests students have a weaker understanding of the place value of the numbers. Again, using the place value grid and a number line will help them to position the number mentally.
Struggling to round up when there is a 9-digit that requires rounding to 10 (and hence an effect on the next column)	Start by asking students to consider the nearest multiples. For example, to round 4798 to the nearest 10, we are choosing between 4790 and 4800. The key to eliminating this error is ensuring enough exposure to examples where the digit to be rounded up is a 9.
Incorrectly rounding when the answer should be 0	Exposure to examples where the answer could be 0. For example, round 42 to the nearest 100

Developing conceptual understanding

7Np1 Interpret decimal notation and place value; multiply and divide whole numbers and decimals by 10, 100 or 1000.

- FIX: Encourage students to represent numbers using a place value grid (Resource 2) so that they can easily read and compare numbers.

1 000 000	100 000	10 000	1 000	100	10	1	.	0.1	0.01	0.001
millions	hundred thousands	ten thousands	thou-sands	hundreds	tens	units		tenths	hundredths	thou-sandths
							.			

- When multiplying and dividing numbers by 10 (and then 100 and 1000), encourage students to see that each element of the number becomes 10 times bigger or smaller. This will help them understand why the shortcut of moving the digits to the left or the right works and make it more memorable.

> TIP: Encourage students to estimate the size of the answer they are expecting to check whether their answer is reasonable.

STRETCH: Students working at greater depth could suggest calculations that are equivalent to discover the structure of these calculation families.

For example, given 46 × 10:

46 × 10	4600 ÷ 10
4.6 × 100	46 000 ÷ 100
0.46 × 1000	460 000 ÷ 1000
0.046 × 10000	4 600 000 ÷ 10 000
...	...

7Np2 Order decimals including measurements, changing these to the same units.

- FIX: When ordering, it can be useful to add placeholder 0s to numbers that are of different lengths as some students find it hard to align decimals otherwise.

  For example, 2.3, 2.409 and 2.39 would become 2.300, 2.409 and 2.390 which makes them easier to compare.
- FIX: Recap unit conversions first to support students who are struggling to work with multiple units.
- Use the decimals cards in the photocopiable resources. Ask students to position these numbers in order from smallest to largest.

7Np3 Round whole numbers to the nearest 10, 100 or 1000 and decimals, including measurements, to the nearest whole number or one decimal place.

- FIX: When rounding, encourage students to start by finding the nearest multiples of 10, 100, 1000 (or whole numbers etc.) to the given number first. They can then use a number line to show these multiples, the halfway point between them and the actual number. For example, when rounding 17.411 to one decimal place, you would show:

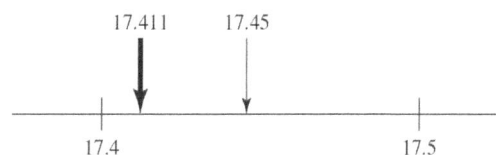

STRETCH: Students could explore which numbers round to the same result to discover that there is a range (or interval) of numbers. For example, the numbers that round to 240 to the nearest 10 lie in a range from 235 to 245 (not including 245). You could even show students how to record this algebraically as $235 \leq x < 245$.

- Use the decimals cards in the photocopiable resources. Ask students to sort them out into groups of numbers that round to the same number to 1 decimal place.

End of chapter mental maths exercise

1. Write this number in numerals:

   Three million, two hundred and seven thousand, three hundred

2. Write this number in numerals:

   Zero point two four seven

3. Calculate   8.7 × 1000

4. Calculate   54 ÷ 100

5. Which of these numbers is greater?

   0.68 or 0.673

6. Which of these measurements is greater?

   471 cm or 4.8 m

7. Round 0.456 to the nearest whole number.

8. Round 0.456 to one decimal place.

9. A runner completes a race in a time that is recorded as 13.59 seconds. Round this time to the nearest tenth of a second.

10. Jemma threw the javelin a distance of 71.19 m in a competition. Kaye threw her javelin a distance of 7120 cm.

    Who threw the javelin further?

Technology recommendations

- There are a range of electronic versions of base 10 apparatus, place value counters, number lines and place value grids to support place value development as per the approaches shown in this chapter.

  For example, you can quickly produce numbers using this artificial apparatus and ask students to produce the number they represent, say which is greatest/greater or order the numbers.

  You could use these electronic resources for your own modelling or enable the students to produce diagrams to support their responses to the Convince Me ... questions above more rapidly than they could by hand.

- You could explore rounding using a spreadsheet to see how it automatically rounds numbers and predict what the output will be.

  For example, if you enter 23.795 into the spreadsheet, what will the cell convert this to? How do you change the accuracy? What will the number change to? If a number is showing as 24 to the nearest whole number, what could the actual (typed) number be?

Investigation/research tasks

- Investigate the effect of rounding measurements on the accuracy of answers.

  You could start by showing students a rectangle of length 6.4 cm and width 2.3 cm.

  Ask them to measure the sides and round the lengths to the nearest whole number of centimetres.

  Now ask them to find the perimeter of the rectangle.

  How much have we underestimated the real value of the perimeter?

  You can then ask them to find the worst case scenario.

> TIP: You can extend this task by exploring the effect on the accuracy of the calculation of the area of the rectangle

- Research: where is rounding used in real life? Try to find four examples of situations where data is rounded to make calculations easier or the numbers clearer.

> TIP: You could start by investigating how measurements are recorded in sport.

- **Game/investigation**
  - How many different numbers can I make with these five number cards?

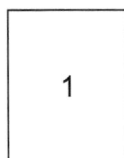

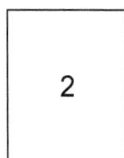

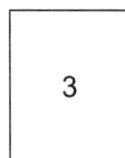

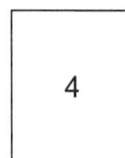

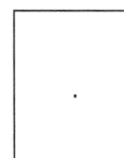

| 1 | 2 | 3 | 4 | . |

  (see photocopiable online resources)
  - Answer: 72

    For example, here are all the options starting with the 4 card (so there are 4 times as many as this!)

    4.321 4.312 4.231 4.213 4.132 4.123
    43.21 43.12 42.31 42.13 41.32 41.23
    4.321 4.312 4.231 4.213 4.132 4.123

This assumes that we do not allow a number to start or end with a decimal point without a preceding or following digit.

Possible questions/prompts

o   How many of them have a 3 in the tenths column?

o   Can you put them in order from smallest to largest?

o   What if I add another number card, for example, 5. How many different numbers will there be now? Can you predict the largest? The smallest?

o   **Support:** What if you were only allowed to use two number cards and the decimal point card each time?

o   **Challenge:** What if you did not have to use all the cards each time (so could have numbers like 3.2 as well as those with all four digits above)?

Multiplying and dividing

Learning objectives

Learning objectives covered in this chapter: 7Nc1, 7Nc2, 7Nc3, 7Nc4

- Consolidate the rapid recall of number facts, including positive integer complements to 100, multiplication facts to 10 × 10 and associated division facts.
- Use known facts and place value to multiply and divide two-digit numbers by a single-digit number, for example, 45 × 6, 96 ÷ 6.
- Know and apply tests of divisibility by 2, 3, 5, 6, 8, 9, 10 and 100.
- Use known facts and place value to multiply simple decimals by one-digit numbers, for example, 0.8 × 6.

Key terms

- multiple
- partition(ed)
- recombine(d)
- product
- quotient
- divisible
- divisibility tests
- dividend

Prior knowledge assumptions

- Students are familiar with the multiplication tables up to 10 × 10.
- Students know that multiplication is commutative.
- Students recognise and can use the distributive law to simplify a calculation (for example, they know that (4 × 3) + (5 × 3) = 9 × 3).
- Students can find related multiplication and division facts given one multiplication or division fact (the fact family).
- Students can multiply a single digit by a multiple of 10 mentally, for example, 3 × 60.
- Students can multiply and divide two-digit numbers by a single-digit number in writing.
- Students can instantly recognise odd and even numbers, multiples of 10 and multiples of 5.
- Students can explain the value of each digit in a decimal and represent it using place value equipment.
- Students know that ten tenths is the same as 1 unit and so can convert larger numbers of tenths to decimals, for example, 15 tenths to 1 unit and 5 tenths or 1.5.

Guidance on the hook

Problem solving

Purpose: this hook is designed to revisit prior knowledge of multiplication facts and begin to explore the common features of multiples.

Use of the hook: Give pairs of students a copy of the multiplication grid shown and ask them to see if they can deduce the missing headings for the columns and rows containing 2 multiples, before students then find some additional missing numbers in the main grid.

Once the grid is complete, ask the students what they notice about the different types of multiple in their table.

For example, 'what do you notice about the digits of the multiples of 9? of 3?'.

Adaptation: If students get stuck, or if they complete the challenge totally, review with the whole class how they can progress step by step.

For instance, you could start by asking 'which multiplication tables contain the numbers 20 and 35 (in the third column)?'. You can then prompt students to complete the 5 in the top row to correspond with this column. Then prompt students to find the multiplication tables containing, for example, 72 and 27 and so on.

Extension: Students could design their own similar challenge, by producing a full grid to start with and then removing enough numbers to make a challenging but solvable problem.

You could encourage students to use numbers that are in more than one multiplication table to make this more challenging.

Starter ideas

Mental maths starter

8 × 7	9 × 6	6 × 8	8 × 8
42 ÷ 6	72 ÷ 9	36 ÷ 9	48 ÷ 4
50 × 6	40 × 8	30 × 7	9 × 40
28 + ? = 100	614 + ? = 1000	? + 56 = 100	172 + ? = 1000
Double 29	Double 8.5	Double 9.4	Double 0.74
Halve 14.8	Halve 1.5	Halve 13.2	Halve 22.7

Start point check

Give pairs of students a set of these number and symbol cards.

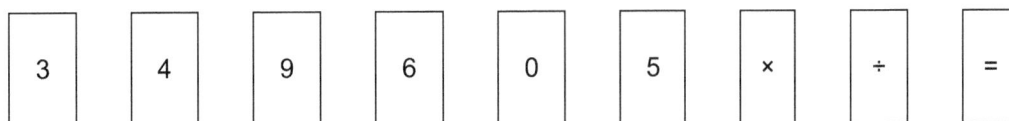

3	4	9	6	0	5	×	÷	=

1. Ask students to use the cards to make as many different multiplication and division facts as possible using these digit cards. They should record their facts in a list once they have made them.
   Go through the students' facts with the whole class to produce an exhaustive list.
   Ask students how they know that they have found all the possible facts.

2. **Fact Families:**
   Give students a multiplication fact (or a division fact) using the digit cards, for example, 9 × 4 = 36
   Ask them to rearrange the digit cards to produce an equivalent fact.
   For example, for 9 × 4 = 36 you would give:

   > 4 × 9 = 36
   > 36 ÷ 9 = 4
   > 36 ÷ 4 = 9

   TIP: Give students a false example such as 9 ÷ 4 = 36 and ask them to explain whether it is correct or not.

   You could also ask students to represent these facts visually using a diagram (for example, a bar model).

3. Ask students to make numbers that are

      a) multiples of 2

      b) multiples of 5

      c) multiples of 10

using their number cards.

You can make this more challenging by asking them to find ALL the possible numbers that are multiples of 2/5/10 using the cards.

You can also extend this to other multiples once you have covered the tests of divisibility that are covered later in the chapter.

Estimating game

Tell students that you are going to give them a series of multiplications and divisions that they must do in their head. If they cannot do the question exactly then they can estimate. The person who gets the closest to the exact answer is the winner.

For example, 5 × 3 × 6 × 10, divide by 5, multiply by 2.5, halve it, multiply by 3.1, divide by 9.9.

Write final answers – the student with the closest answer is the winner.

Encourage them to discuss strategies.

Fizz buzz game

Stand the students in a circle.

Explain that they must work together to count, taking it in turns to say the next number.

Whenever a number is a multiple of 3, they should say 'Fizz' instead of the number. Whenever a number is a multiple of 5, they should say 'Buzz' instead of the number. If a number happens to be both a multiple of 3 and of 5, then they should say 'Fizz Buzz'.

Students continue to count until someone says the wrong number or says/fails to say Fizz/Buzz correctly. This person then sits down, is 'out' and play continues.

Discussion ideas

Probing questions	Teacher prompts
Convince me that 28 × 7 = 20 × 7 + 8 × 7.	You may wish to name this as the distributive law for students.
	Try representing the calculation with place value counters in an array to show why you can calculate in this way.
	You can also ask the students to simplify a calculation the other way round by recombining, for example, to represent 8 × 3 + 5 × 3 and show that this is equal to 13 × 3.
When is it more useful to partition 78 as 60 – 18 than 70 – 8?	Encourage students to recognise that it can be useful to separate known multiples out when you are trying to divide mentally.
	For example, to calculate 78 ÷ 6 it is more useful to partition 78 into 60 – 18 as we can easily divide both of these numbers by 6 (whereas 70 – 8 gives us two numbers that we cannot!).
	You could get students to use place value equipment (such as place value counters) to show why 60 – 18 is easier to divide by 3 than 70 – 8.

Probing questions	Teacher prompts
True or False? Every number is divisible by 0.	Encourage students to consider what happens when we divide a number by 0 (i.e. the answer is infinite). You could use the idea of repeated subtraction to show that you can keep on removing 0 from the starting number forever without 'running out'. You can also show that the answer cannot be 0, which many students believe, using this method.
True or False? Numbers that contain only one digit that is repeated are divisible by 9.	Encourage students to test this statement for different numbers. They may need prompting to extend their tests to three-digit numbers. Encourage students to explain their final conclusions clearly by stating that the statement is generally false e.g. for 22 or 77 but true for some examples e.g. 99 or 333.
True or False? Numbers that contain a digit of 5 are divisible by 5.	Again, encourage students to test different numbers to deduce whether this statement is true. You may need to prompt them to try a number such as 52, which has a 5 in the tens (or hundreds) position. Once students have established that the statement is false, you could encourage them to refine the statement to make it true. For example, "numbers that end in a digit of 5 are divisible by 5". Focus then on getting students to show their reasoning. It is crucial that for true statements they can show why it is always true, rather than just one true example.
How many different ways can you show that $0.6 \times 6 = 0.9 \times 4$	Students could show this directly by calculating both sides. Alternatively they could construct 0.6×6 as an array using place value counters and then rearrange the counters to show they also form an array for 0.9×4.
Convince me that $0.8 \times 4 \neq 0.32$.	Students could show this directly by calculating the correct answer as 3.2 Alternatively they could show that the value of 0.8×4 should be close to 4 because this is nearly 1×4. They could do this with a paper strip to represent a practical bar model.

Common errors/misconceptions

Misconception	Strategies to address
Forgetting to apply a multiplication or division to both parts of a partitioned number For example, saying incorrectly that $24 \times 6 = 20 \times 6 + 4 = 120 + 4 = 124$	Start by showing students an example that has been incorrectly calculated $24 \times 6 = 20 \times 6 + 4 = 120 + 4 = 124$ and asking them to check whether this is correct and, if not, where the error appears. To avoid this error, encourage students to represent the initial number using place value apparatus and show the multiplication/division as an array or a grid multiplication. This will help them to see why we must apply the multiplication (or division) to both parts of the partitioned number.

Misconception	Strategies to address
Believing that numbers containing or ending in a 3 are multiples of 3	Ask students whether this statement is true or false (numbers containing or ending in a 3 are multiples of 3). They could test different numbers to produce a list of counterexamples and a list of those for which it is true. Ask students what the numbers that ARE multiples of 3 have in common.
Believing that numbers that are divisible by 2 and 4 will divide by 8	Start by showing students that this statement isn't true using a counterexample, for example, with 84. You can then encourage students to refine the rule to being divisible by 4 and the result of this being divisible by 2 (or even).
Thinking that numbers cannot be divided by a number they are not divisible by For example, saying that 24 cannot be divided by 5 rather than recognising that any number can be divided by 5, but only multiples of 5 will have a whole number answer.	Start by showing students using a calculator that the division can be done but the answer is just not a whole number. You could use counters to explore remainders practically if necessary.
Positioning the decimal point incorrectly when multiplying a decimal by a single digit For example, incorrectly saying $0.9 \times 3 = 0.27$	Start by asking students why this statement cannot be true using their checking skills. For instance, encourage them to estimate the answer as $0.9 \times 3 \approx 1 \times 3 = 3$. Students could then represent 0.9 using place value counters and replicate this 3 times to show why the result is 2.7 (and not 0.27).

Developing conceptual understanding

7Nc1 Consolidate the rapid recall of number facts, including positive integer complements to 100, multiplication facts to 10 × 10 and associated division facts.

- FIX: You could give students empty multiplication tables to complete to improve their recall of these key multiplication facts.

STRETCH: To make this more challenging you can reorder the multiplication tables in the grid so that the numbers cannot simply be filled in using a pattern.

- FIX: You can use the bar model to represent a single addition/subtraction or multiplication/division fact and use it to find associated facts.

For example, this bar shows the facts:

$38 + 62 = 100$, $62 + 38 = 100$, $100 - 38 = 62$ and $100 - 62 = 38$

Similarly, this bar shows the facts:

$38 \times 4 = 152$; $4 \times 38 = 152$; $152 \div 4 = 38$ and $152 \div 38 = 4$

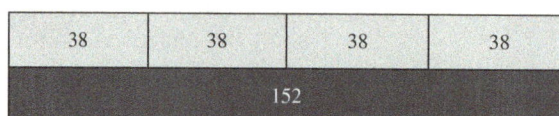

7Nc2 Use known facts and place value to multiply and divide two-digit numbers by a single-digit number, for example, 45 × 6, 96 ÷ 6.

- FIX: You could use the part–part–whole model to help students to partition a number and then recombine it (for multiplication or for division).

7Nc3 Know and apply tests of divisibility by 2, 3, 5, 6, 8, 9, 10 and 100.

- FIX: You can encourage students to explore the properties of numbers divisible by 3 (and other single digits) using a 100-square.

  Students can colour the multiples in and then try to identify things they have in common.

Part–part–whole Model

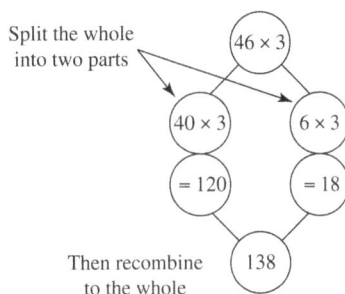

TIP: It can be helpful to use a different grid for each multiple to show the pattern more clearly. However, try to get students to compare their grid for 6, for example, with their grids to for 2 and 3 to identify the overlap and the link between the multiplication tables.

1	2	3	4	5	6	7	8	9	10
11	12	13	14	15	16	17	18	19	20
21	22	23	24	25	26	27	28	29	30
31	32	33	34	35	36	37	38	39	40
41	42	43	44	45	46	47	48	49	50
51	52	53	54	55	56	57	58	59	60
61	62	63	64	65	66	67	68	69	70
71	72	73	74	75	76	77	78	79	80
81	82	83	84	85	86	87	88	89	90
91	92	93	94	95	96	97	98	99	100

STRETCH: Students working at greater depth could explore numbers that are divisible by 6 and why they must also be divisible by 3 and 2. They could then apply this to other numbers e.g. divisibility by 15 or divisibility by 12.

7Nc4 Use known facts and place value to multiply simple decimals by one-digit numbers, for example, 0.8 × 6.

- FIX: You could use place value equipment to help students represent a decimal multiplied by a single digit.

For example, here is a representation of 0.3 × 4 as an array with every row worth 0.3:

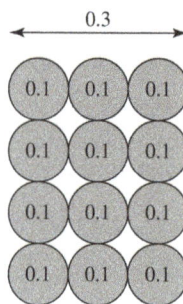

STRETCH: Students working at greater depth could also find related calculation families including decimals. For example, given 23 × 9 = 207, they could suggest groups of calculations that are linked, including 207 ÷ 9 = 23, 2.3 × 9 = 20.7, 2070 ÷ 230 = 9.

BEWARE: Be aware that this task may lead students to some examples of numbers with 2 decimal places multiplied by a single digit, such as 0.23 × 9 = 2.07, which are beyond the scope of Stage 7 but may follow logically.

End of chapter mental maths exercise

1. Find the product of 7 and 7.	7. Emma has 78 sweets. She shares them with her two friends fairly. How many sweets does each person get?
2. Find the quotient of 48 and 8.	
3. Calculate 1000 – 127.	8. Give two possible answers to complete this sentence: 105 is divisible by … (and …).
4. Calculate 23 × 6.	
5. Pens cost 67 cents. Paolo buys 3 pens. How much does this cost?	9. Calculate 0.7 × 5.
	10. Calculate 0.6 × 9.
6. Calculate 92 ÷ 4.	

Technology recommendations

- Use a calculator to test whether numbers are divisible by a given number to help deduce the rules.

  For example, ask students to find out which numbers 360 is divisible by (1–10).

  Then ask students if they could have predicted any of their answers (especially 2, 5 and 10 using the final digits and 3 and 9 by adding the digits).

  You can then give students a number, ask them to predict the numbers it is divisible by, before testing their answer using a calculator.

- Students could create a spreadsheet (or simple computer program if appropriate) that calculates whether a number is divisible by each of the digits 1–9.

  Encourage students to use formulae to automatically calculate the quotient of the number and 1, 2, 3, 4, 5, 6, 8, 9 and 10. Some students may be able to then convert the result to a Yes/No using an 'integer' formula too.

Investigation/research tasks

- Investigate the sum of three consecutive numbers. What numbers is it divisible by? Why does this happen?   *Problem solving*

  Start by asking students to pick three consecutive numbers, find their sum and then say which of the numbers 1–10 it is divisible by.

  They can repeat this for a number of different sets of numbers to deduce that the sum will always be a multiple of 3.

  Students can begin to explain this by considering what happens when you add the smallest and the largest number (they even out to give two copies of the middle number). Therefore, the sum of all three numbers will always be three times the middle number (and so a multiple of 3!).

  You could help students to show why this happens using algebra:

  Let n be the first number. The next number is then $n + 1$ and the last number is then $n + 2$.

  If we find the sum of these three numbers, we get:

  $n + \quad n + 1 \quad + \quad n + 2 = 3n + 3 = 3(n + 1)$ which is a multiple of 3 (in fact, it is 3 times the middle number).

- **Multiples Investigation**   *Problem solving*

  How many numbers between 200 and 250 are multiples of 9?

  What strategy could you use?

  Write them all down. What do these numbers have in common?

  > TIP: The first multiple of 9 is the first number after 200 where the digits sum to 9.

  Teacher Note: Students may just list the multiples of 9 first and then count them (207, 216, 225, 234, 243 → total of 5 numbers).

  However, encourage them to think about how they can predict how many multiples of 9 there will be i.e. how many multiples of 9 will come up in a range of 50 numbers? They can link this to 50 ÷ 9 to see that the answer has to be 5 or 6.

  To decide if it is 5 or 6, they need to know where the first multiple is – for us this is 207. So we have 43 places left and 43 ÷ 9 = 4.7777... so only 4 more can be fitted in, which makes 5 in total.

  Can the students now find the number of multiples of 9 between 600 and 750?

  STRETCH: Can you use your answer to find how many numbers between 200 and 250 are multiples of 3? Explain your answer.

  Ask students how the number of multiples of 3 relates to the number of multiples of 9. How will they deal with what happens at the end points?

  Can the students now find the number of multiples of 3 between 600 and 750?

- Here are five numbers: 4, 6, 7, 9, 10

  Pick three of the numbers to add up to a multiple of 3.

  Now generate five numbers of your own and find three that add up to a multiple of 3.

Can you find five numbers where no combination of three will add up to a multiple of 3?

Investigate   *Problem solving*

Answer:

For example: 4, 7 and 10 have a sum of 21, which is a multiple of 3.

The answer to the broader problem, is no, there is no set of five such numbers.

Any number you choose will either be a multiple of 3, one more than a multiple of 3 or two more than a multiple of 3.

- o If we have three of any one of these types, then we can add them to make another multiple of 3. (You can show this algebraically.)
- o If we have one of each type, we can also add them to make another multiple of 3.
- o If we have two of one type and two of another type above, we have to pick either a third one from the same type or one from the final type to make a triple. Either way, we will be able to produce a multiple of 3.

STRETCH: Research divisibility tests for 7 – is there a way to tell whether a number will divide by 7? What about 13? 11?

Answer:

For example, Remove the last digit, double it, subtract it from the truncated original number and continue doing this until only one digit remains. If this is 0 or **7**, then the original number is **divisible** by **7**. For example, 1617:

The last digit is a 7, which doubled is 14. If we subtract 14 from the truncated original number, 161, we get 161 – 14 = 147. Repeating, we calculate 14 – 14 = 0, so 1617 is a multiple of 7.

Equivalent fractions

Learning objectives

Learning objectives covered in this chapter: 7Nf1 and 7Nf2

- Recognise the equivalence of simple fractions, decimals and percentages.
- Simplify fractions by cancelling common factors and identify equivalent fractions.
- Change an improper fraction to a mixed number, and vice versa.
- Convert terminating decimals to fractions,

  e.g. $0.23 = \dfrac{23}{100}$.

Key terms

- fraction
- decimal
- percentage
- equivalent
- cancel down
- denominator
- numerator
- simplify (fully)
- proper fraction
- improper fraction
- mixed number
- terminating decimal

Prior knowledge assumptions

- Students know the decimals and percentages equivalent to $\dfrac{1}{2}, \dfrac{1}{4}, \dfrac{1}{10}$ and $\dfrac{1}{100}$.
- Students can find common factors of numbers.
- Students can explain the value of each digit in a decimal up to 3 decimal places.

Guidance on the hook

Purpose: To revisit the concepts of fractions as parts of the whole and begin to explore equivalent fractions by seeing the whole as different numbers of parts.

Use of the hook: Look at the images of the fractions shown in the Student's Book with the whole class.

Ask the students what fraction is shaded in each case and how they know, emphasising the number of shaded parts and the number of parts in the whole.

BEWARE: Students may see the fractions in simplified form (e.g. $\dfrac{1}{2}$) or in a larger form by considering each triangular section as one part (e.g. $\dfrac{9}{18}$)

Then give each student a selection of blank grids.

Ask them to try to shade different unit fractions from this list:

$$\frac{1}{2}, \frac{1}{3}, \frac{1}{4}, \frac{1}{5}, \frac{1}{6}, \frac{1}{7}, \frac{1}{8}, \ldots, \frac{1}{24}$$

They should make a note of any fractions that they cannot shade.

Once this is complete, explore the different solutions with the whole class (making sure that the correct number of triangles out of the 18 available are shaded each time, wherever they are placed).

Discuss which fractions were not possible and why this might be. Encourage students to consider the relationships between the denominators and 18 where the fractions can and cannot be shaded.

Ask students to record how many triangles out of 18 have been shaded for each fraction. Then ask them how the fraction they have recorded relates to the fraction they were trying to shade.

Adaptation: Produce grids containing a different number of parts, for example, 24 and repeat the task, this time asking students to predict in advance which fractions will be possible and not possible.

Extension: Students could consider how many different ways there are of shading, for example, $\frac{1}{3}$ of the shape.

Starter ideas

Mental maths starter

Write 50% as a fraction	Write $\frac{1}{5}$ as a percentage	Write 0.7 as a fraction	Write 0.24 as a fraction
State the value of the 4 in 0.34	State the value of the 4 in 5.491	State the value of the 4 in 12.354	State the value of the 4 in 0.004
Which is greater, 0.3 or 0.28?	Which is greater, 3.48 or 3.4?	Which is greater, 0.07 or 0.09?	Which is greater, 1.034 or 1.34?
I have 20 sweets and 7 of them are red. Write the fraction of the sweets that are red.	I have 30 sweets and 11 of them are red. Write the fraction of the sweets that are red.	I have 12 sweets and 5 of them are red. Write the fraction of the sweets that are red.	I have 16 sweets and 4 of them are red. Write the fraction of the sweets that are red.
Find a common factor of 15 and 25	Find a common factor of 18 and 12	Find a common factor of 21 and 24	Find a common factor of 28 and 49

Start point check

Give each student a mini-whiteboard and give them the following tasks:

1. a) Write $\frac{1}{2}$ as a percentage and a decimal.

    b) Write 25% as a fraction.

    c) Write 0.75 as a percentage.

    d) Write $\frac{1}{10}$ as a decimal.

2. Write down a number that has 7 tenths. (Try to give a number that no one else will have!)

3. Draw a picture to show the meaning of $\frac{1}{10}$.

4. Draw a picture to show the meaning of 20%.

5. Which is greater: $\frac{1}{5}$ *of* 100 or $\frac{1}{20}$ *of* 100?

6. Give a common factor of 24 and 18 … and another … and another …

After each question ask students to hold up their whiteboards to help you see who has the prior knowledge. You can also then discuss specific answers with the whole class, particularly where students may have different answers for Q2–4.

Paper strip and paperclip

The aim of this activity is to develop students' number sense and proportional reasoning to help them use the bar model confidently.

You should be able to see which students are confident in doing this by both the accuracy and speed of their responses.

Give each student a strip of paper and a paperclip.

Tell the students the paper strip represents the number line from 0 to 100.

Ask them to position their paper clip at

* 50
* 25
* 75
* 10
* 3
* 90
* 33 etc.

and then hold their strip up for you to see.

> TIP: It is useful to have your own large strip and marker at the front to share key ideas and answers with the whole group.

Then change the scale on their paper strip number line, for example, from 0 to 200 or 500, and ask students to position the same numbers (and more!) once again.

You can also try using a smaller scale, for example, from 0 to 50.

Finally, use a scale from 0 to 1 and ask students to position simple fractions and decimals, for example, $\frac{1}{2}$, 0.9, $\frac{1}{4}$, 0.05, etc.

Discussion ideas

Probing questions	Teacher prompts
True or False? You can order unit fractions from smallest to largest just by putting the denominators in order from largest to smallest.	You could encourage students to try out ordering some sets of unit fractions, such as $\frac{1}{3}, \frac{1}{5}$ and $\frac{1}{4}$. They may want to represent these fractions visually or concretely to help them. Try to get the students to see that if the numerator is always 1, then the size of the denominator will determine the size of the fraction.
Show that $\frac{2}{12}$ and $\frac{5}{30}$ are equivalent fractions.	Students could do this problem concretely using paper strips or visually using a drawn bar. However, the size of the numbers in the denominator is such that this problem is best done abstractly by dividing numerator and denominator by a common factor.
How many equivalent fractions are there to $\frac{5}{6}$?	Encourage students to list their equivalent fractions systematically to show why there must be an infinite number.
Convince me/a partner that 12 hundredths is the same as 0.12.	You could encourage students to use place value counters to represent 12 hundredths and then exchange ten of these for one tenth, before recording using place value columns.

Probing questions	Teacher prompts
How would you go about finding which of these numbers is closest to one third? $\frac{10}{31}, \frac{100}{301}, \frac{1000}{3001}$	Encourage students to describe what the representation of these fractions would look like (although it is too onerous to actually produce it!) and hence the value of the difference between each of them and $\frac{1}{3}$ to help them identify which is the closest. Students could also use a calculator to convert these fractions to decimals to compare them.
Convince me/a partner that $\frac{3}{20}$ is the same as 15%.	Encourage students to make reference to parts per hundred and find an equivalent fraction with a denominator of 100 to make the comparison. You could then ask them what they would do if the denominator was greater than 100, for example, $\frac{14}{200}$. Finally, ask the students what they would do if the denominator was not a factor or a multiple of 100, for example, $\frac{14}{40}$.

Common errors/misconceptions

Misconception	Strategies to address
Applying a general 'whatever you do to the top you must do to the bottom' rule when simplifying fractions, which can appear additively rather than multiplicatively	Start by showing a counterexample to make students realise that this rule cannot work. For example, explore whether $\frac{2}{5}$ equals $\frac{1}{4}$ using a bar model (based on the idea of subtracting one from both the numerator and denominator). To solve the issue, it is important to develop a stronger understanding of the meaning of fraction and the student would benefit from going back to representing fractions concretely to explore equivalent fractions practically.
When simplifying fractions, many students tend to prefer dividing both numerator and denominator by 2 repeatedly. Hence you may notice that they fail to completely simplify fractions where the common factor is 6 or even 7 etc.	You could use a calculator to simplify a fraction like $\frac{6}{15}$, which students may think cannot be simplified to help them realise that you do not always need to divide by 2. This issue tends to arise from weaker times table knowledge and lack of awareness of divisibility tests (such as adding the digits to check for a multiple of 3) so reinforce these points to support them.
Making errors when simplifying or finding equivalent fractions, such as saying that $\frac{7}{8}$ is equivalent to $\frac{42}{56}$	Again, this is related to times table knowledge as shown above, so encourage students to check their answer by multiplying back (inverse operations).
Not linking the denominator and numerator to the number of parts in the whole and the number of parts we have respectively Believing that fractions with larger denominators are greater than those with smaller denominators, saying for example that $\frac{2}{6} < \frac{2}{7}$	Representing the fractions visually or concretely using a bar model will help to challenge this idea as will exploring what happens when we divide by a bigger number as an investigation. *Problem solving.*
Believing that longer decimals are greater than shorter ones, rather than looking at the place value of the numbers concerned	Ask students which they would prefer? 0.09 or 0.1? Represent the numbers using place value equipment to help students see why 0.09 < 0.1

Misconception	Strategies to address
	Encourage these students to use their place value chart to identify the true value of the digits presented in a decimal.
Believing that there is an equivalence between decimals and percentages of the form $\frac{1}{x} = x\%$	Start by exploring whether this is true for an example such as $\frac{1}{5}$ and 5% (to discover that it is not!). Most commonly this occurs with fifths and twentieths where students believe that $\frac{1}{5} = 5\%$ and $\frac{1}{20} = 20\%$. This is incorrect and stems from not having a clear visualisation of the relative size of $\frac{1}{5}$ and $\frac{1}{20}$ compared to 0% and 100%. The starter using paper strips and paperclips above is a good way to develop this number sense to avoid this issue.
Making errors with converting decimals with no hundredths to percentages or fractions e.g. writing 0.6 as 6% or 0.05 as $\frac{5}{10}$	Ask students whether it is true that 0.6 = 6%, using a visual representation compared to a whole if necessary. Then ask students why this error may have occurred and the percentage that 0.6 is really equivalent to.

Developing conceptual understanding

7Nf1 Recognise the equivalence of simple fractions, decimals and percentages.

- Emphasise the meaning of a fraction as a number of parts of a whole, where the denominator represents the number of parts in the whole and the numerator represents the number of parts we have.

- FIX: Use place value equipment and charts to help relate decimals (tenths and hundredths) to simple fractions and percentages. You could use the matching fraction, decimal and percentage cards provided in the online photocopiable resources for this chapter to help students explore equivalence.

7Nf2 Simplify fractions by cancelling common factors and identify equivalent fractions; change an improper fraction to a mixed number, and vice versa; convert terminating decimals to fractions, for example, 0.23 = $\frac{23}{100}$.

- Use the bar model shown in the examples in the Student's Book to represent fractions of a whole and to explore which fractions are equivalent (and then to compare those that are not to say which is greater). You can use the fraction wall from the online photocopiable resources for this chapter to support students in finding equivalent fractions by comparing the different lines.

- FIX: You could give students equal length strips of paper to fold into thirds, quarters, fifths and so on to test out equivalences.

  For example, you could ask students to convince you that $\frac{3}{9}$ is equivalent to $\frac{1}{3}$.

  Students could show this using two equal length strips of paper folded into thirds and ninths respectively:

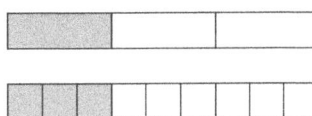

Alternatively, they could represent $\frac{1}{3}$ as a bar model and then sub-divide it vertically to show how this is equivalent to $\frac{3}{9}$:

- Students should identify the abstract rules from this work (such as if I multiply or divide the numerator and denominator by the same number I will have an equivalent fraction) and then go on to use these rules thereafter.

STRETCH: Students working at greater depth could find more obscure equivalent fractions such as $\frac{3}{7} = \frac{?}{651}$ or simplify more complex fractions such as $\frac{112}{392}$.

- They could also try to identify fractions that lie between two given fractions, for example, find a fraction that lies between $\frac{1}{5}$ and $\frac{1}{6}$.

- Represent mixed numbers using whole bars and fractions of bars that are divided up to represent their equivalent improper fraction.

  For example, $2\frac{1}{4}$ can be represented as:

  and then divided into quarters as:

  to show that it is equivalent to $\frac{9}{4}$.

- FIX: Use place value counters to represent terminating decimals and help convert them to fractions and vice versa.

- Ensure that students are confident in converting fractions to decimals by converting to a denominator of tenths, hundredths or thousandths without a calculator.

STRETCH: Challenge students working at greater depth to identify fractions that lie between two given decimals such as 'Find a fraction that lies between 0.3 and 0.35' or, more difficultly, 'Find a fraction that lies between 0.31 and 0.32.' This would also work by asking for a decimal lying between two fractions.

TIP: Students also need experience in using the fraction key on a calculator to enter a fraction and read it as a decimal from the display.

End of chapter mental maths exercise

1. Find 25% of 340.	7. Write a fraction that is equivalent to 0.3.
2. State the value of the 7 in 0.172.	8. Simplify $\frac{18}{30}$ fully.
3. Write $\frac{3}{5}$ as a percentage.	9. Find an equivalent fraction to $\frac{5}{6}$ with denominator 24.
4. Which is greater, 0.69 or 0. 8?	
5. I have 21 sweets and 14 of them are red. Write the fraction of the sweets that are red.	10. Find an equivalent fraction to $\frac{3}{8}$ with numerator 18.
6. Find a common factor of 27 and 45.	

Technology recommendations

- You can use a virtual maths environment to produce bar models to represent fractions. You could use these bar models for your own modelling or to let the students to produce diagrams to support their responses to the Convince me... questions above more rapidly than they could by hand.

- Use scientific calculators to convert fractions to decimals and to simplify fractions.

  This is a good way of discovering the relationships between simple fractions and their equivalent decimals. This can also help students realise that fractions can be cancelled down by dividing by numbers other than 2.

  You may wish to use a calculator emulator to model these calculations to students.

- Design a spreadsheet to convert a fraction to its simplest form, its equivalent decimal and its equivalent percentage (automatically using formulae). You could use the fractions, decimals and percentages matching cards from the online photocopiable resources for this chapter as a stimulus for this task.

Investigation/research tasks

- **Investigation:** In Between   *Problem solving*
  Find a fraction that lies between:

  a) $\frac{1}{4}$ and $\frac{1}{5}$　　　b) 0.6 and 0.63　　　c) 0.35 and 0.36.

  BEWARE: Students may naturally suggest $\frac{1}{4.5}$ as a fraction for part (a) above, without realising that the denominator needs to be a whole number.

  How can you be certain that your fraction is definitely between the 2 numbers given?
  Can you do this for any two fractions?
  Any two decimals?

TIP: Encourage students to convert the decimals to fractions first to help them find a fraction that lies between them.

  Investigation: Samira is buying pizzas for her family. If pizzas can only be spilt into halves and she wants everyone to have exactly the same amount of pizza with no pizza left over, she would have to buy 2 pizzas for 4 people or 3 pizzas for 6 people. Investigate the smallest number pizzas she would need for 5 people and all the different numbers of people up to 10.

How many whole pizzas would she need for all the different numbers of people up to 10 if she were also allowed to cut the pizzas into quarters and everyone had to have exactly the same amount of pizza? Are any answers the same for halves as for quarters? Can you explain why? Investigate your idea if Samira could also cut the pizzas into eighths.

> TIP: You will need to explain why 3 people means 3 pizzas in the first part of this investigation as students may want to just halve the number of pizzas.

STRETCH: Investigate Farey sequences, named after John Farey.   *Problem solving*

These are sequences of every fraction with a denominator of up to a given number, written in order. The fractions should be written in their simplest form, with any duplicates removed.

To find the fourth Farey sequence you first need to write all the proper fractions with denominators which are less than or equal to 4. These are:

$$\frac{0}{1}, \frac{1}{1} \text{ and } \frac{0}{2}, \frac{1}{2}, \frac{2}{2} \text{ and } \frac{0}{3}, \frac{1}{3}, \frac{2}{3}, \frac{3}{3} \text{ and } \frac{0}{4}, \frac{1}{4}, \frac{2}{4}, \frac{3}{4}, \frac{4}{4}$$

Next cross out duplicates – fractions which are the same as another fraction when simplified. These are shown in bold below:

$$\frac{0}{1}, \frac{1}{1} \text{ and } \mathbf{\frac{0}{2}}, \frac{1}{2}, \mathbf{\frac{2}{2}} \text{ and } \mathbf{\frac{0}{3}}, \frac{1}{3}, \frac{2}{3}, \mathbf{\frac{3}{3}} \text{ and } \mathbf{\frac{0}{4}}, \frac{1}{4}, \mathbf{\frac{2}{4}}, \frac{3}{4}, \mathbf{\frac{4}{4}}$$

Now write out a list, in order of size, of the fractions which remain:

$\frac{0}{1}, \frac{1}{4}, \frac{1}{3}, \frac{1}{2}, \frac{2}{3}, \frac{3}{4}, \frac{1}{1}$ and this is the fourth Farey sequence.

Can you work out the first, second and third Farey sequence?

Now write down how many fractions are in the first second, third and fourth Farey sequence. How many fractions do you think that there will be in the fifth Farey sequence? Work out the sequence and see if you are correct.

> TIP: Students will need this explained clearly on the board. You may want to work through F_4 in detail on the board. Ask them how they know that $\frac{2}{3}$ comes between $\frac{1}{2}$ and $\frac{3}{4}$. Does this mean that $\frac{7}{8}$ comes between $\frac{6}{7}$ and $\frac{8}{9}$?

Negative numbers

Learning objectives

Learning objectives covered in this chapter: 7Ni1

- Recognise negative numbers as positions on a number line.
- Order, add and subtract positive and negative integers in context.

Key terms

- positive
- negative
- integer
- zero
- ascending order
- descending order

Prior knowledge assumptions

- Students have encountered negative numbers in context (such as temperature).
- Students can mentally add and subtract positive whole numbers.
- Students are familiar with the number line (marked and unmarked) and can use it to find the difference between two numbers.

Guidance on the hook

Purpose: This hook links negative numbers to the real-life context of temperature and introduces students to the difference between negative numbers.

Use of the hook: Discuss the places listed in the task with the students as a whole group as well as the meaning of 'average temperature'.

Ask the students to work in pairs to position the destinations on the scale.

They can then attempt the questions provided, before sharing their answers as a whole class.

> TIP: It is useful to have your own scale on display on the board to share these answers and help mode finding the difference.

BEWARE: Look out for students not counting 0 as a position when finding the difference. Also be aware that students may not consider the sign of the number and just find the difference between the positive versions of the numbers.

Adaptation: You could add other destinations into the activity by giving their relationship to others in the list.

For example, you could say: "Winnipeg has an average temperature in January that is 18 °C warmer than Yakutsk. Where should we position Winnipeg?"

Extension: Students could convert their warmer/colder statements to number sentences using addition and subtraction.

Starter ideas

Mental maths starter

What comes next? −6, −12, −18, …	What comes next? −9, −18, −27, −36, …	What comes next? −45, −50, −55, −60, …	What comes next? −5, −8, −11, −14, …
Give a number that lies between −10 and −20	Give a number that lies between −18 and −22	Give a number that lies between −55 and −60	Give a number that lies between −74 and −84
What number is halfway between 0 and −2 on a number line?	What number is halfway between 0 and −4 on a number line?	What number is halfway between 2 and −2 on a number line?	What number is halfway between 4 and −2 on a number line?
What is one degree warmer than a temperature of −7°?	What is one degree warmer than a temperature of −15°?	What is one degree warmer than a temperature of −1°?	What is one degree warmer than a temperature of −20°?
What is one degree colder than a temperature of −12°?	What is one degree colder than a temperature of −10°?	What is one degree colder than a temperature of −9°?	What is one degree colder than a temperature of −50°?

Start point check: washing line

Put up a washing line or piece of string across the classroom.

Use paperclips to attach numbers at each end to show the range of the number line. For example, −20 and 20.

Give each student a number to attach in the right place on the line.

TIP: It is a good idea to start with 0.

Ask the students questions such as:

* what is the difference between these two numbers?
* how far is this number from 0?
* complete this sentence: my number … −10

Then change the numbers at the ends of the line (for example, to −50 and 50) so that students have to rethink their positioning.

Ask them what is the same and what is different now that the line has changed.

(**Note:** you can draw this also on the board.)

Words for add and subtract

Ask students to work in groups to create a list of words that mean add and subtract.

For example:

Add: plus, and, as well, extra, more than, total, altogether, higher than, sum

Subtract: less, take away, remove, fewer, minus, lower than, difference, below.

Counting in negatives

Practise counting on but using negative numbers.

You can count on in −2s (−2, −4, −6, −8, …) or count in −5s (−5, −10, −15, …).

You could also count forwards and backwards from a given start numbers in 2s, 3s, etc. to include negative numbers.

For example, counting forwards in 3s from −22.

−22, −19, −16, −13, ...

Negative number loop cards

- Give pairs of students a shuffled set of the negative number loop cards provided in the online photocopiable resources for this chapter.
- Ask them to work together to find a question and answer that match to form a complete chain of all the cards.

> Tip: If they get stuck, prompt students to find another card and to work backwards to find the missing answer.

Discussion ideas

Probing questions	Teacher prompts
Convince me/a friend that −42 is less than −1.	Students could use a number line to position these values to help them explain this. TIP: Ensure students understand that 'less than' refers to position rather than magnitude of the number.
True or False? Ordering negative numbers is just the same as ordering positive numbers but backwards.	You could give students a set of negative numbers to order as a starting point. Encourage students to see that the magnitude of negative numbers help us put them in order but larger negatives are lower (less) than smaller negatives.
Is January the coldest month in every city in Europe? The world?	Use the internet to display the average temperatures for a city and look at the warmest month. You could then prompt them to look at other cities in Europe and then look at cities in the southern hemisphere.

Common errors/misconceptions

Misconception	Strategies to address
Thinking that large negative numbers are greater than small ones For example, believing that 82 > 20	Ask students which temperature is colder (or lower): −82 or −20 Then ask them whether −82 can be called greater than −20 (or −20 less than −82). You could use a marked number line to show that −82 is positioned further to the left than −20. It can be helpful to explain that since 82 is greater than 20, −82 is more negative than −20.

Misconception	Strategies to address
Thinks that 5° warmer than −8° is −13°	Show the number line with colder and warmer arrows below it
Thinks that −20 is bigger than 5	Explain the importance of the negative sign and the places of the numbers on the number line
Mixing up 'negative', 'minus' and 'subtract' and hence struggling to know how to solve a problem	This is probably a matter of policy within your school so that all teachers are consistent. One model is to use the word negative as the way to describe a number and subtract as the way to describe the operation of taking away.

Developing conceptual understanding

- **7Ni1 Recognise negative numbers as positions on a number line, and order.**

- **Add and subtract positive and negative integers in context.**

- Encourage students to use marked and then unmarked number lines to find and position negative numbers first.

- FIX: Try using a vertical number line (like a thermometer) to help students see why, for example, −9 is less than 4

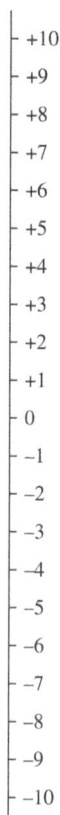

```
+10
+9
+8
+7
+6
+5
+4
+3
+2
+1
0
−1
−2
−3
−4
−5
−6
−7
−8
−9
−10
```

STRETCH: Students working at greater depth could begin to work with negative numbers that are not whole.

For instance, they could find numbers that lie between −2 and −3 on a number line or between −2.4 and −2.5.

They could also find differences in temperature, money etc using decimal values.

End of chapter mental maths exercise

1. Give a whole number that appears between −5 and −10 on a number line.	5. The floors of a building are labeled −2, −1, 0, 1, 2, 3, 4, 5 and 6. Jana's car is parked on floor −2. Her office is on floor 4. How many floors below her office is her car?
2. Give a whole number that appears between −23 and −27 on a number line.	
	6. On Monday, the temperature was −4°. On Tuesday it went down by 3° On Wednesday it dropped another 2°. On Thursday it went back up 1°.
3. What temperature is 7° warmer than −2°?	
4. What temperature is 8° colder than −4°?	What was the final temperature on Thursday?

Technology recommendations

* Research inhabited places whose height above sea-level is negative and find how much lower they are than your current location.

* How can you input negative numbers onto a calculator? Explore the similarities and difference between the negative number key and the subtract key.

Investigation/research tasks

1. Research the uses of negative numbers in real life contexts on the internet.

   Students should come up with examples such as handicaps and scores in golf, labelling of lifts/elevators in buildings with floors below ground, heights above and below sea level, temperatures. Avoid subjects which may be sensitive − bank statements, weight loss in humans, etc.

2. Get students to write a question involving negative numbers in contexts that you give them. Again avoid subjects which may be sensitive – bank statements, weight loss in humans etc.

   Contexts could include:

   a. temperature

   b. lifts in buildings with floors below ground

   c. heights above and below sea level

   d. scores above and below an average

3. Research the history of negative numbers.

   Students could produce a presentation or poster to explain why negative numbers were first introduced and how they have been integrated over time.

Units of measurement

Learning objectives

Learning objectives covered in this chapter: 7GI1

- Choose suitable units of measurement to estimate, measure, calculate and solve problems in everyday contexts.

Key terms

- distance
- mass
- capacity
- millimetres
- centimetres
- metres
- kilometres
- miles
- grams
- kilograms
- tonnes
- millilitres
- litres
- cubic metres

Prior knowledge assumptions

- Students can read, choose, use and record standard units to estimate and measure length, mass and capacity.
- Students recognise and use the units for time.

Guidance on hook

Pupils will need a sheet of plain, unlined paper, a ruler and a sharp pencil.

Purpose: The purpose of this hook is to help pupils in drawing lengths accurately, estimating lengths and getting a 'feel' for a centimetre and which lengths are most appropriately measured in centimetres. They may need help in realising that 1 cm is going to be the shortest line on the page if all lines are an exact number of centimetres long.

Use of the hook: Let them know that the 10 lines should not just be 1, 2, 3, 4 … 10 cm but up to whatever length they can fit on the page they have been given and that the lines can be at different angles as they are in the example in the student book.

Extension: Repeat the exercise without the 1 cm line drawn.

Starter ideas

Mental maths starter

A book has a mass of 250 g. What is the mass of 5 of these books?	Write 378 g correct to the nearest 10 grams.	Estimate the mass of a tennis ball – is it less than 100 g, 100–500 g or more than 500 g?	Which unit is the odd one out? litres, grams, kilograms, tonnes
A piece of ribbon is 714 cm long. It is cut into 7 equal pieces of ribbon. How long is one piece of ribbon?	Write 1.7 cubic metres correct to the nearest cubic metre.	Estimate the length of a lorry. Is it less than 1 m, 1 m–3 m, longer than 3 m?	Which unit is the odd one out? centimetre, kilometre, cubic metre, millimetre

A school buys 34 bottles of water to take on a school trip. Each bottle of water is 50 centilitres. How many centilitres of water do they buy in total?	Write 9.09 millimetres correct to the nearest $\frac{1}{10}$ of a millimetre.	Estimate the capacity of your mouth? Is it less than 50 millilitres, between 50 and 150 millilitres, more than 150 millilitres?	Which unit is the odd one out? cubic metre, litre, centilitres, millimetre
A marathon is 26.2 miles. A runner completes 3 marathons. How far did they run in total?	Write 9178 tonnes correct to the nearest hundred tonnes.	Estimate the circumference of the earth. Is it less than 1000 km, between 1000 and 10 000 kilometres, more than 10 000 kilometres.	Which dimension is the odd one out? length, width, height, mass, depth

Start point check

Give each student a set of cards from Card Set A. Check student's understanding of the prerequisite knowledge by asking them to sort the cards in a variety of ways.

- Sort the cards by units. Ask them to name each unit. Can they spell each unit? Can they give an indication of its size?
- Separate cards into those for mass, and those for weight. Can they order the measurements within each group – which is larger km or m?
- Highlight the two measurements with decimal places. What is the value of each decimal digit. Remind students of the relationship between the different units (100 cm in a metre) and explain that measurements such as 2 metres 50 centimetres can also be written in a decimal form 2.5 m.

TIP: write the units in full on the board so that students can see the correct spelling

Estimation game

Select a container that holds between 10 ml and 1 litre. Ask students to individually estimate the capacity of the container. Work together as a class to measure the capacity (you can do this by filling the container with water, and then decanting the water into a measuring jug). The students who has the best estimation receives 5 points. Any students within 5% receives 3 points, and any students within 10% receives 1 point. Keep playing with different containers until one student has 10 points.

Mental maths – quiz maker

Students are told that they are going to write their own mental maths quiz. All their questions must be set in a context, or have a 'story'. This allows the opportunity to check that students can identify realistic contexts for each unit.

Each student writes five mental maths questions. The first question must have an answer in units of grams; the second question must have an answer in the units of centimetres; for the third the units must be litres; for the fourth the units must be kilograms, and for the final question the units must be millilitres.

It may help to give an example of a context/story questions before they start: encourage students to write questions such as, John is running a 400 m running race, he has run 125 m, how many metres has he left to run? rather than, for example, 400 m – 125 m.

When students have finished, students swap papers and complete the quiz. Alternatively, select some of the questions to give to the whole class.

TIP: Look out for students who have created inappropriate contexts for the questions, for example, A book weighs 3 grams, how many grams do 20 books weigh?

Where in the world am I?   *Problem solving*

Students will need access to a map of the world, and this task would work particularly well on an online interactive map.

Tell students that you are 7140 km from Sydney, 2900 km from Tokyo and 8100 km from Cairo. Can they use the map to work out where you are?

At the end of the task, discuss with students any strategies they may have used.

Discussion ideas

Probing questions	Teacher prompts
Can you give me an example of when it is important to measure accurately?	Consider a wide range of contexts that will be meaningful to students, for example, when making medicines. As students offer examples, discuss the consequences of inaccurate measurements for example, if the gas/petrol isn't measured accurately when filling the car up you may pay more/less.
What is the difference between 3.50 kg, 3.05 kg and 3.005 kg?	Prompt students to consider the place value of each '5'. It may be helpful to write them all to 3dp, i.e. 3.500 kg, 3.050 kg, 3.005 kg.
What are the different ways we can measure the size of a person? Which is the best measurement?	Discuss the usual measurements, such as height, weight. Students may also offer more unusual measurements such as waist or head circumference. Encourage students to think about some different reasons why they might be measuring a person, for example, if it is for clothes then a length may be more appropriate, Challenge students to think about whether shoe size is a measurement – does it have units? Is it possible to have a shoe size of 7.1 (US size)?

Common errors and misconceptions

Not giving units with answers	Model good practice in your teaching, always giving units in solutions to worked examples. Insist students give units with their answers. Emphasise to students that a measurement is meaningless without its unit.
No relational understanding of how long a kilometre is, how heavy a gram is, how much is a litre	Offer students practical opportunities to engage with a range of different weights and measures to become familiar with their relative sizes. Encourage students to compare unknown measures to those they may know –for example, if they know they are 1.5 m tall, is it taller or shorter?

© HarperCollins*Publishers* 2018

When solving problems, calculating with measurements in different units For example, two pieces of string of length 20 cm and 2 metres are added together to give a length of 220 cm	Relate the units to place value. Discuss how the 2 units in 12 cm means 2 units of cm, while 2 in 12 metres means 2 units of m. Wherever possible, demonstrate the different measures using measuring equipment, for example, show students 2 ml of water and 2 litres of water. When solving word problems, encourage students to underline the different units in the question as a prompt to check the units used.
Errors in the place value of decimals For example, 1 metre 5 cm is 1.5 metres.	Check first that students are able to tell you that a centimetre is a <u>hundredth</u> of a metre, and a metre is a <u>thousandth</u> of a kilometre. Relate this to place value in a decimal measurement to make the link between $\frac{1}{100}$ th of a metre, and the hundreds place in a decimal. Encourage students to use decimal notation to record measurements, ensuring they have the opportunity to record measurements with a 0 in the tens or hundreds column (for example, 3.05 kilos, 1.007 litres), watching out for students who make this mistake.

Developing conceptual understanding

7GI1 Choose suitable units of measurement to estimate, measure, calculate and solve problems in everyday contexts.

* FIX: Students who have difficulty in estimating the length/mass or capacity of an object will benefit from practical experiences of different measurements. This is particularly important for mass and capacity which they may have had less exposure to. Allow students to pour litres of water into different containers to become familiar with 1 litre, and allow them to hold different weights in their hands to become familiar with 1 gram/1 kilogram.

* FIX: Give students the opportunity to solve problems that involve more than 1 unit, for example,1 m – 45 cm. For students who find this difficult, provide them with cm cubes and a 1 metre ruler so that they can model the problem.

STRETCH: Encourage students to think about the accuracy of measurements. Is it possible to measure length/mass/capacity exactly? Link this to their work on rounding. Thinking about this will be helpful when they come to learn about continuous data in subsequent years.

End of chapter mental maths exercise

1. Which of these could be the weight of an adult? 1 kg, 7 kg, 70 kg, 700 kg	5. Which units would you use to measure the mass of a suitcase?
2. A tonne is a unit of measurement for what? length, mass or capacity	6. Here are 5 units: milligrams, tonnes, grams, centilitres, kilograms. Which is the odd one out?
3. Yasmin is taking a 1-hour hike. Which of these is a reasonable distance to walk in this time? 5 m, 500 m, 5 km or 500 km	7. Write down a measurement that is lighter than 1 kg.
4. Which units would you use to measure the width of a computer screen?	8. Spell 'centilitres' in full.

Technology recommendations

* Use online maps with distance measuring functionality (for example, https://www.gmappedometer.com) to plan a sightseeing walk around the local town that is approximately 5 kilometres long. Ask students to write instructions for their sightseeing route, to include distances. You could adapt this by asking to students to plan a sightseeing bus tour that is 30 km.

* Students will be most familiar with measure distance using a ruler, but this is not the most effective way to measure distance in many cases – particularly when working in a practical context. Ask students to name any technologies that they may know of that measure distance – for example, odometer in a car, or laser rangefinders.

Investigation/research task

* **Olympic weights and measures**

  The purpose of this activity is to check that students can estimate the lengths and weights of familiar objects/distances. The context of the activity – weights and measures of the Olympics – also provides a good opportunity to discuss the accuracy in measurement in real life.

  Start by discussing when and how weights and measures are used in the Olympic games. Encourage students to reflect on

  o Which weights and measurements must be precise, and which may be approximate? For example, a rugby ball can be 410–460 grams, but a 400 m running track must be exact.

  o What would the consequences be if measurements were not sufficiently precise?

  o What challenges do the Olympic hosts face in ensuring their measurements are accurate – for example, a different venue every games, a different swimming pool, different race track. Precise distances are essential when races are won and lost on a thousandth of a second.

  o The accuracy of the measurements taken, and how this might have improved over time.

Provide students with card Set A – they may already be familiar with these measurements from earlier work in the chapter. Give students a card Set B and ask them to match the two sets. The solution is given below.

During the activity, prompt students to think about the relative sizes of each length or mass. For example, if they think that the height of a hurdle is 1.067 then how could they use this information to decide on the width of a lane in the swimming pool – is it more or less?

15 kg	1.83 metres	1.067 metres	2.5 metres	70 metres
(the steel bar (bar bell) used in women's weight lifting)	(the width of a goal in a hockey match)	(height of a hurdle)	(width of one lane in Olympic-sized swimming pool)	(distance to the target in archery)
10 cm	2 kg	2 km	10 m	42 mm
(width of a balance beam in gymnastics)	(the mass of a discus (men))	(the distance of rowing race)	(the height of the highest diving board)	(the diameter of a table tennis ball)
2.7 grams	5.6 metres	57 grams	425 grams	42.195 kilometers
(the mass of a table tennis ball)	(the distance between the two posts in rugby)	(mass of a tennis ball)	(approximate mass of a soccer ball)	(distance of a marathon)

- **Very small measurements and very large measurements**

  Remind students that there is structure to the prefixes of the units system, for example, kilo-relates to thousand, centi to hundreths, milli to thousandths. They may also be familiar with giga, nano and mega from everyday language. Ask students to research these prefixes. Can they find examples of things that are measured in units of this size. For example, a Yottagram is equal to 1000 000 000 000 000 000 000 000 grams. The mass of the earth is 5.972 Yg. Students could record their findings in a table.

- **Paperclip investigation**   *Problem solving*

  Set your students the task of calculating the number of paperclips required to create a perimeter around the classroom or the playground, if the paper clips are linked together. Students should work in small groups of three or four. Start by encouraging them to discuss strategies they could use to find the answer. Make measuring equipment available to students, as well as a reasonable number of paperclips per group. Students should be allowed to measure the playground/classroom and the paperclips themselves. At the end of the task, ask each group to share their findings with the group, encouraging them to explain all of their calculations.

Algebra

Learning objectives

Learning objectives covered in this chapter: 7Ae1, 7Ae2, 7Ae3, 7Ae4

- Use letters to represent unknown numbers or variables; know the meanings of the words *term, expression* and *equation.*
- Know that algebraic operations follow the same order as arithmetic operations.
- Construct simple algebraic expressions by using letters to represent numbers.
- Simplify linear expressions, for example, collect like terms; multiply a constant over a bracket.

Key terms

- expression
- term
- equation
- operation
- bracket
- constant
- like terms
- collect(ing) (like terms)
- simplify(ing)
- expand

Prior knowledge assumptions

- Students know that addition and multiplication are commutative so the order does not matter.
- Students know that the order you carry out a subtraction or division in does matter as they are not commutative.
- Students understand how a bracket works with a numerical calculation such as $2(4 + 3) = 2 \times (4 + 3) = 2 \times 7 = 14$.

Guidance on the hook   *Problem solving*

Purpose: This task encourages students to explore a mathematical trick to think about why it works for any number. It helps students see that one purpose of algebra is to allow us to generalise a statement. This also leads to forming an expression using a letter to represent any number.

Use of the hook: Give students the instructions for the trick shown in the Student's Book. They could either read these, and carry them out or you could carry out the trick yourself using a number that one of them gives you.

Once students are convinced that the trick always works, ask them to explore why this is.

You could prompt students to record the operations as a sequence of steps (like a function machine).

You could also get them to write what has happened to a specific number.

For example, if we start with 11, we get $(11 + 3) \times 2 + 4 - 10$.

They could refine this to the more conventional $2(11 + 3) + 4 - 10$.

Students may then spot that adding 4 and then subtracting 10 has the net effect of subtracting 6

They may also notice that $2 \times + 3$ from the bracket results in +6 which is the opposite.

Students working at greater depth may already be able to use algebra to explain the trick by using a letter as the start number and expanding the bracket.

Adaptation: You could explore tricks where the answer is always fixed to see why this is happening.
For example:

Think of a number between 1 and 10.
Multiply it by 3.
Add 10 to your answer.
Multiply this number by 3.
Subtract 30.

Add the digits together.

Do you have 9?

Extension: Ask students to come up with their own tricks of the same type.
When they have produced one, they can partner with another student to test out each other's tricks to see if they work.

Starter ideas

Mental maths starter

I think of a number, f.	I think of a number, g.	I think of a number, h.	I think of a number, j.
I add 10 to my number. Write an expression for the number I now have.	I multiply my number by 3. Write an expression for the number I now have.	I subtract 4 from my number. Write an expression for the number I now have.	I subtract my number from 20. Write an expression for the number I now have.
Calculate $11 + 11 + 11 + 11 + 11 + 11$	Calculate $7 + 7 + 7 + 7 + 7 + 7 + 7$	Calculate $13 + 13 + 5 + 5 + 5 + 5 + 5$	Calculate $100 - 9 - 9 - 9 - 9$
Simplify $3x + 2x + 2x$	Simplify $9y + 10y - 4y$	Simplify $3x + 2y + 5x$	Simplify $2y + y + 3z + 7z$
Expand $2(a + 5)$	Expand $3(b - 3)$	Expand $10(c + 11)$	Expand $5(10 - d)$
Draw a shape with a perimeter of $3x$	Draw a shape with a perimeter of $2x + 2y$	Draw a shape with a perimeter of $3x + 2y$	Draw a shape with a perimeter of $x + 20$

I think of a number

Given each student a mini-whiteboard.

Describe a number, n to the students and ask them to write an expression for it on their whiteboard and then reveal this at the end.

For example:

I think of a number, n. I double my number and add 4 to it. What number do I have now?

You could also include examples where students could suggest a value for your number to develop their sense of letters as numbers in algebra.

For example:

I think of a number, n. When I double it, I get a number greater than 10 but less than 20. What could my number, n, be?

> TIP: You could use the matching cards in the photocopiable resources for this chapter to help students to match up word descriptions with their equivalent algebraic expressions.

What was the question?

Give students one of these terms/expressions and ask them each to suggest an expression that could be simplified to produce it.

> TIP: This could be run as a game with students playing in teams with 1 point being awarded for each unique solution.

Examples:

- $4x$
- $7y$
- $2x + 8$
- $x + y$
- $2x + 3y$
- $3x - y$

Discussion ideas

Probing questions	Teacher prompts
Show me an expression that is also a term Can an equation be made of just one term?	Encourage students to produce any expression to start with and then ask them how many terms their expression has. They can then remove extra terms to leave just one. Prompt students to realise that by having an equals sign this forces there to be at least one term of each side of it.
Always, Sometimes, Never? $$x \div y = y \div x$$	You could simplify this initially to $x \div 2 = 2 \div x$ to help students explore the statement in a more specific way. Encourage them to try different numbers as x to see whether the two calculations are equal (which in general they will not be). If necessary, ask them whether there are any values where they are equal. Students can then think about the more general statement $x \div y = y \div x$. and the conditions where they would be equal to realise that if $x = y$ then the result will be the same.
Convince me that there are an infinite number of expressions that simplify to $4a + b$	You could ask students to simplify this expression first: $2a + a + b + a$ before asking them whether they can write their own expression that simplifies to $4a + b$. They can then consider how many ways this can be done to respond to the probing question.
Which is the odd one out? Explain your answer $3a + b$; $9x$; $7y - 1 = 15$; f; $20 - g$	Ask students to describe each of the 5 items to help spot that only one of those listed is not an expression (and is an equation). You could follow up by asking 'are all terms expressions?' to check whether students understand that terms are a subset of expressions.
How many possible shapes can you find with a perimeter of $3x + 2y$?	Give students this pentagon and ask them how they could label the sides to make the perimeter $3x + 2y$. Then ask them to produce their own shape with the same perimeter. You may need to prompt them to consider shapes that are not pentagons too.
Always, Sometimes, Never? $$2a = a + 2$$	Encourage students to try different numbers out to see if this statement is true. They should be able to show an example where it is true and one where it is not to illustrate their choice of 'Sometimes'. You could then ask them to think about other similar statements such as $$3a = a + 3$$

Common errors/misconceptions

Misconception	Strategies to address
Believing that certain letters always have certain values, especially linked to the alphabet position For example, students may believe that $a = 1$, $b = 2$ and so on.	Give students examples where these values cannot apply to expose this misconception. It is also useful to use examples where the letter could take more than one different value. For example, I'm thinking of a number a. It is greater than 100 but less than 120. What could this number be? Using the word version of an unknown or variable first of all and then later replacing it with a letter to save time can help to eliminate this issue.
Feeling that an answer must be a number and so a question is not finished when the answer still contains a letter This can lead to combining letters when collecting terms. For example, students may say that $3x + 2y = 5xy$	Students often show this when simplifying by collecting or expanding brackets. In particular, they may try to collect up unlike terms to 'finish' the question. Use algebra tiles to build the expression to ask them whether these items can be added together (to show that they cannot). E.g. $3x + 2y$ x x y x y Only the light grey and dark grey terms can be combined together so we will have to end up with two separate terms in our answer.
Forgetting the multiplication operation between two letters or a number and a letter in maths For example, thinking that $5x$ means 53 when $x = 3$ rather than seeing it as $5 \times x$.	Build the expression using algebra tiles to show why $5x$ means 5 lots of x: x x x x x
Struggling to work with terms without coefficients (i.e. with coefficients of 1) such as x Students may forget that x represents $1x$ and so say, for example, that $4x - x = 4$ rather than $3x$.	Again, you can represent the expression visually using algebra tiles (either real or drawn) as $4x$ with one x removed to leave $3x$ x x x x (crossed out)
Not taking account of the signs of terms when collecting For example, students may say that $7x + 2y + 4x - 3y = 11x + 5y$. Alternatively, they may apply an earlier sign to a later term	It can help students to circle each separate term in an expression including the sign before it as part of the term: i.e. $7x$ $+ 2y$ $+ 4x$ $- 3y$

Misconception	Strategies to address
For example, $10x - 3x + 2x$ may be wrongly interpreted as $10x - 5x$	Again, using algebra tiles either visually or practically can help to combine the terms. Students need to see negative terms in their own right as terms that 'neutralise' other positive terms of the same size For example: $5x + 2y - 2x - 3y$ is represented as: The two $-x$ terms 'neutralise' or cancel out two of the $+x$ terms to leave: or $3x + 2y - 3y$. Two of the $-y$ terms 'neutralise' or cancel out the two $+y$ terms. However, there isn't a third term for the last $-y$ to neutralise, so it remains, leaving: or $3x - y$.
Not applying the constant term outside a bracket to all the terms inside. Most commonly students do not apply it to the last term. For example, they may write that $2(x + 7) = 2x + 7$.	Students can check whether their expansion works by picking a number to be x. For example, if $x = 5$ is $2(5 + 7) = 2 \times 12 = 24$ the same as $2 \times 5 + 7 = 10 + 7 = 17$? Representing a bracket visually as an array or grid multiplication can help eliminate this error. Again, you can use algebra tiles for this purpose: For example: $2(x + 7)$ would look like: which shows why the answer has to be $2x + 14$ and cannot be $2x + 7$.

Developing conceptual understanding

7Ae1 Use letters to represent unknown numbers or variables; know the meaning of the words *term, expression and equation.*

- FIX: BEGIN writing expressions about an unknown or variable by using the word description of the number.

   For example, 'mystery number + 1' or 'age of Pedro × 3' before replacing these with letters as a shorthand

   For example, '$n + 1$' or '$p \times 3$'

7Ae2 Know that algebraic operations follow the same order as arithmetic operations.

- FIX: SHOW students that the rules of arithmetic are simply generalised to work for any number to make the rules of algebra.

  For example: we can add numbers by grouping them together or collecting them.

  We might calculate

  12 + 12 + 7 + 12 + 7 + 12 + 12 + 12 + 12 + 7 + 7 + 12 + 12 + 12 as

  10 lots of 12 and 4 lots of 7 or

  $10 \times 12 + 4 \times 7$

  This is just the same as saying that

  $x + x + y + x + y + x + x + x + x + y + y + x + x + x$ is

  10 lots of x and 4 lots of y or

  $$10x + 4y$$

- FIX: STUDENTS could explore whether the order of addition, subtraction, multiplication and division matters by trying them out with different numbers before writing this algebraically.

STRETCH: Students working at greater depth could try to find cases where the order of subtraction and division does not matter, for example, $a - b = b - a$ when $a = b$.

7Ae3 Construct simple algebraic expressions by using letters to represent numbers.

- FIX: TRY writing expressions using words to represent the unknown or general number first and then replacing this phrase with a letter as a shorthand.

  For example, to represent 'I think of a number then double it then add 3 to the result' you might write

  my number × 2 + 3

  before shortening to

  $m \times 2 + 3$

  or $2m + 3$

TIP: Try using algebra tiles to build expressions from directions.

For example, you might say

I'm thinking of a number x

I add 1 to it:

I then multiply the result by 3:

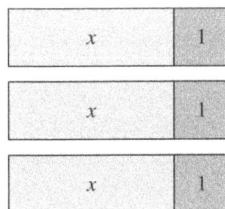

to show why the result is $3x + 3$.

You could use the matching cards in the photocopiable resources to help students pair up expressions with their word descriptions.

> TIP: If you use algebra tiles you will need different positive letter tiles of different lengths as well as +1 tiles to represent numbers. Make sure the number +1 tiles are squares with the same width as the letter tiles so that they can be arranged as arrays.

7Ae4 Simplify linear expressions, for example, collect like terms; multiply a constant over a bracket.

- FIX: USE algebra tiles either practically or visually to construct expressions to show how and why collecting terms works

For example:

Here is $3x + y + 2x + 2y$:

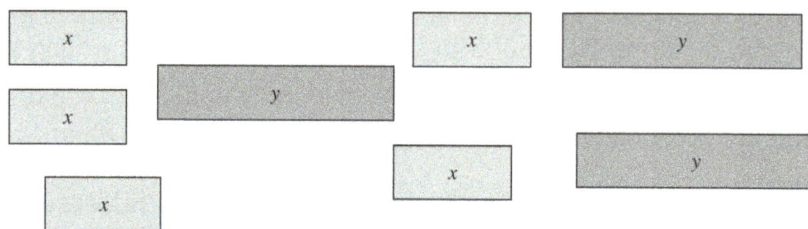

which simplifies to $5x + 3y$:

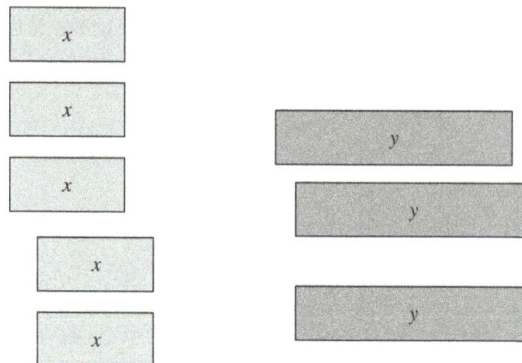

- FIX: When subtracting, use negative tiles to produce the expression and then 'neutralise' or cancel out any available equal and opposite positive tiles.

For example: $2x + y - 3y$ is represented as:

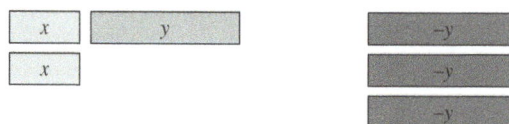

One of the $-y$ terms 'neutralises' or cancels out one of the $+y$ terms to leave $2x - 2y$:

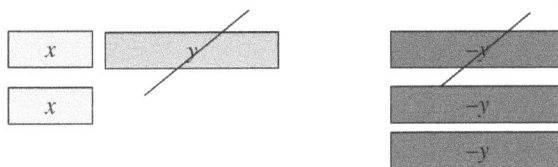

STRETCH: Students working at greater depth can suggest expressions that simplify to a given answer.

STRETCH: These students may also be able to apply these ideas to perimeter, for example, and generate shapes whose perimeter is a given expression.

- FIX: Liken expanding a bracket to partitioning a number when multiplying.

  For example, students should be happy that 23×4 can be calculated by finding $20 \times 4 + 3 \times 4$.

  So similarly $(x + 3) \times 4$ or $4(x + 3)$ can be found by finding

  $x \times 4 + 3 \times 4$, which is $4x + 12$.

STRETCH: Students working at greater depth could try to find different brackets which expand to the same result such as $12x + 20$. Can they find all the possible solutions (using whole numbers only)?

End of chapter mental maths exercise

1. I think of a number, m.
   I add 4 to my number and then multiply the result by 3.
   Write an expression for the number I now have.
 	
2. Amy eats x sweets. Bethany eats twice as many sweets as Amy.
   Carla eats 10 sweets more than Bethany. Form an expression for the number of sweets that Carla eats.
 	
3. The perimeter of a square is y cm.
   Write an expression for the length of one side of the square in cm.
	4. A shape has a perimeter of $4x + 2y$.
	   Draw two possible shapes that this could be. You should label the sides.
	
	5. Expand $3(x + 7)$.
	
	6. A bracket is expanded to give an answer of $25x + 15$.
	   What was the bracket?
	
	7. Simplify $7m + 2n - 3m - n$.
	
	8. An expression was simplified to give an answer of $2a - b$. What could the expression have been?

Technology recommendations

- Using a spreadsheet to carry out different operations to a number that can then change or take many values.

  For example, students might create the following table and use formulae to calculate the results for each line.

	A	B
1		
2	Number, n	
3		
4	n+1	
5	3n	
6	n+n	
7	20-n	
8	n - 3	
9	n ÷ 4	
10	3n + 4	
11	50-2n	
12		
13		

Solution:

	A	B
1		
2	Number, n	
3		
4	n+1	=B2+1
5	3n	=B2*3
6	n+n	=B2+B2
7	20-n	=20-B2
8	n - 3	=B2-3
9	n ÷ 4	=B2/4
10	3n + 4	=3*B2+4
11	50 - 2n	=50-2*B2
12		
13		

- Using a spreadsheet to investigate whether the order of calculations matters and test statements like
  - $a + b = b + a$
  - $a - b = b - a$
  - $a \times b = b \times a$
  - $a \div b = b \div a$

  Students could create a box to represent each of the numbers a and b and experiment with changing these to see what happens to the two answers. Can they find any times when the subtractions and division are equal?

Investigation/research tasks

- **Opposite corners**   *Problem solving*

  Take a hundred-square and lay a three-square over the top.

  Find the sum of the numbers in opposite corners of your overlay.

  For example, on this hundred-square the opposite corner totals are

  13 + 35 = 48

  and

  15 + 33 = 48:

1	2	3	4	5	6	7	8	9	10
11	12	13	14	15	16	17	18	19	20
21	22	23	24	25	26	27	28	29	30
31	32	33	34	35	36	37	38	39	40
41	42	43	44	45	46	47	48	49	50
51	52	53	54	55	56	57	58	59	60
61	62	63	64	65	66	67	68	69	70
71	72	73	74	75	76	77	78	79	80
81	82	83	84	85	86	87	88	89	90
91	92	93	94	95	96	97	98	99	100

Move the overlay and repeat – what do you notice?

Why is this happening?

How can you use algebra to show that this will always happen?

Students should be able to use algebra to generalise a 3 by 3 grid and show why the sum of the values in opposite corners is equal.

For instance, they may produce a general 3 by 3 square like this:

x	$x + 1$	$x + 2$
$x + 10$	$x + 11$	$x + 12$
$x + 20$	$x + 21$	$x + 22$

and show that

$$x + x + 22 = 2x + 22 = x + 2 + x + 20$$

BEWARE: You may need to prompt students to think about how the number on the next row relates to the one directly above in a 100 square.

TIP: You could encourage students to consider alternative shapes to lay on the grid to test whether the same thing happens.

Good shapes to try include rectangles and crosses.

STRETCH: Students working at greater depth could consider crosses with only two lines of symmetry i.e. where the length is not equal to the width.

- **Number hops**   *Problem solving*

Choose a number, for example, 34.

Now hop over the next number and find the number after, for example, 36.

Find the sum of these two numbers and halve your answer.

Now choose your own number, hop over the next number and find the next one.

Add your numbers and halve the answer.

What do you notice?

Can you use algebra to show why this is happening?

Students should discover by trying this with numbers that the answer is always the middle number that has been 'hopped' over.

Students should be able to write expressions to represent the two numbers.

For example, they may say that the first number is n, the one that has been hopped over is therefore $n + 1$ and the second number is $(n + 1) + 1$ or $n + 2$.

They can then show that $\frac{n+(n+2)}{2} = \frac{2n+2}{2} = n + 1$ which is the same as the middle number.

You could extend students by asking them to think about hopping a different amount between the first number and the second number.

BEWARE: Encourage students to stick to an odd number of hops, at least at first, as this problem is harder when there is an even number and a decimal is generated. For example, for 4 hops, the result will be $\frac{n+n+5}{2} = \frac{2n+5}{2} = n + 2.5$, which is harder to identify.

- **Perimeter and area challenge**   *Problem solving*

  Here is a rectangle:

  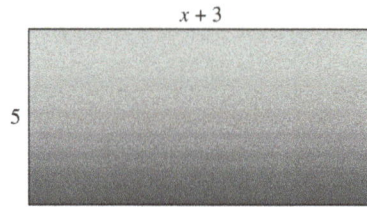

  - o   Can you find an expression for its perimeter?
  - o   What about the area?
  - o   Can you draw a rectangle with a perimeter of $2x + 12$?
  - o   Are there are any other possible solutions?
  - o   Can you draw a rectangle with an area of $10x + 20$?
  - o   Are there any other possible solutions?
  - o   Can you find a rectangle with a perimeter of $4x + 14$ and an area $8x + 12$?

  > TIP: You may need to remind students of how to find the perimeter and area of a rectangle first with a numerical example.

  Students should be able to form expressions for the perimeter and area by adding the four sides and multiplying the length and width respectively.

  Encourage students to expand their brackets when finding the area.

  BEWARE: Students may forget to add all four sides when finding the perimeter.

  Encourage students to find multiple solutions for rectangles that could give a certain perimeter or area. When they are then given both the perimeter and the area this pinpoints just one of these possibilities.

STRETCH: Students who finish could then make up their own problem with a perimeter and area for others to produce a suitable rectangle. They can swap over to try each other's problems out.

Sequences

Learning objectives

Learning objectives covered in this chapter: 7As1, 7As2

- Generate terms of an integer sequence and find a term given its position in the sequence; find simple term-to-term rules.
- Generate sequences from spatial patterns and describe the general term in simple cases.

Key terms

- sequence
- term
- position number
- term-to-term rule
- general term
- position-to-term rule

Prior knowledge assumptions

- Students know the meaning of the word 'integer'.
- Students can count in whole numbers from any given number for example, in 6s from 4.
- Students have explored patterns of numbers including times tables in number squares.

Guidance on the hook

Purpose: This task gives students a chance to generate and investigate sequences from a simple number context. The aim is for them to notice the patterns being created and begin to describe these mathematically.

Use of the hook: Ask students to try Kate's investigation on some numbers.

It is helpful to start with the examples given in the Student's Book, that is

1. 15
2. 24

Solutions:

1. 15, 30, 15, 30, ...
2. 24, 30, 15, 30, 15, ...

Encourage students to explain what they have found and to say which number is the first number that repeats as well as its position in the pattern.

Students should also try to think about other numbers that will behave similarly.

For instance, numbers whose digits add to 6 or 3 will join the repeating 30, 15 pattern or 15, 30 pattern respectively.

Numbers whose digits add to 9 will join the 45 repeating pattern.

Adaptation: Students could make a list of all possible digit sums and what the result will be like this:

Digit Sum	Pattern
1	5, 25, 35, 40, 20, 10, ...
2	10, 5, 25, 35, 40, 20, 10
3	15, 30, ...
4	20, 10, 5, 25, 35, 40, ...

Digit Sum	Pattern
5	25, 35, 40, 20, 10, 5
6	30, 15, ...
7	35, 40, 20, 10, 5, 25, ...
8	40, 20, 10, 5, 25, 35, ...
9	45, 45, ...
10	**50**, 25, 35, 40, 20, 10, 5, 25, ...
11	**55, 50,** 25, 35, 40, 20, 10, 5, 25, ...
12	**60,** 30, 15, ...
13	65, 55 ....
14	**70,** 35, 40, 20, 10, 5, 25, ...
15	**75, 60,** 30, 15, ...
16	**80,** 40, 20, 10, 5, 25, 35, ...
17	**85,** 65, 55 ....
18	**90,** 45, 45, ...

(**Note:** the bold numbers are not part of the repeating patterns).

TIP: Students could then highlight which patterns are related to each other (despite having different starting points) as shown in the table.

Extension: Students could consider other multiplication and the patterns created. For instance, what happens when you multiply the digit sum by 3 each time? Or 9? Or 7?

Starter ideas

Mental maths starter

What comes next in this sequence? 10, 16, 22, ...	What comes next in this sequence? 19, 30, 41, ...	What comes next in this sequence? 8, 15, 22, ...	What comes next in this sequence? 17, 25, 33, ...
What comes next in this sequence? 12, 7, 2, ...	What comes next in this sequence? 14, 6, -2, ...	What comes next in this sequence? 8, 5, 2, ...	What comes next in this sequence? 21, 12, 3, ...
Which number is the odd one out in this sequence? 2, 4, 7, 8, 10, 12, ...	Which number is the odd one out in this sequence? 3, 6, 9, 11, 15, ...	Which number is the odd one out in this sequence? 1, 4, 6, 10, 13, ...	Which number is the odd one out in this sequence? 20, 18, 16, 15, 12, ...
The position-to-term rule of a sequence is 'divide by 4'. Find the 18th term.	The position-to-term rule of a sequence is 'multiply by 3'. Find the 18th term.	The position-to-term rule of a sequence is 'add 4 and divide by 10. Find the 18th term.	The position-to-term rule of a sequence is 'subtract 5 and multiply by 6. Find the 18th term.

The term-to-term rule of a sequence is add 7 and the first term is 11. Find the 5th term.	The term-to-term rule of a sequence is multiply by 3 and the first term is 4. Find the 4th term.	The term-to-term rule of a sequence is divide by 2 and the first term is 12. Find the 5th term.	The term-to-term rule of a sequence is subtract 9 and the first term is 11. Find the 5th term.
The first two terms of a sequence are 7 and 10. What could the term-to-term rule be?	The first two terms of a sequence are 4 and 11. What could the term-to-term rule be?	The first two terms of a sequence are 20 and 30. What could the term-to-term rule be?	The first two terms of a sequence are 15 and 13. What could the term-to-term rule be?
The first two terms of a sequence are 5 and 10. What could the position-to-term rule be?	The first two terms of a sequence are 4 and 5. What could the position-to-term rule be?	The first two terms of a sequence are 12 and 24. What could the position-to-term rule be?	The first two terms of a sequence are 0 and 1. What could the position-to-term rule be?

Sequence builders

Put the students into two teams and stand them in two lines, preferably facing each other.

Give one team a first term and a term-to-term rule.

The students in that team must then recite the terms of the sequence aloud using the first term and the rule to find them. They must stop when the first person makes a mistake or if someone takes too long to say a term. Once they have stopped, they receive a point for every correct term they have said.

Play then passes to the other team.

Repeat these turns as many times as you wish to produce a final score for each team and identify a winning team.

Possible sequences:

* first term 8, term-to-term rule of add 6
* first term 11, term-to-term rule of add 8
* first term 200, term-to-term rule of subtract 11
* first term 2, term to term rule of multiply by 2
* first term 10, term-to-term rule of multiply by 3 and subtract 10.

What comes next in this sequence?

Show students these sequences and give them each a mini-whiteboard.

Ask them to suggest what comes next in each sequence and to be ready to explain their answer

1. 21, 29, 37, 45, ... (53 – adding 8)

2. 256, 128, 64, ... (32 – halving)

3. 301, 201, 101, ... (1 – subtracting 100)

4. 100, 91, 82, 73, ... (64 – subtracting 9)

5. 1, 3, 9, 27, ... (81 – multiplying by 3)

6. 1, 2, 4, ... (could be 8 if doubling or 7 if increasing the difference by 1)

7. 1, 1, 2, 3, 5, ... (8 – Fibonacci-type sequence where previous 2 terms added)

8. 1, 4, 9, 16, ... (25 – square numbers or difference increasing by 2 each time)

TIP: You could play this game in teams and award 1 point for each correct answer or, where appropriate, possible answer.

Discussion ideas

Probing questions	Teacher prompts
Create a sequence with a 3rd term of 7. Explain the term-to-term rule and/or the position in your sequence. How many possible answers are there?	Prompt students to suggest a number of different sequence with a 3rd term of 7 and then share their responses to develop a sense of the infinite number of possibilities.
How many terms of the sequence with first term 2 and term-to-term rule will be below 100? • add 10 • add 4 • multiply by 3	Students may start by finding the first few terms to help them get a sense of the sequence. Encourage them to think about the structure of what is happening rather than just continuing this to find all the terms below 100. For example, how many times can they add 10 to 2 before getting beyond 100?
How many terms of the sequence with position-to-term rule will be below 100? • divide by 2 • add 7 • multiply by 5 and add 3	Again, prompt students to think about the structure here and find the first term that goes beyond 100 to work out how many lie below it. This is a good way for students to start to understand the value of a position to term rule, which is much easier in this sort of question than a term-to-term rule.
True or False? The 35th term of the sequence 7, 11, 15, 19, ... is 144.	Encourage students to think about the types of number in this sequence (i.e. odd numbers due to a term-to-term rule of add 4 and a first term that is odd) rather than simply to continue the pattern all the way to the 35th term!
Always, Sometimes, Never? The 10th term of a sequence will be double the 5th term.	Students could check this directly for a sequence like 7, 10, 13, ... to show that in general it is not true. They could then think about any possible situations where it is true also, such as when the sequence is of the type *an*, for example, 2, 4, 6, ... or 11, 22, 33, 44, ... They might want to consider why this rule works for times tables but not for other sequences. It is useful for them to see that it is not the term-to-term rule only that decides this but the first term too.

Common errors/misconceptions

Misconception	Strategies to address
Thinking that you need a first term to be given with a position-to-term rule	It is useful to give students a position-to-term rule and a first term that does not match and ask them to generate the sequence. Once produced, they should realise that the first term does not 'fit' and so is extra information they do not need. You can model how to calculate the first term using a position number of 1 also.
Believing that the (2*n*)th term is double the *n*th term	Students should try this out with a sequence like 10, 14, 18, ... to show that it is not true.

Misconception	Strategies to address
For example, that the 8th term will always be double the 4th term.	Usually this idea comes from times tables (where it is true) as students have sometimes found multiples by doubling earlier multiples and so on. It is important to show students that most sequences are not like times tables in that they do not start on the first multiple.
Believing that all sequences are linear	Students need exposure to a range of sequences including those with term-to-term rules involving multiplication and division or combinations of the four operations. They could also explore sequences like the Fibonacci sequence where the term-to-term rule is based on two previous terms to widen their understanding of what a sequence is.
Producing or continuing a visual pattern incorrectly by failing to apply the same rule each time they create a new term For example, students may say that this pattern reflects the sequence 1, 2, 3, 4, ... but it does not grow in a uniform way and so is not a sequence.	Ask students to describe how the pattern grows from term to term. Ensure they describe the images and not the numbers. If necessary, ask them whether it is the same between each pair of terms to help see that it is not and so the visual pattern is incorrect (even though it has the right number of squares in each term).

Developing conceptual understanding

7As1 Generate terms of an integer sequence and find a term given its position in the sequence; find simple term-to-term rules.

- FIX: Use arrows to link each term of the sequence, labelling them with the calculations for the term-to-term rule.

  For example: For a sequence with term-to-term rule 'multiply by 2 and add 1' with first term 3:

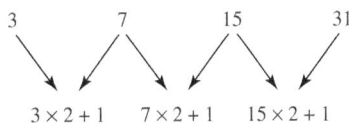

  $$3 \qquad 7 \qquad 15 \qquad 31$$
  $$3 \times 2 + 1 \qquad 7 \times 2 + 1 \qquad 15 \times 2 + 1$$

- FIX: Use a table to relate the position to the term to help with generating sequences using a position-to-term rule.

  For example, for a position-to-term rule of 'add 3 and multiply by 4' could look like this:

Position Number	1	2	3	4	5
	$(1 + 3) \times 4$	$(2 + 3) \times 4$	$(3 + 3) \times 4$	$(4 + 3) \times 4$	$(5 + 3) \times 4$
Term	= 16	= 20	= 24	= 28	= 32

- FIX: When finding term-to-term rules, it can help to write the sequence first and continue it, before naming the rule.

  For example, if the first 3 terms are 1, 4, 10 ... can the student suggest the next term? If so, they can then work backwards to see what operations they used.

TIP: Try matching sequences and their rules first before trying to come up with their rules. The matching cards in the online photocopiable resources are a good way of doing this.

STRETCH: Students working at greater depth can suggest multiple term-to-term rules that could relate the first two terms of a sequence.

For example, given the first two terms of 7 and then 10 the term-to-term rule could be:

- Add 3
- Multiply by 2 and subtract 4
- Subtract 2 and multiply by 2
- Multiply by 3 and subtract 11
- Add 13 and divide by 2
- and so on …

7As2 Generate sequences from spatial patterns and describe the general term in simple cases.

- FIX: Show students a range of visual sequences and get them to

  a) convert these into numbers to help them see how they are growing numerically

  b) look for the position numbers in each pattern.

- FIX: Use concrete objects such as counters or cubes to build patterns directly. Students can then find the next term in the pattern before counting the key parts of the pattern to find a number sequence. They can also move the objects together to see how they relate to the position number.

STRETCH: Ask students to find the general term in more complex sequences, where the position number is not just multiplied by a constant or added to a constant.

For example, for this pattern:

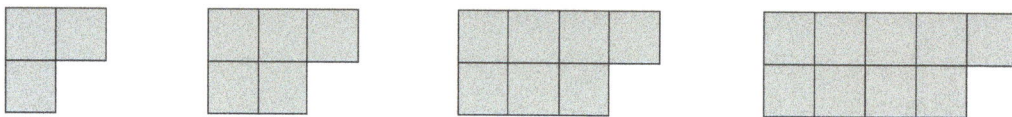

students might separate the 'extra 1' out each time to help them see the pattern as a rectangle of position number x 2 attached to a single extra 1.

End of chapter mental maths exercise

1. Give the next 3 terms of this sequence: 17, 24, 31, ...	6. The position-to-term rule of a sequence is 'divide by 3'. Find the 42nd term.
2. Give the next 3 terms of this sequence: 33, 23, 13, ...	7. The position-to-term rule of a sequence is 'add 5 and multiply by 2. Find the 42nd term.
3. Give the next term in this sequence: 1, 3, 6, 10, ...	8. The first two terms of a sequence are 9 and 13. Give two possibilities for what the term-to-term rule could be.
4. The first term of a sequence is 7 and the term-to-term rule is 'multiply by 2'. Give the next 3 terms of the sequence.	9. The 3rd term of a sequence is 12. Give two possibilities for what the position-to-term rule could be.
5. The first term of a sequence is 7 and the term-to-term rule is 'add 3 and divide by 2'. Give the next 3 terms of the sequence.	

Technology recommendations

- Use spreadsheets to generate the next terms of a sequence using either a term-to-term rule.

  For example, here is a spreadsheet to generate the sequence formed using a term-to-term rule of 'multiply by 2 and subtract 3':

	A	B
1	Position	Term
2	1	10
3	2	=B2*2-3
4	3	=B3*2-3
5	4	=B4*2-3
6	5	=B5*2-3
7	6	=B6*2-3
8	7	=B7*2-3
9	8	=B8*2-3
10	9	=B9*2-3
11	10	=B10*2-3
12	11	=B11*2-3
13	12	=B12*2-3
14	13	=B13*2-3

  Students can edit the first term, which is currently 10, to see the effect on the rest of the sequence.

- Similarly, use spreadsheets to generate the next terms of a sequence using a position-to-term rule.

  In this case, students do not need to enter a first term (since it will be calculated by the rule). However, it can be useful to let them discover this in contrast to the term-to-term rule above.

Investigation/research tasks

- **1, 2, ...**   *Problem solving*

  How many different sequences can you find that begin 1, 2, ...?

  For each sequence:

  o write the number pattern
  o write the term-to-term rule
  o draw a visual sequence representing the numbers that shows how the pattern grows using your term-to-term rule.

BEWARE: Students may produce visual diagrams that do not actually form a sequence. If this happens, ask them to explain the term-to-term rule of their visual pattern and also to show how it grows in the same way between each pair of terms.

TIP: Get students to draw at least four terms of the visual sequence so you can see how it is growing.

Here are four possible examples:

Sequence	Term-to-term rule	Visual example
1, 2, 3, 4, ...	Add 1	
1, 2, 4, 8, ...	Multiply by 2	
1, 2, 3, 5, 8, ...	Add two previous terms together	
1, 2, 4, 7, 11, ...	Add 1 more than previous difference	

- Use the internet to investigate the Fibonacci sequence, which was first documented by Leonardo Fibonacci.

  Write the sequence when the first two terms are 1 and 1.

  What if the first two terms are 10 and 12?

  What is the term-to-term rule?

  Why is the Fibonacci sequence so interesting?

  Give some examples of where the sequences or its terms are found in nature. For instance, you could investigate flower petals, bees or rabbit populations.

- **Challenge: Bacteria Multiplying**   *Problem solving*

  In biology bacteria reproduce through the process of binary fission. This is where one cell copies its DNA and simply splits into two cells.

  The new cell is identical to the original cell.

  We say that each time the cells split a new 'generation' is made.

  If you start with one cell, how many generations will it take to get

  a) 16 cells?
  b) 128 cells?
  c) 1024 cells?
  d) over 50 000 cells?

  What is the term-to-term rule for this sequence?

BEWARE: This task is a challenging sequence because it is based on a term-to-term rule of multiplying by 2. This generates large numbers quickly and so students need to be disciplined about recording them carefully.

Once students have listed the first few terms of the sequence and continued it, they could think about the structure more carefully to help them work out when the number of cells will be greater than 50 000. In particular, they could use a calculator to try multiplying by different powers of 2. For example, if they know that 1024 cells is the 11th generation, then what will happen if we multiply by 1024 by another 1024 or another 11 generations later? Can they predict what the number of cells at the 22nd generation will be?

TIP: Students would benefit from a calculator once the initial small calculations are complete to help them quickly test combinations.

2D shapes

Learning objectives

Learning objectives covered in this chapter: 7Gs1, 7Gs2, 7Gs3

- Identify, describe, visualise and draw 2D shapes in different orientations.
- Use the notation and labelling conventions for points, lines, angles and shapes.
- Name and identify side, angle and symmetry properties of special quadrilaterals and triangles, and regular polygons with 5, 6 and 8 sides.

Key terms

- polygon
- triangle
- quadrilateral
- pentagon
- hexagon
- heptagon
- octagon
- regular
- irregular
- parallel
- equilateral, isosceles, scalene, right-angled
- square, rectangle, rhombus, parallelogram, trapezium, kite, delta dart

Prior knowledge assumptions

- Students are familiar with the meaning of polygon.
- Students understand the difference between a regular and an irregular polygon.
- Students know the names of polygons with 3, 4, 5, 6 and 8 sides.
- Students understand the meaning of sides and vertices.
- Students know the names and features of common 2D shapes, such as equilateral triangles, squares, rectangles and parallelograms.
- Students can recognise a right angle.
- Students can recognise parallel lines.
- Students can find lines of symmetry.

Guidance on the hook   *Problem solving*

Purpose: This task is designed to revise students' knowledge of shape names and properties as well as challenge them to use their creativity and systematic problem solving skills.

Use of the hook: Give students cut outs of six equilateral triangles (see photocopiable resources online).

Ask them to use as many of them as they wish to produce a polygon (closed shape).

Ask them to draw their shape using isometric paper and then rearrange the triangles to produce another shape and so on.

Once students have exhausted their lists of possible shapes, bring the class back together to discuss and share their answers.

Ask students to categorise the shapes they have made as triangles, quadrilaterals, pentagons and so on. Are all of these possible? What is the largest number of sides that can be made using the triangles?

Ask students whether they can name all the different types of quadrilateral that they have made. Are there any quadrilaterals that they cannot make?

Adaptation: You could restrict students to having to use exactly one triangle, then two triangles, then three triangles and so on to help them work more systematically.

Alternatively, you could start by asking students to produce a list of shape names that they can remember. They can then try to make as many of them as possible. You could discuss any that cannot be made as well as any shapes that they can make that they do not know the name of.

Extension: Students working at greater depth could classify their shapes (using their own criteria or those that you give them) to produce a 'shape family tree'. They should label the sections of the tree to show the categories as well as individual shape names.

Starter ideas

Game: Describe it!

Select a student to be the describer. Give them the pack of vocabulary cards made from the template in the online photocopiable resources.

The student must describe as many of the words as possible during 30 seconds using mathematical language, while the rest of the class must guess the word being described.

The student must not say the word on the card!

Keep score of the number of words correctly described and guessed by the group.

Then give other students turns as the describer to see who can achieve the highest score.

Start point check: Guess my shape

Play 20-questions style game where students must guess the teacher's shape using yes/no questions. For example: Does the shape contain a right angle? Does the shape have more than five sides? Does the shape have a line of symmetry?

The teacher can only answer yes or no and the students have to try to work out the shape in fewer than 20 questions.

I like …

Give the students a property of shapes that you like.

For example, I like shapes with a right angle or I like shapes with one line of symmetry.

Students must then try to draw (or name) as many shapes as they can that meet this criterion.

You can share these shapes on the board to produce a class collection and to find out how many are possible.

> TIP: You can make this more challenging by giving two criteria for your shape to restrict the number of shapes that are possible.

Discussion ideas

Probing questions	Teacher prompts
What kinds of triangle can be right-angled? How do you know?	Ask students to try to draw: – an equilateral triangle that has a right angle – an isosceles triangle that has a right angle – a scalene triangle that has a right angle. BEWARE: Students may assume that isosceles is not possible. You could try thinking about the angles in a triangle to ask them what the other two angles could be if one has to be 90 degrees. Students should realise that the definitions of scalene, isosceles and equilateral cannot overlap but that both scalene and isosceles triangles can be right-angled, whereas equilateral triangles cannot.
Is a square a parallelogram? Is a trapezium a parallelogram? Explain.	Encourage students to start by reviewing the definition of a parallelogram: a quadrilateral with 2 pairs of parallel sides. Then ask them whether this applies to a square too? Does it matter that a square has extra features? What about a trapezium? Ask similar questions to get students to begin to form the 'family-tree' of shapes.
What's the same and what's different? • scalene, isosceles, equilateral, right-angled triangles • square and rectangle • trapezium, rectangle, parallelogram, kite	Use these questions to encourage students to articulate the specific properties of each shape first, before saying which of them are shared and which are specific to one shape only. You could encourage students to use a Venn diagram to record their properties. TIP: It can help for them to draw a diagram of each to annotate.
What is the difference between a regular polygon and an irregular one?	You could ask students to draw a regular polygon and then to make it irregular by a small alteration. This helps them see that irregular shapes do not have to be really far from regular shapes to still be described as irregular – these just need not all sides equal or not all angles equal. Ask whether a rhombus is regular as a follow up.
Why do we label angles like this? *ABC* Can you draw this angle?	Try to get students to draw the lines *AB* and then *BC* first to establish the angle. Also ask them 'why do we not just say angle B?' to get them to see that there can be multiple angles at vertex B. TIP: It can help students to trace the letters in the angle around the diagram to form the lines of the angle.

Common errors/misconceptions

Misconception	Strategies to address
Thinking that categories of shapes do not overlap For example, thinking that a square cannot be a rectangle.	Define a rectangle first and then ask students whether a square also fits this definition. You could ask students to try building a set diagram to show quadrilaterals and how they overlap.
Being imprecise with language For example, referring to 'a parallel side' rather than a pair of parallel sides. Similarly, not stating whether equal length sides are opposite or adjacent. For example, saying 'a kite has 2 pairs of equal length sides' is correct but to be more precise 'a kite has 2 pairs of equal length *adjacent* sides' (rather than a parallelogram which has 2 pairs of equal length *opposite* sides).	Ask students to draw 'a parallel line' to help them realise that this does not mean anything without a second line. Model accurate mathematical language. Ask students to rewrite or re-attempt their explanations where the language needs refinement.
Believing that irregular shapes must be asymmetrical	Recap the definition of regular and then irregular. Ask students to show that an isosceles trapezium or an isosceles pentagon are irregular. Also consider a rhombus to show that a shape having all equal sides is not sufficient to be regular.
Giving too much or too little information to define a shape For example, defining a square as having 4 sides. Or defining an isosceles triangle as having two equal sides <u>and</u> two equal angles.	Draw a shape that meets the students' definition (for example, that has 4 sides but is not a square, for example, a kite) to show them that they need to say more.
Identifying the wrong angle in a diagram or mislabelling a given angle, usually by putting the letters in the wrong order	Encourage students to draw along the sides of the angle in order to help identify it on a diagram.
Believing a shape has a line of symmetry where in fact it does not For example, saying that the diagonals of a rectangle are lines of symmetry.	Give students shapes to fold to test whether a possible line is in fact a line of symmetry.

Developing conceptual understanding

7Gs1 Identify, describe, visualise and draw 2D shapes in different orientations.

* Provide students with cut-out shapes made of paper or card so that they can manipulate them, rotate them, turn them over and so on to recognise the same shape in different positions (see shape cut-out sheet in the online photocopiable resources).

- FIX: Use geoboards and elastic bands to help students make their own shapes on a grid and adjust these as they go. For example, students could make a rectangle on the grid and then adjust this to form a parallelogram (not a rectangle).

> TIP: Alternatively you can use dotty paper to sketch these shapes instead of making them practically. It is a good idea to use both square and isometric dotty paper to give students experience of both grids.

- Ask students to sketch shapes with given features to help them to recall the key terms and explore the range of shapes that meet these names.

    For example: Sketch:

    a) a rectangle of length 7 units and width 3 units

    b) a quadrilateral with four equal sides

    c) a triangle with all sides of different length

    d) a hexagon

    e) a quadrilateral with all sides of different length

    f) a heptagon

    g) a shape that is not a polygon

    h) a semicircle with the straight edge **parallel** to the side of your page

    i) a quadrilateral that does not have opposite sides of equal length

    j) a triangle with an obtuse angle

7Gs2 Use the notation and labelling conventions for points, lines, angles and shapes.

- FIX: Ensure students are confident in labelling a shape, line and an angle using the vertices (capital letters).

    For example:

    o Shape $ABCD$ is the shape made by connecting vertex A to vertex B to vertex C to vertex D and then back to vertex A.
    o Line AB is the line made by connecting vertex A to vertex B.
    o Angle $\angle ABC$ is the angle formed by connecting vertex A to vertex B to vertex C.

STRETCH: Give students instructions to sketch a shape using this notation. For example:

Shape $ABCD$ is a kite. $\angle DAB = \angle DCB = 130°$, $AB = BC = 3$ cm.

7Gs3 Name and identify side, angle and symmetry properties of special quadrilaterals and triangles, and regular polygons with 5, 6 and 8 sides.

- FIX: Provide students with cut-out shapes made of paper or card so that they can manipulate them, measure the sides, fold them and so on to discover their properties (see shape cut-out sheet in the online photocopiable resources).

    Use the cut-out shapes to classify and categorise shapes using Venn diagrams and Carroll diagrams.

- FIX: Use a geoboard with elastic bands or a square-dotty grid to produce as many different shapes as possible

---

STRETCH: Students working at greater depth could design a quadrilateral diagnosis machine using yes/no questions. The aim is to take any shape and use yes/no questions to determine its identity. You could start by doing this for triangles to get the idea.

STRETCH: Explain why is it not possible to sketch the following:

a) a rectangle with an acute angle

b) a triangle with parallel sides.

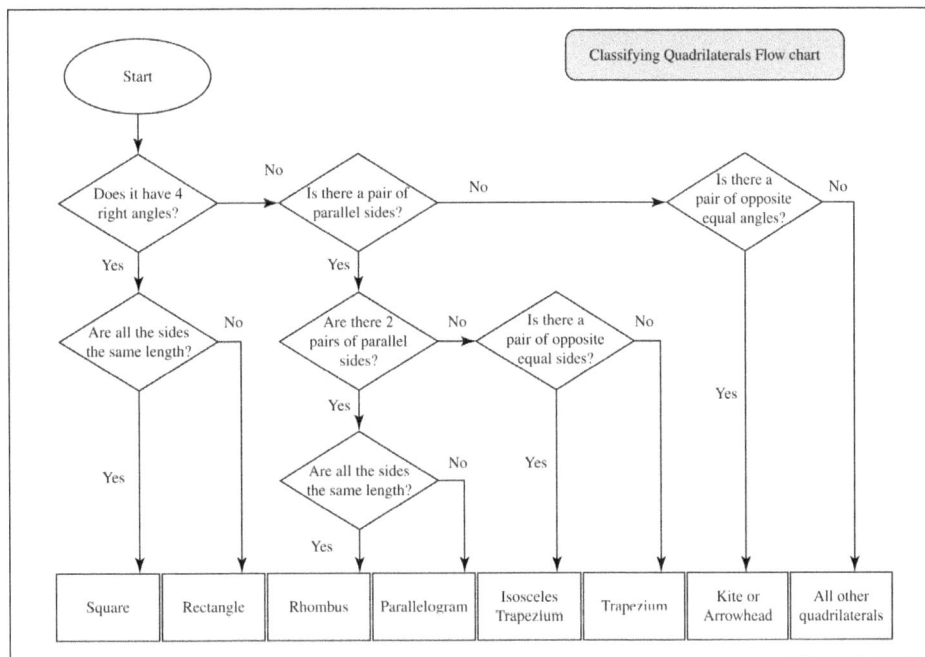

Classifying Quadrilaterals Flow chart

End of chapter mental maths exercise

1. A quadrilateral has two pairs of equal length, adjacent sides. Draw a sketch of the shape and name it.	5. Write down the number of lines of symmetry of a parallelogram.
2. Sketch a decagon.	6. Visualise a rectangle in your head. Fold the rectangle along the diagonal. Sketch the resulting shape.
3. A quadrilateral has diagonals that meet at right angles. Sketch three possible shapes.	7. *Challenge:* Sketch a trapezium. Rotate the trapezium half a turn around the midpoint of one of its sides. Sketch the new shape. What shape has been formed by the original and new trapezium together?
4. Visualise a square in your head. Fold it once along the diagonal to create a triangle. Write down whether the resulting triangle is isosceles, scalene or equilateral.	

Technology recommendations

- Use dynamic geometry software to produce shapes, for example, to produce the different types of quadrilateral.

  Students can then go on to identify the similarities and differences between their shapes.

  For example, they could explore draw a square just by positioning four points and connecting them, then manipulate the locations of these vertices to change the shape and turn it into a different shape.

TIP: Use a grid layout on the software to help students position their vertices to make the different quadrilaterals etc. Usually the points will snap to the grid to make things easier.

Challenge: Can the students produce a square that cannot be changed when one of the vertices is moved?   *Problem solving*

• Using the internet, research less familiar 2D shapes to find out what they look like and their features. For example, students could investigate an isosceles trapezium, an annulus or an isosceles pentagon.

Can the students find any other shapes that they have not yet studied? Which of these are polygons?

Investigation/research tasks

• **Tangrams**   *Problem solving*

Here is a tangram:

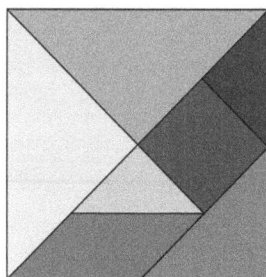

Which shapes can you see here individually?

If you cut the shapes out, which other shapes can you make by putting two or more pieces together? Draw the shapes you can make and name these.

How do you know you have found all possible shapes?

Categorise the shapes you have made. You could use a diagram to do this.

TIP: Give students a cut-out copy of the tangram shown. These are available in the online photocopiable resources. They can then draw round their pieces to record their findings or produce smaller sketches.

• Research the names of polygons with different numbers of sides.

Make a list of polygon names for sides up to 12. What about the names of polygons with twenty, fifty or one hundred sides?

Where do these names link to words in real life?

• **Right-Angled Triangle Building Blocks**   *Problem solving*

Try fitting two right-angled triangles together to make a rectangle, a kite, a parallelogram, a pentagon, a hexagon, an isosceles triangle, another quadrilateral, ...

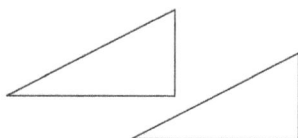

Which other shapes can be made?

Are there any shapes that cannot be produced?

Why is this?

> TIP: Give students two identical right-angled triangles as cut outs to help them investigate this initially.

> TIP: Ask students to consider which sides could be joined and what the result of this is.

You could give students further triangles to then investigate the shapes that can be made from three, four and five right-angled triangles and so on.

Estimating angles

Learning objectives

Learning objectives covered in this chapter: 7Gs4

- Estimate the size of acute, obtuse and reflex angles to the nearest 10°.

Key terms

- estimate
- measure
- degree(s)
- acute
- right (angle)
- obtuse
- straight (line)
- reflex

Prior knowledge assumptions

- Students understand that an angle is a measure of turn and know that it is measured in degrees.
- Students can confidently recognise and draw right angles; they know that a right angle is 90°.
- Students are familiar with acute and obtuse angles and can say whether a particular angle is acute or obtuse.

Guidance on the hook

Purpose: To relate angles to real-life measures of turn and direction using compass points.

Use of the hook: Ask the students to stand up and face the same direction. Call this direction North.

Now ask the students to start from North each time and:

- turn to face East. How many degrees have you turned? Did it matter which way you turned?

- turn to face South? How many degrees have you turned? Did it matter which way you turned?

- turn clockwise to face North-East (halfway between North and East). How many degrees must this be?

- turn clockwise to face North-North-East (halfway between North and North-East). How many degrees must this be?

Give students a copy of a compass to label with the degrees for each turn from North.

Discuss the number of degrees for each quarter turn.

Then discuss the number of degrees for each halfway point (eighth of a turn).

Extension: You could ask students to calculate the number of degrees to turn between two directions: for example, from NE to SSW. They could also explore the number of degrees needed to turn clockwise and anticlockwise to see if there is a link.

Starter ideas

Mental maths exercise

What is halfway between 90° and 180°?	What is halfway between 180° and 360°?	What is halfway between 180° and 270°?	What is halfway between 270° and 360°?
Calculate 180 + 38	Calculate 180 + 54	Calculate 180 + 126	Calculate 180 + 157
Calculate 180 – 24	Calculate 180 – 37	Calculate 180 – 98	Calculate 180 – 87
Calculate 360 – 35	Calculate 360 – 42	Calculate 360 – 145	Calculate 360 – 168
I am thinking of an acute angle. It is a multiple of 5 and greater than 50°. What could my angle be?	I am thinking of an obtuse angle. It is divisible by 3 and its last digit is 2. What could my angle be?	I am thinking of an obtuse angle. It is a prime number. What could my angle be?	I am thinking of a reflex angle. It is divisible by 10 and by 7. What could my angle be?

Start point check: Angle family

Ask the students to use their arms to form a right angle (an acute angle, an obtuse angle, a straight line, a 45° angle and so on).

Practical angles

Stand the students in a circle and place yourself in the middle.

Use some string to form a line between you and one student.

Then, use another piece of string to form a second line, which revolves around the circle by passing the end from one student to the next.

Get the students to stop at various points and ask them:

* Do we have an acute/obtuse/reflex angle?
* Roughly how many degrees is our angle?
* Is our angle close to a right-angle/straight line?

TIP: If students find this hard, you can also encourage them to count in 10s as the angle changes from 0° to 360°.

Estimate my angle

Split the students into teams.

Draw an angle on the board and ask each team to estimate the value of the angle.

They could write their solutions of mini-whiteboards and then reveal at the same time.

You can measure the angle with a protractor to check its value or, if you are using electronic resources, you can measure it directly.

The team that is closest to the real value gets a point.

Alternatively, you could award 3 points for an exact answer, 2 points for being up to 10° away and 1 point for being up to 20° away.

Discussion ideas

Probing questions	Teacher prompts
Always, Sometimes, Never? Reflex angles have an acute angle on their 'other side'.	Encourage students to draw some reflex angles to investigate the size and type of angles that are left to make up the full turn. This will help them discover that it is possible to have an obtuse angle paired with a reflex angle to make whole turn too.
Is an angle of 260° more or less than a three-quarter turn? Explain how you know.	Prompt students to recall the values of quarter turns in degrees rapidly. They could relate this to the 9 times table to help them find multiples of 90 quickly. Follow up with other angle values and ask them to think which multiples of 90 they are close to and hence what the approximate size must be.
True or False? You cannot have an angle of more than 360°.	Look for students recognising that any angle greater than 360° will appear the same as one that is smaller than 360°. However, also look for them recognising that you can turn more than 360°, by turning more than one full turn. BEWARE: Students may think you have to stop turning at a full turn or 360°. Try asking them to turn 1 and a half turns clockwise from a given starting direction to help them to realise that it is possible to turn more than 360°.
What's the same and what's different? 15° and 345° How many pairs of angles are there like this?	Look for use of descriptor of acute and reflex as well as recognition that the angles form a pair to make 360°. Encourage students to list their angle pairs systematically to help them realise that there is a pattern. You could allow only whole numbers of degrees or decimals too.

Common errors/misconceptions

Misconception	Strategies to address
Misconstruing an angle as a measure of distance rather than of turn For this reason, some students do not recognise equal angles drawn with different length line and they may say that an angle is bigger because it has longer lines. For example, students might say that these angles were not equal: 	Act out the process of an angle being formed by turning using string and a circle of people as explained above. Explicitly do this with different sized circles/string to help students realise that it is the turn that matters, not the length of the string or the distance between each piece.
Finding it hard to work with a scale centred around 90 and 360 For example, some students cannot quickly find half of 90 or a quarter of it to use their sense of the size in a numeric way. Reflex angles are particularly challenging because they cover an area twice the size of acute and obtuse.	Work with mental maths strategies based on factors and multiples of 90 to develop number sense that supports this work.
Being unsure which angle is being referred to where there is a choice of a reflex and an acute/obtuse	Ask students, 'What is the size of angle C on this diagram?' This should help them realise that we don't know which of the two angles is required. Check students are using the correct vocabulary and marking angles correctly. You could refer back to the notation and identification of angles in Ch8 to help here.
Forgetting to use units	Prompt to include units at the end of each answer.

Developing conceptual understanding

7Gs4 Estimate the size of acute, obtuse and reflex angles to the nearest 10°.

- FIX: Students who are struggling to get a sense of the size of an angle could work with an overlay of an angle measurer showing angles in multiples of 10°. This can help them develop a sense of the size of angles prior to estimating abstractly.

TIP: Give students angles in increasing size to begin with to help them use their previous answer to help them estimate the next angle.

TIP: Encourage students to turn their images to help them if necessary – it is often easier to estimate an angle where one of the lines is either horizontal or vertical.

STRETCH: Students could estimate angles within known shapes, bringing in their knowledge of shape properties to help. For example, they could estimate the interior angles of a kite and then check whether this makes a total of 360°.

STRETCH: Students working at greater depth could also begin to estimate angles to a greater accuracy than the nearest 10° where they can relate the angle to a property, for example, 135°.

End of chapter mental maths exercise

1. Find 4 factor pairs of 90.	6. I turn angle of 20°. I then turn a quarter turn – how many degrees have I turned altogether?
2. What is halfway between 90 and 180?	
3. Find the angle that pairs with 285° to make a full turn.	7. I turn angle of 72°. I then turn a three quarter turn – how many degrees have I turned altogether?
4. Find the angle that pairs with 93° to make a straight line.	8. How many degrees will I have turned if I complete two full turns?
5. Calculate 360 – 112.	

Technology recommendations

- Use dynamic geometry software to produce and then measure angles accurately to aid discussion and practice of estimation.

  For instance, draw an angle, then ask students to predict its size before revealing the answer using the measuring tool.

- Use a simple programming language such as LOGO to recreate shapes such as hexagons, and stars.

  To do this successfully they will have to estimate the angles first and then programme them in.

  See photocopiable resources, available online, for examples of shapes that could be produced.

Investigation/research tasks

- Estimate each of the angles in this pentagon.

  Use these to estimate the total of the angles in the pentagon.

  You could average your class's estimates to see if you can find the true total!

Is this always true? Investigate further!

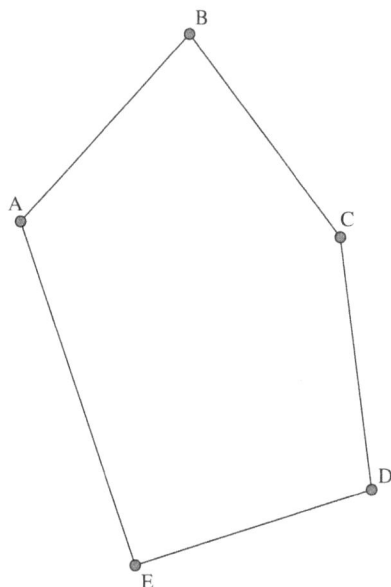

Students could then go on to investigate other polygons, for example, octagons.

- Research the role played by angles in different sports.

  Find some photos of sports being played and estimate the angles that you see in them.

- Directions challenge:

  Take the students to a large space like a hall or playground.

  Spread the students out so they have space between them.

  Give them directions to follow with their eyes shut to see if they can end up the same relative distance from the others.

  For example: walk forward 2 metres, turn clockwise through an angle of 90°, walk forward 3 metres, then turn anticlockwise through an angle of 120°.

  Then ask students to come up with their own directions to get from a given start point to an end point. They should include angles and turns in their instructions.

  Swap over the students' instructions and test them out to see if they work.

  Ask the students, 'how many different sets of instructions are there to get from point *A* to point *B*'?

Data collection

Learning objectives

Learning objectives covered in this chapter: 7Dc1, 7Dc2

- Decide which data would be relevant to an enquiry and collect and organise the data.
- Design and use a data collection sheet or questionnaire for a simple survey.

Key terms

- questionnaire
- data
- data collection sheet
- table
- frequency table
- biased
- representative
- leading (questions)

Prior knowledge assumptions

- Students are familiar with data as shown in a list or in a frequency table, and have experience of producing such tables to collect data themselves.
- Students have used questionnaires and surveys and can begin to structure one themselves.
- Students have experience of collecting data, although this may have been recorded on a given data collection sheet.

Guidance on the hook

Purpose: This task is a practical opportunity to apply the data handling cycle.

Use of the hook: Begin by asking the students what they know about pulse rates and what they could hypothesise.

Ask them to list data that would be relevant.

They can also design the data collection sheets: at this stage, enable students to experiment to work out what is important.

Students can then collect the data: Show students how to measure their own pulse at the wrist. Ask all the students to calculate an estimate of their pulse rate at the same time and write this down.

Then set a timer for 1 minute and ask the students to run on the spot throughout that time. Ask the students to calculate their pulse rate again straight afterwards and to write it down.

Now ask the students to work in groups to collate their data. How useful is their data collection sheet? Are there any issues? Would it work if they had to collect hundreds of people's pulse rates?

Discuss what the pulse rates were before and after exercise. Was there a change? Why might this be?

What data might you collect next to investigate further?

Adaptation: You could collect the data centrally using a list and a table and add some additional information, for example, gender, asking students to complete their own entry to see which is the most useful format.

Extension: Students could suggest information that is best obtained from an experiment and information that is best obtained from a questionnaire. Why are pulse rates difficult to capture using a questionnaire?

Starter ideas

Start point check

Ask the students to imagine that the school is going to open a café for the students to use after school. Tell them they will need to decide what items to sell and how much to stock. They will be able to complete a questionnaire with a large number of students to help them.

Ask the students to work in groups to decide:

1. decide the data they need to find from their questionnaire
2. draft the specific questions they could ask
3. design the data collection sheet for the questionnaire
4. who they will ask to complete the questionnaire.

> TIP: Emphasise with students the importance of checking if their answer makes sense.

Alternatively, you could bring the groups together to arrive at a whole class questionnaire that amalgamates their ideas.

Vocabulary

Put the students in pairs.

Read each sentence below with a missing word/phrase and ask the students to complete the missing word/phrase in their pairs. You could get them to record their word/phrase on a piece of paper or mini-whiteboard and then reveal their answers at the same time. Award each pair 1 point if they have chosen a suitable word/phrase.

The most common ways to collect your own data is to complete a .... or perform an .... (questionnaire or survey/experiment)

Questions should not be .... (leading/biased)

If you use response boxes, then it must be possible for everyone to .... (select a box)

Questions in a questionnaire could include .... (tick boxes, yes/no answers, rankings, written answers).

Questionnaires should be detailed enough to .... (collect the data you need) but not so detailed that .... (they take too long to collect the data).

Before you survey people you should .... (design your questionnaire carefully/complete a pilot questionnaire/think about which data you actually need to collect/test your questions out).

Game: Data sort

Split the students into two teams.

Give the students a hypothesis or question and ask one student from each team to come to the board to give an example of relevant data for this inquiry. Continue with another student from each team until the students run out of ideas. Award 1 point per relevant piece of data.

For example:

'Do older people walk more than younger people?'

'Do people in towns earn more than people in the countryside?'

'Do students who are punctual do better academically?'

'Are people who are good at estimating lengths, also good at estimating weights?'

> BEWARE: Students may suggest data that could be useful but do not directly relate to the hypothesis or question.

They may do this because they want to check they have a representative sample but they may just be listing information that could be found, rather than relevant information.

Discussion ideas

Probing questions	Teacher prompts
Explain why these questions are leading: Questions that begin "Do you agree that ...." "Do you think like me that...." "Are you in favour of ...."	It can be useful to actually ask students a question like this to enable them to see how they might respond. You could then ask students to come up with some other question stems that are leading.
Dana is investigating people's opinions about the theatre. Why would it not be a good idea to collect data in a theatre lobby?	Encourage students to explain that asking people in a theatre may not be typical members of the public because they are likely to be regular theatre users. They can then come up with similar examples where the location/timing may affect the answers to a questionnaire.
How likely are people to tell the truth when completing a questionnaire? Suggest some situations or topics where they are less likely to be honest.	Encourage students to think about examples where the person's answers may affect someone's view of them (for example, health issues, political viewpoints) and/or where people know a questionnaire is not anonymous.
Jemma is investigating whether males are quicker at mental arithmetic than females. She conducts an experiment with 50 males and 50 females. Why might Jemma want to collect information about the age of the people completing her experiment?	Encourage students to explain that, while this data is not relevant to Jemma's question, she also wants to check that her two samples of males and females are similar in other ways (including age) to rule out any effect from other variables.

Common errors/misconceptions

Misconception	Strategies to address
Being unable to identify relevant data for an inquiry	Take the students forward to the processing of their data (making calculations, drawing graphs) to help them see why they do not need this data (and hence why it is a waste of time to collect it).
Not considering whether a questionnaire sheet a used to collect the information of just one person at a time (for example, a postal survey) or to collect the information of many people on the same sheet (for example, a questionnaire on the telephone)	Encourage students to think about how they will complete their data collection sheets in practice, using a pilot if necessary to spot these issues. Doing the questionnaire themselves can help identify any issues.
Questionnaires: – writing leading questions – writing questions that lack a time period (for example, how many hours of television do you watch rather than how many hours of television do you watch at the weekend?) – using response boxes that overlap – using response boxes that do not cover all possible answers (omitting an 'other' box or 0 or a 'more than' box)	Provide an example of their questions and ask them to answer it themselves. This will help students realise that this cannot be answered! Encourage students to think about the range of expected responses they will get to each question.
Recording too specific an answer on a data collection sheet For example, recording someone's age exactly so that all the data is in a list, rather than using categories.	It can be useful to collect data like this initially to discover why it is not helpful directly. Show students how to use categories (classes) to group data.

Developing conceptual understanding

7Dc1 Decide which data would be relevant to an enquiry and collect and organise the data.

- FIX: Encourage students who are struggling with constructing questionnaires to answer their questionnaires themselves. This will help them recognise the weaknesses. You can also respond to their questionnaire with a deliberately challenging answer (for example, a response not catered for) to encourage them to edit their questions

> TIP: It is useful to provide the opportunity for students to complete the full cycle of data handling at least once. This will help them to see why some data is not relevant or not useful in the form it is collected.

- Use extreme examples initially to help students understand how to choose who to ask. For instance, discuss making a decision about the quality of the school food by asking the school catering staff to answer a questionnaire.

STRETCH: Students working at greater depth can begin to think about other ways that data can be collected. For example, using data used when signing up for a new email address, using information collected by loyalty cards in supermarkets, and so on.

7Dc2 Design and use a data collection sheet or questionnaire for a simple survey.

- FIX: You can provide templates for frequency tables to students who are struggling to construct these. The students then need only fill in the categories and complete the tally/frequency.

- Students should also begin to consider how to group data to make data collection easier. For example, if they are investigating the amounts of pocket money received, they may want to create groups or categories for their data collection sheet. You could use the secondary data in the photocopiable resources section online as a starting point for constructing tables and so on.

End of chapter mental maths exercise

1. Find the total of these frequencies: 7, 11, 14, 21 2. 132 people complete Amy's survey. One quarter of them are children. How many are children? 3. Joseph surveys 29 students in each of Year 7, Year 8, Year 9 and Year 10. How many students does he survey altogether? 4. Bill has carried out an experiment with 81 participants. He needs to complete the experiment with 220 people altogether. How many more people does Bill need to complete the experiment?	5. In a survey about the number of hours they work each day, 11 people said they worked 10 hours and 5 people said they worked 8 hours. How many hours did they work altogether? 6. What is halfway between $35 and $75?

Technology recommendations

- Use a spreadsheet to create and dynamically edit data collection sheets. You can model this as a teacher or ask students to use the spreadsheet themselves.

- Use word processing programs to produce questionnaires to investigate a given hypothesis. These can then be tested out or piloted before being refined and amended.

Investigation/research tasks

- Use the internet to find out about some real surveys that take place, such as a national census or a poll.

  What data is collected?

  How is it collected?

- "More children are born in the first half of the year than the second half."

  Investigate.

  What data will you need to collect?

  Design a data collection sheet and complete your survey.

  How can you find out whether the statement is true?

  How reliable are your results?

Give students the opportunity to collect primary data themselves, for example, collecting birthdays of their classmates.

> TIP: Secondary data could also be used, such as the number of births per month/per quarter from national and international records.

- "Older people walk for longer each day than younger people."

  Investigate.

  What data will you need to collect/find?

  Look at the secondary data sheet provided.

  How can you organise the data to make it more useful?

  How can you find out whether the statement is true?

  How reliable are your results?

> TIP: Give students copies of the secondary data provided in the photocopiable resources section online as a starting point to focus on organising the data.

Probability 1

Learning objectives

Learning objectives covered in this chapter: 7Db1, 7Db2, 7Db3

- Use the language of probability to describe and interpret results involving likelihood and chance.
- Understand and use the probability scale from 0 to 1.
- Find probabilities based on equally likely outcomes in simple contexts.

Key terms

- outcome
- event
- probability
- probability scale
- likely
- unlikely
- evens
- at random
- notation: P(event)
- fair

Prior knowledge assumptions

- Students can use the language of probability, for example, words like chance, certain, impossible and likely.
- Students know how to write fractions and decimals.
- Students can position numbers on number scales.

Guidance on the hook   *Problem solving*

Purpose: A game to help students recognise that not all outcomes are equally likely and to develop a strategy to improve their chance of winning.

Use of the Hook: Play the Dice Bingo activity from the Student's Book.

Students need to start by drawing a 3 by 3 bingo grid each.

Ask students to pick their own numbers from 1 to 12 for their first go without explaining any further.

Discuss what happened with the students afterwards: they should discover that not all totals are equally likely and begin to work out which totals are the most likely. You can also ask students which numbers are best avoided and which should be used in the middle of the grid.

Then ask students to repeat the game but this time to select their numbers to maximise their chance of winning.

Adaptation: You could play the game as a whole class, with each student working on their own grid using numbers rolled by one pair of dice at the front. This can allow you to intervene and discuss certain outcomes as they appear.

Extension: You could ask students to predict what the most likely scores are from totalling the scores on <u>three dice</u>. Which number(s) would be best to use in the middle of the grid? Are there any numbers that should be avoided?

What if you were just using one dice?

Starter ideas

Mental maths starter

Give the decimal that lies halfway between 0.5 and 1	Give the decimal that lies halfway between 0.4 and 0.5	Give the decimal that lies halfway between 0.1 and 0.3	Give the decimal that lies halfway between 0.2 and 0.5
Simplify $\frac{8}{12}$	Simplify $\frac{3}{15}$	Simplify $\frac{8}{20}$	Simplify $\frac{21}{28}$
Find an equivalent fraction to $\frac{3}{4}$ with denominator 20	Find an equivalent fraction to $\frac{1}{3}$ with denominator 18	Find an equivalent fraction to $\frac{4}{5}$ with denominator 20	Find an equivalent fraction to $\frac{5}{6}$ with denominator 42
Give the decimal that is equivalent to $\frac{1}{4}$	Give the decimal that is equivalent to $\frac{2}{5}$	Give the decimal that is equivalent to $\frac{3}{10}$	Give the decimal that is equivalent to $\frac{17}{100}$
Give the simplest fraction that is equivalent to 0.1	Give the simplest fraction that is equivalent to 0.05	Give the simplest fraction that is equivalent to 0.8	Give the simplest fraction that is equivalent to 0.24

Start point check: Probability washing line

Create a washing line with string and pegs to represent a probability scale (note: you can simply draw this on the board if preferred).

Ask the students what each end point represents and label these.

Mark the midpoint on the line and ask the students what this represents.

Ask the students to describe the probability in words at each position on the line for example, certain or unlikely.

Give each student an event and ask them to position it on the correct place on the washing line.

Possible events:

- It rains tomorrow.
- It snows tomorrow.
- You go to bed before 11 p.m. this evening.
- You have school tomorrow.
- You have maths tomorrow.
- You eat breakfast tomorrow.
- You go to the Moon tomorrow.
- You walk to school tomorrow.
- You drop a drawing pin and it lands point up.
- A baby will be born in China today.
- It is someone in this class's birthday tomorrow.

Game/investigation: Higher or lower

Take a set of 0–9 digit cards.

Shuffle them.

Turn the top card over and ask students to predict whether the next card will be higher or lower.

Encourage them to reason based on
a) the position of the card turned over (for example, a 3 implies that the next card is likely to be higher)
b) the cards they know are left (if a 5 is turned over but the only cards left are a 2 and a 3 then this means the next card is certain to be lower).

Discussion ideas

Probing questions	Teacher prompts
Describe an event which has a probability of • 0 • 1 • 0.5 • 0.2 • $\frac{1}{3}$ • $\frac{1}{7}$	Encourage students to get used to assigning a number (fraction or decimal) to probabilities in situations where they have equally likely outcomes. Students could create spinners or bags of counters to help them. Days of the week are useful for sevenths. You could also relate this to the probability scale by asking students to position the fractions on the scale first, before they then finding an event with this probability.
I am rolling a dice. I have just rolled two 6s. What is the probability that I roll a 6 next?	Try to get students to see that these events are independent and (unless the dice is biased) the probabilities will be the same each time it is rolled. It can be useful to refer the dice as having 'no memory' to help students understand that the coin cannot take previous outcomes into account to even things out. TIP: It is worth considering the possibility of whether the coin is biased and if three 6s in a row is enough to suggest this.
Convince me that an impossible event will have a probability of 0.	Encourage students to express the probability as $\frac{0}{total\ number\ of\ outcomes}$ and realise that this always has value 0, regardless of the denominator.
I roll a dice. True or False? The probability I roll a 2 = 0.5 as either I either get a 2 or I don't get a 2.	Look for students explaining that these outcomes are not equally likely (such as, there are 5 ways to not get a 2 but only 1 way to get a 2). You could relate this to the chance of picking one student's name out of a hat from the class. You will either pick that name or not pick that name, but the chance of picking it is much smaller than the chance of not picking it.

Common errors/misconceptions

Misconception	Strategies to address
Being reluctant to use numbers to describe probabilities and still using words like likely, unlikely etc. instead of a fraction or a decimal	Discuss two events that are 'likely' but with different numerical probabilities, for example, getting a 3 or higher when you roll a dice versus getting a 2 or higher when you roll a dice. This should help students see that we need a way to show that rolling a 2+ is more likely than rolling a 3+.
	Try to get students to see that we can calculate the probability as a number in some cases because we know how many outcomes there are and they are all equally likely.
	However, there are other cases where we don't know all the outcomes and/or they are not equally likely and so we cannot calculate it.
Believing that some outcomes are less likely than others For example, when rolling a dice, pupils may think that the $P(3) > P(6)$	Try listing all the outcomes to show that each one has a probability of 1/total number of outcomes. This will also show that the favoured outcome only appears once in the list like the others.
Believing that all outcomes are equally likely in every situation For example, students may think that that P(it rains tomorrow) = 0.5 because there are only 2 options, not realising that they are not necessarily the same likelihood.	Put red and blue counters in a bag. Make sure there are more reds than blues. Then select one at random. Discuss that there are 2 outcomes: red and blue... ... but they are not equally likely because there are more reds than blues in the bag. Also consider a football match between Manchester United and the school football team. What is the probability that the school team will win? There are three outcomes – does this mean that the school team have a $\frac{1}{3}$ chance of beating them. For every three games they play, can they expect to win one?
Expressing a probability as a ratio or as 'odds' rather than as a fraction or decimal (or percentage)	Reinforce need for fraction or decimal. You could show that a ratio of 1 : 4 for example actually represents a probability of $\frac{1}{5}$ because the total number of parts is 5.
Believing that the next outcome will be influenced by the previous outcomes For example, students may believe that if they are tossing a coin and have had 3 heads in a row then the next one is likely to be a tail to 'even things out'. Or they may believe that the next one is likely to be a head because there is a 'run' of heads.	Carry out some practical probability experiments to see how runs of this type can occur in real life and to see that the experimental values are not always exactly the same as the theoretical values (but that they approach them as you repeat the experiment). You could also discuss the equipment having 'no memory' to help explain this.

Developing conceptual understanding

7Db1 Use the language of probability to describe and interpret results involving likelihood and chance.

* Try to give students some practical experience with chance and probability alongside the theoretical work. For example, get them to roll a dice repeatedly or spin a spinner repeatedly and record their outcomes. This will help them realise that some outcomes are not equally

likely and that past events do not affect the next event (as we are only looking at independent events).

7Db2 Understand and use the probability scale from 0 to 1.

- Students could begin to assign numbers by trying to place an event using their instincts onto the probability scale and then using their knowledge of fractions/decimals to estimate the value.
- FIX: Try labelling a probability scale with fractions/decimals first to help students relate these values to physical positions on the scale.

STRETCH: You could ask students to position outcomes on the scale in complex situations, such as selection of an item from a bag without replacement.

7Db3 Find probabilities based on equally likely outcomes in simple contexts.

- FIX: Listing the possible outcomes can help students to identify the number of possible outcomes more easily as well as the number of favourable outcomes to help them write the probability as a fraction.
- You could use the matching statement and probability cards in the online photocopiable resources for this chapter as a task to support this process.

TIP: Although we want students to calculate probabilities in situations where the outcomes are equally likely, it is worth exposing students to examples where the outcomes are not equally likely (such as a spinner where the sections are not of equal size) to show them that the theory does not work in this situation.

STRETCH: Students working at greater depth can begin to extract information from other settings and use it to find a probability. For example, they can read data from frequency tables, charts and Venn diagrams.

STRETCH: These students can also begin to consider events with combined outcomes. For example: the outcomes of rolling two dice or the outcomes of tossing a coin and rolling a dice.

End of chapter mental maths exercise

1. Give the decimal that lies halfway between 0.3 and 0.6.	6. I roll a 10 sided dice. Find the probability that I roll a multiple of 3.
2. Simplify $\frac{24}{30}$	I randomly select a counter from a bag of red and blue counters. There are 9 red counters and 6 blue counters.
3. Find an equivalent fraction to $\frac{5}{8}$ with denominator 32.	7. Calculate the probability that I select a red counter. Simplify your answer.
4. Give the decimal that is equivalent to $\frac{27}{100}$	8. Calculate the probability that I select a blue counter. Simplify your answer.
5. Give the simplest fraction that is equivalent to 0.18.	

Technology recommendations

- Use a spreadsheet to record outcomes from experiments.

  Students can then use formulae to calculate the total number of each outcome as well the totals before calculating the probabilities. They could also draw a chart to show the distribution.

- Use a simulator of a dice and a biased dice to show how the distributions of the outcomes are different. Students can explore whether a dice is fair by assessing the distribution of its outcomes. This can also be applied to other equipment e.g. coins, spinners. There are a number of virtual experiments that can be done using apps online to simulate these items.

Investigation/research tasks

- Investigate the truth of this statement:

  "You are more likely to score 9 when rolling two dice than 10."

  Can you find the probability of each score when rolling two dice?

  What if there were three dice?

  > TIP: Students could start by producing a list of outcomes for two dice, as well as their totals, to help them test the statement.

  They can then repeat this with three dice.

- **Stick or Twist?**

  Play the game Stick or Twist in pairs:

  > Take two sets of 0–9 digit cards and shuffle them.
  >
  > Player 1 turns over the top card and keeps turning cards for as long as they like. They add together the scores of the cards they have turned to get their first score.
  >
  > Player 1's turn stops when they choose or stop (stick) OR when they turn over a 0 or a 9 card. If they get a 0 or a 9 they get no points for that turn and play passes to the next player.
  >
  > Player 2 now takes their turn.
  >
  > The winner is the first player to reach 50 points.

  When is the best time to stick?

  When should you definitely turn over another card (twist)?

  Can you find a strategy to help you win this game?

  For example, what is the probability of a 0 or 9 on the first turn? So is it better to stick or twist?

  Then on the second turn?

  And so on.

Time and scales

Prior knowledge assumptions

- Students can read an analogue and a digital clock (12-hour and 24-hour).
- Students know the relationship between the different units of time, for example, there are seven days in a week.
- Students can read a scale using marked intervals.

Guidance on the hook

Purpose: This hook gives students the opportunity to measure time in a practical context. Students will develop a greater sense of time, as well as gain practical experience of using measuring equipment.

Use of the hook: Students will need stopwatches, or a watch with a second hand. They should work in pairs and record their results in a table. If students are using a stopwatch with split seconds, this provides a good opportunity to practise rounding – students should record the time to the nearest second.

Discuss with the students whether a digital or analogue device is more accurate for measuring time.

Extension: ask students to reflect on how they could estimate the number of hours that have passed by in a day. For example, look at the way the sun has moved.

Starter ideas

Mental maths starters

Write a quarter of an hour in minutes	Write 7.5 hours in hours and minutes	How many days are in November and December altogether?	Write the time shown on a 24-hour digital clock 1 minute after midnight
Write 2 minutes 30 seconds in seconds	Write 1.25 hours in hours and minutes	How many days are in March, April and May?	Write the time shown on a 24-hour digital clock 1 hour before midnight
Write 3 days in hours	Write 4.75 hours in hours and minutes	How many days are in the first 11 months of the year?	Write 'a quarter to three' as a digital clock time
Write 8 weeks in days	Write 8.2 hours in hours and minutes	How many days are in July and January?	Write five thirty in the afternoon as a 24-hour digital clock time

Start point check: What's my error?

Start by showing students two times:

| 23:15 | and | 17:20 |

Check students understanding of the 24-hour clock by asking:

* Are these 24-hour clock, or 12-hour clock?
* Can you tell me this time in a different way, i.e. quarter past 11 in the evening, twenty past 5 in the afternoon?
* What would the time be 1 hour later than 23:15? What would the time be 15 minutes earlier than 17:20?

Don't tell students you are going to calculate the time interval between these two times.
On the board complete a subtraction for the two four-digit numbers, explaining your steps.

> TIP: If students are more familiar with a different written algorithm for subtraction, for example, borrow and pay back', then use this method instead.

$$
\begin{array}{r}
2\overset{12}{\cancel{3}}:{}^{1}1\,5 \\
1\,7:2\,0 \\
\hline
5:9\,5
\end{array}
$$

"The time difference is 5 hours 95 minutes"

Ask students to explain what you mistake you have made.

Identify the point that you 'borrowed' 1 hour from the hours and continued the subtraction with 115 minutes, instead of 75 minutes.

Ask students to find the time difference using their own method. Observe the different methods that students use. Look out for students who do not find a correct time of 5 hours 55 minutes.

Make a ruler   *Problem solving*

Give students a strip of paper 100 cm long. Challenge them to mark the scale out of the 100 cm ruler by folding – no measuring or guessing!

Students should be able to find 25, 50 and 100 cm easily by folding in half, and in half again. Students can find 20, 40, 60 and 80 by folding into fifths – although this may take several attempts to do accurately!

They may add lengths together, for example, if they've found 20 cm, they can add this to 50 cm to make 70 cm.

Discussion ideas

Probing questions	Teacher prompts
Which digits stay the same and which change when 3:30 p.m. is converted to the 24-hour clock? Is this the same for all times?	Look at a range of times. Ask students to generalise. Which times of the day does the time always stay the same?
	Remind students of the need to place a leading zero in the time before 10 a.m., for example, 9:50 a.m. must be written as 09:50.
What is the difference between 9:50 and 09:50?	Prompt students by asking them 'what might you be doing at ten to ten each day' – to help them realise it is not clear if 9:50 is in the morning or the evening.

Probing questions	Teacher prompts
What would happen to the dial on an analogue scale if I changed the scale, for example, from 100 200 to 100 500 What about if I changed the scale by adding more intervals? 100 500 to 100 500	In each example encourage students to consider what each interval represents. Ask students to estimate where the arrow on the 2nd diagram would be.

Common errors/misconceptions

Incorrectly believing that there are 100 seconds in an hour and 100 seconds in a minute	Avoid reinforcing this misconception by writing time using a colon ':' and not a decimal point '.'. Students will confuse 4.35 with the decimal number 4.35 leading to the belief that there are 100 seconds in a minute. Writing the time as 4:35 or 4 35 will help students make the necessary distinction.
Incorrect interpretation of the decimal part of a time, for example, 4.5 hours = 4 hours 50 minutes	This misconception arises because students are more familiar working in metric units where 1.25 m is easily interpreted as 1 m 25 cm. Remind students that a decimal represents <u>part of a whole</u>. Ask students to compare 1.25 m and 1.25 hours. What does the .25 represent in each case? Be explicit that it is 25 cm because 1 m = 100 cm. In the case of an hour we need to find .25 of 60. Encourage students to convert common decimals to a fraction form – for example, writing 4.5 as $4\frac{1}{2}$ hours will remind them that the decimal represents part of 60, and less likely to make this error. Discuss '4.75 hours' with students – ask them, is this more or less than 5 hours? Is it 4 hours 75 minutes?
Interpreting the interval marks on a scale incorrectly, for example, reading this scale as 61 instead of 62 60 70	Encourage students to label every unmarked interval on the scale, as this will often help them identify their error. For very weak students, it may be beneficial to compare the scale to a more familiar number line, and practise counting in steps, for example, counting in 5's, 50's etc.
Reading and interpreting the decimal part of the scale incorrectly, for example, 4.05 kg as 4 kg and 5 grams	Students need to know metric conversions in order to read digital scales correctly. Remind students of these conversions and take any opportunity to reinforce these facts. The prefixes, 'centi' 'kilo' etc. are helpful reminders. Encourage students to use these facts to re-write the measurement to the appropriate number of decimal places, for example, 4.6 metres as 4.60 metres, and 4.05 kg as 4.050 kg to help reduce these errors.

Developing conceptual understanding

7Mt2 Know the relationships between units of time; understand and use the 12-hour and 24-hour clock systems; interpret timetables; calculate time intervals.

- FIX: Students may find local timetables with familiar place names more accessible than examples given in a textbook. Source examples from your local towns. Focus on the journey a bus makes, tracing the route on a map and highlighting the stops. Be explicit about the difference between the time it takes to travel between the two stops – the time interval, and the time it stops given on the timetable.

- FIX: When calculating time intervals, encourage students to consider the best strategy, particularly when calculating intervals that go over the hour. Often a mental strategy is more effective and results in less errors.

For example, the difference in time between 1050 and 1122:

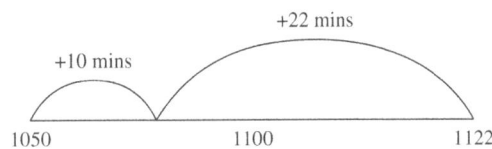

STRETCH: Source examples of more complex 1100 timetables, for example, train timetables with missing times.

DARLINGTON	1040	1140	1240	1340	1440	1540	1640	1740	1840	1940	2040	2140	...	2240
Aycliffe Village	1055	1155	1255	1355	1455	1555	1655	1755	1855	1955	2055	2155	...	2255
Newton Aycliffe	1103	1203	1303	1403	1503	1603	1703	1803	1903	2003	2103	2203	...	2303
Greenfield Way	1106	1206	1306	1406	1506	1606	1706	1806	1906	2006	2106	2206	...	...
Rushyford	1111	1211	1311	1411	1511	1611	1711	1811	1911	2011	2111	2211	...	2316
Chilton	1113	1213	1313	1413	1513	1613	1713	1813	1913	2013	2113	2213	...	2318
Feeryhill Village	1119	1219	1319	1419	1519	1619	1719	1819	1919	2019	2119	2219	2249	2324
Wood Lane Estate	1122	1222	1322	1422	1522	1622	1722	1822	1922	2022	2122	2222	2252	...
West Cornforth	1131	1231	1331	1431	1531	1631	1731	1831	1931	2031	2131	2231	2301	...
Coxhoe	1139	...	1339	...	1539	...	1739	...	1939	...	2139	...	2309	...
Bowburn	1144	...	1344	...	1544	...	1744	...	1944	...	2144	...	2314	...
Sherburn Village	1154	...	1354	...	1554	...	1754	...	1954	...	2154	...	...	...
Pittington	1159	...	1359	...	1559	...	1759	...	1959	...	2159	...	...	...
West Rainton	1206	...	1406	...	1606	...	1806	...	2006	...	2206	...	...	...
Houghton-le-Spring	1213	...	1413	...	1613	...	1813	...	2013	...	2213	...	...	...
SUNDERLAND	1229	...	1429	...	1629	...	1829	...	2029	...	2229	...	...	...

7MI3 Read the scales on a range of analogue and digital measuring instruments.

- FIX: When reading analogue scales, students will need to be familiar with common fractions of 100 and 1000, for example, $\frac{1}{4}$ of 1000 is 250. Consolidate these number facts through routine practice. Students who continue to find this difficult can find some fractions through finding half, and then finding half again – although this will not work in all cases.

End of chapter mental maths exercise

1 What is 30 + 45?	1 What is 75 − 15?	1 What is 125 + 30?	1 What is 75 − 15?
2 How many seconds in 3 minutes?	2 How many minutes in 2 ½ hours?	2 How many seconds in 15 minutes?	2 How many minutes in 5 hours?
3 How many days in March, April and May in total?	3 How many days in November, December and January in total?	3 How many days in February, March and April in a leap year in total?	3 What is the difference in days between March, April and May in total, and September, October and November in total?
4 Convert 5:45 p.m. to the 24 hour clock	4 Convert 2:40 a.m. to the 12-hour clock	4 Convert 11:52 a.m. to the 12-hour clock	4 Convert 11:43 p.m. to the 12-hour clock
5 Convert 03:20 to a.m. or p.m. time	5 Convert 21:40 to a.m. or p.m. time	5 Convert 10:06 to a.m. or p.m. time	5 Convert 19:31 to a.m. or p.m. time
6 What is the difference in time between 4:15 p.m. and 7:10 p.m.?	6 What is the difference in time between 03:25 and 06:15?	6 What is the difference in time between 9:45 p.m. and 11:30 p.m.?	6 What is the difference in time between 23:15 and 02:30?

Technology recommendations

- Use a spreadsheet to calculate a time interval in days, months or years: for example – ask a student how old they are in days.

TIP: Ask students to calculate these values using a pen/paper/calculator first, and check their answers on a spreadsheet.

The following formulas may be helpful:

- =datedif(A1,A2,"d") will return the number of full days
- =datedif(A1,A2,"m") will return the number of full months
- =datedif(A1,A2,"y") will return the number of full years

where A1 contains the start date, and A2 contains the end date.

This can be extended by asking students to research how they can find out how to calculate their age in years and months, for example, 11 years 6 months. There are many ways to do this – one option is to use the formula =datedif(A1,A2,"y") to give the full years, combined with the formula =datedif(A1,A2,"ym") to give the number of remaining months.

Investigation/research tasks

- **Timetable logic**   *Problem solving*

  Students work in small groups of two to four to solve the logic problem in the online photocopiable resource.

  Each group will need one blank timetable, one set of times and Clue Set A.

TIP: Allow students to cut out the times so they can easily try different options.

Students must complete the timetable using the clues provided, and their knowledge of timetables.

The solution is shown below:

	Bus A	Bus B	Bus C	Bus D	Bus E	Bus F
Fleckley	0903	0918	1040	1210	1321	1410
Sandy	0942	0946	1101	1245	1352	1427
Foxton	1002	1003	1112	1300	1403	1438
Maytown	1015	1045	1145	1315	1445	1515
Tynwade	1059	1122	1210	1439	1520	1555

The logic problem can be solved using Clue Set A only. However, you may choose to use all or some clues from Set B to differentiate the task for different learners, or to enable students to complete the task quicker.

- **Metric time**

  Students can research the question 'why is time not metric'. Remind students that most of our measurement systems used in the modern day are metric – length, weight and capacity, as well as others. Long ago, there were a wide variety of different measurements in place, some of which can still be seen today (for example, a pes (food) was a unit of length dating back to the Roman empire, which was divided into 12 *unciae* ('inches'). Over time countries adopted the metric system of measuring lengths weight and capacity – and money. Time, however, has not made this transition to metric.

  Their research could consider

  - Units of time 'year', 'month' relate to real world facts, such as revolutions of the planet, and are not arbitrary. There is not a nice relationship between them.

  - The numbers 24 and 60 are convenient for breaking down into many parts, because it has so many factors. On the other hand, 10 is divisible by just 2 and 5.

  - Our system for measuring time is already used worldwide – so there is no need to create a standardised system as there was for other measurements.

Numbers

Learning objectives

Learning objectives covered in this chapter: 7Ni2, 7Ni3

- Recognise multiples, factors, common factors, primes (all less than 100), making use of simple tests of divisibility.
- Find the lowest common multiple in simple cases; use the 'sieve' for generating primes developed by Eratosthenes.
- Recognise squares of whole numbers to at least 20 × 20 and the corresponding square roots; use the notation 7^2 and $\sqrt{49}$.

Key terms

- multiple
- factor
- prime number
- tests of divisibility
- common factor
- lowest common multiple (LCM)
- square number
- square root

Prior knowledge assumptions

- Students are confident in their multiplication and division facts up to 10 × 10.
- Students know the meaning of a prime number and say if a number up to 20 is prime or not.

Guidance on the hook

Purpose: This hook introduces one of the most notable practical applications of prime numbers: cryptography, while also providing an opportunity to use tests of divisibility.

Use of the hook: Introduce students to the context of the hook. If students have no prior knowledge of codebreaking, discuss as a class what it means to 'encrypt' a message. Introduce the vocabulary 'key'; 'public key' and 'private key'.

The numbers given in the book are semi-prime (that is, they are the product of two prime numbers). Set students the challenge of finding the two prime factors. Encourage students to be systematic in their approach. They can start with checking whether numbers are divisible by 2, then 3, then 5, then 7 etc. You could ask students to record their results in a table. The task gives students a good opportunity to practise using their tests of divisibility. Do not permit calculators initially. Students should be able to identify the majority using mental methods.

When students have completed the task discuss with students which of the semi-prime numbers took the longest to factorise. Explain to students that there is no method to find the two prime numbers – it is a trial and error process. The more primes that need to be attempted, the longer the process will take. Encryption methods use the semi-prime to encrypt a message and the two prime factors to decrypt the message. The semi-prime can be released to the world as the public key, confidently knowing that finding the two prime factors, and hence the decryption key, will be very hard to crack.

Extension: You could extend the hook by giving some larger semi-primes to factorise, 4387 (107 × 41), 5429 (61 × 89), 17287 (59 × 293). This will provide good consolidation of prime numbers under 100, while also illustrating the point further.

Starter ideas

Mental maths starter

Write three multiples of the number 9.	Write a four-digit multiple of 50.	Write down a multiple of 3 between 340 and 350.	117 is a multiple of 9. Write the next biggest multiple of 9.
Write the factors of 16.	A number has exactly 4 factors. Two of the factors are 5 and 3. What is the number?	Write 4 factors of the number 100.	Which of these is not a factor of 18? 1, 2, 6, 18, 36
Write the next prime number after 23.	Write the prime number that comes before 43.	Write a prime number between 70 and 80.	Which of these is prime? 36, 37, 38, 39
What is the square root of 81?	What is 6 squared?	Write the square number between 60 and 70.	How many square numbers are there that are less than 20?

Start point check: Prime-master!

Use this activity to check students' knowledge of the basic multiplication and division facts, and to consolidate knowledge of primes (and squares if appropriate).

Give each student a set of digit cards from 2 to 20.

Call out a number between 2 and 100.

> TIP: Use a random number generator on the board for greater engagement.

Students race to hold up two numbers that multiply together to give that number. For example, call out the number 20. Students can hold up either 1 and 20, 2 and 10, 5 and 4. After each number ask students to look around the room – How many different solutions are there?

> BEWARE: Look out for students who do not demonstrate good knowledge of the number facts. These students are likely to need additional support to access the content of this chapter.

Throughout the activity, model the language of the chapter. For example, "*Pierre has shown me 7 × 6 = 42. The numbers 7 and 6 are both factors of 42; Frances has shown me the 21 × 2 = 42, 21 and 2 are also factors of 42. 42 is in the 6 and 7 times table, it is a multiple of 6 and 7.*"

After a few goes, introduce the Prime-master. If a number is recognised as prime they shout 'prime'. The first student to recognise the prime number becomes the Prime-master (you may decide to give the Prime-master a special responsibility, such as calling out the next number or clicking the button to generate the next number, or provide them with a special hat/badge to wear until another student becomes Prime-master).

Extension: Introduce a Square-master, similar to the Prime-master. Students may recognise square numbers, or work out a number is square as they cannot hold up two of the same number.

Adaption: Use mini-whiteboards instead of digit cards.

Go lower

Show students the following set of multiplications:

$4 \times 10 = 40$ $\qquad$ $14 \times 8 = 112$ $\qquad$ $25 \times 6 = 150$ $\qquad$ $48 \times 5 = 240$

Their task is to start by discussing the multiplication statements and how they relate to factors and multiples and common multiples. Ask questions such as:

- 6 is a factor of 150. Can you give me another statement using the word factor or multiple?
- Are 48 and 5 the only factors of 240? How do you know?

TIP: Reinforce the fact that 1 and the number itself are always factors of a number.

- If 14 is a factor, what other two numbers must be factors (2 and 7)?
- Make me a sentence using the phrase 'common multiple' (for example, 150 is a common multiple of 25 and 6).
- Are there more common multiples of 25 and 6? How do you know? Are they bigger or smaller?

Set students the challenge to find a common multiple that is smaller than the one in the multiplication statement, i.e. Is there a common multiple of 4 and 10 that is lower than 40?

As the end of the task, emphasise to students that multiplying two numbers together will give a common multiple, but it may not be the lowest common multiple.

Guess my number

Tell the students you are thinking of a number between 1 and 100. Give students one fact about your number. Select three students to guess your number using the fact you have given. If the number is not correctly guessed, give one more fact about your number before inviting another three guesses. Repeat, until your number has been identified.

Each fact should relate to primes, squares, square roots, multiples or factors. For example:

- My number is 1 more than a prime number.
- My number is greater than the square root of 81.
- 7 is a factor of my number.
- My number and 80 have no common factors.

TIP: Give students a 1–100 grid to help them record the numbers they have eliminated.

Adaption: Students can play this game in small groups of four. One student chooses a number and gives the group members a number fact. After each fact, every group member makes one guess before the next fact is given. The winner chooses the number in the next round.

Discussion ideas

Probing questions	Teacher prompts
Will the lowest common multiple of two numbers Always, Sometimes or Never be a bigger number than both the numbers?	Ask students to consider whether a multiple of a number is always bigger than that number. You may need to remind students that the lowest common multiple is the smallest _positive_ number that is divisible by both numbers.
Do factors always come in pairs?	Students may be familiar with creating spider diagrams that display factors opposite. Ask them to consider the case when a 'pair' of numbers are the same number – what are these numbers called?
Bigger numbers have more factors: True or False?	Ask students to consider which numbers have the least number of factors (primes) to guide their thinking.

Probing questions	Teacher prompts
Are there any numbers that have no factors?	Prompt students to think of the number that goes into every number.

Common errors/misconceptions

Misconception	Strategies to address
1 is a prime number	This misconception arises when students have an imprecise definition of a prime number. Be specific that a prime number must have *two and only two* factors. The number 1 has just 1 factor.
Finding the lowest common multiple by multiplying both numbers together	Students need to understand that multiplying two numbers together will always give a common multiple. The 'Go Lower' starter will help address this error.
Failing to include the number 1 and itself as factors of a number	Encourage students to work systematically to find factor, always starting with 1.

Developing conceptual understanding

Recognise multiples, factors, common factors, primes (all less than 100), making use of simple tests of divisibility; find the lowest common multiple in simple cases; use the 'sieve' for generating primes developed by Eratosthenes.

- FIX: Students need to be able to rapidly recall the multiplication facts up to 10 × 10. Students who are not able to do this must be given opportunity to learn and consolidate these facts. Use a variety of techniques to reinforce these facts through chanting, repetitive practice and number games.

- FIX: Use 'spider' diagrams to record all the factors of a number. This encourages students to find factors in pairs.

STRETCH: After completing the 'sieve of Eratosthenes', students could repeat the activity with a grid that has a different number of columns, for example:

1	2	3	4	5	6
7	8	9	10	11	12
13	14	15	16	17	18
19	20	21	22	23	24
25	26	27	28	29	30
31	32	33	34	35	36

Ask them to record what patterns are the same, and what are different. (For example, in a 5 × 5 grid the multiples of 2 were in alternating columns, but here they are in the same column.)

STRETCH: Students working at greater depth can explore perfect numbers. Illustrate that 6 is a perfect number (the factors excluding itself add up to the number itself (1 + 2 + 3)). Can they find any other perfect numbers?

Recognise squares of whole numbers to at least 20 × 20 and the corresponding square roots; use the notation 7^2 and $\sqrt{49}$.

- FIX: Ask students to draw squares of the different dimensions and calculate the areas to discover square numbers for themselves.

STRETCH: Students can investigate the difference between the square of a number, x, and the product of the two numbers either side. For example, What is the difference between 6^2 and 5×7, 8^2 and 7×9, 13^2 and 12×14? Can they describe their findings? Avoid using algebraic notation with students at this stage.

End of chapter mental maths exercise

1. Write all the factors of 45.	6. What is the lowest common multiple of 10 and 8?
2. What is the square root of 64?	7. Write a square number that is 1 more than a prime number.
3. How many factors does the number 26 have?	
4. Write the even factors of the number.	8. 676 is a multiple of 13. Write down the next biggest multiple of 13.
5. What factors do 20 and 30 have in common?	

Technology recommendations

- How can you calculate a square root using a calculator? Ask all students to demonstrate that they can find and use the $\sqrt{}$ key. Students can investigate what happens if they attempt to take the square root of a number that is not a square number, for example, $\sqrt{59}$. Ask students to explain their findings. They should notice:
    - The solution is not a whole number.
    - The decimal number fills their calculator display.
- Use a spreadsheet to calculate common multiples quickly.

Investigation/research tasks

1. **Rulers** (photocopiable resource)   *Problem solving*

    Give students a 30 cm strip of paper, which they will use to make a ruler. Start by giving the students a smaller 5 cm strip of paper. How can they use the 5 cm strip to start marking the scale on the 30 cm ruler? Elicit from students that they can mark the multiples of 5. For example:

    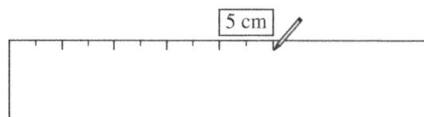

    Now provide the 7 cm strip of paper so that students can mark the multiples of 7.

    Challenge students to use both two strips of paper to mark the rest of scale on the ruler. For example, as 20 cm has been marked, they can use the 7 cm ruler to mark 27 cm.

    When students have completed it, ask them to repeat the activity using the 6 cm and 9 cm strip. Is it possible to mark every centimetre? Why not?

    > TIP: They can use the other side of the 30 cm ruler.

    Students should discover that they are only able to mark the multiples of 3.

Students can investigate further using different combinations of strips. Which combinations of smaller strips will work? The following questions may help guide their thinking:

- If you had two even numbers, could you ever mark an odd number on the scale?
- If you have whole numbers, could you ever mark half a centimetre on the scale?
- Do the two numbers (i.e. 6 and 9) have any common factors?

If appropriate, introduce them to co-prime numbers.

2   **Investigate 'Happy Numbers'**

1. Choose a whole number between 1 and 99.
2. Square each digit, and add them together to create a new number.
3. Repeat with the new number.
4. Continue the process until a pattern emerges or the process leads to 1. Happy numbers are numbers that lead to 1.

Example: 31

$$3^2 + 1^2 \quad = 9 + 1 \quad = 10 \quad 1^2 + 0^2 \quad = 1$$

31 is a happy number!

Note:

Happy numbers between 1 and 100 are:

1, 7, 10, 13, 19, 23, 28, 31, 32, 44, 49, 68, 70, 79, 82, 86, 91, 94, 97, 100

Students will discover that there is a repeating pattern of:

145-42-20-4-16-37-58-89-145

Write these number on the board so that if a student reaches one of these numbers they should stop and try a new number.

Adaptation: Students could try to automate this process using a spreadsheet.

Fractions

Learning objectives

Learning objectives covered in this chapter: 7Nf4

- Add and subtract two simple fractions, for example, $\frac{1}{8} + \frac{9}{8}$, $\frac{11}{12} - \frac{5}{8}$; find fractions of quantities (whole number answers); multiply a fraction by an integer.

Key terms

- fraction
- numerator
- denominator
- equivalent fraction
- simplest form
- improper fraction
- mixed number

Prior knowledge assumptions

- Students should be familiar with the words numerator and denominator.
- They should know how to simplify fractions.
- Students should be able to find equivalent fractions.

The work in this chapter will also be helpful when they consider later Fractions chapters. In Chapter 15, for example, students will explore calculating mentally with fractions.

Guidance on the hook

Students will require a page of centimetre squared paper and two coloured pens or pencils.

Purpose: To remind students of basic addition and subtraction with the same denominator using a block layout for clarity.

Use of the hook: Go through the explanation with students and encourage them to find as many valid calculations as possible.

Extension: Ask students to use three colours and to write down some valid calculations from their coloured diagrams.

Starter ideas

Mental maths starter

I eat $\frac{3}{8}$ of a pizza. What fraction is left?	I watch $\frac{7}{8}$ of a film. What fraction did I not watch?	I drink $\frac{3}{5}$ of a bottle of water. What fraction is left?	I have walked $\frac{3}{4}$ of the way home. What fraction of the journey do I have left?
Write $\frac{11}{4}$ as a mixed number.	Write $\frac{16}{3}$ as a mixed number.	Write $\frac{12}{7}$ as a mixed number.	Write $\frac{19}{5}$ as a mixed number.
Work out $\frac{1}{7} + \frac{1}{7}$	Work out $\frac{1}{5} + \frac{1}{5}$	Work out $\frac{1}{9} + \frac{1}{9}$	Work out $\frac{1}{3} + \frac{1}{3}$

Simplify $\frac{8}{10}$	Simplify $\frac{12}{18}$	Simplify $\frac{15}{20}$	Simplify $\frac{30}{36}$
How many minutes are there in $\frac{1}{3}$ of an hour?	How many seconds are there in $\frac{1}{4}$ of an hour?	How many hours are there in $\frac{1}{8}$ of a day?	How many minutes are there in $1\frac{1}{2}$ hours?

Start point check: Fraction cards

Give students a fraction card (see photocopiable resources online).

1. Ask students to arrange themselves into groups so that everyone in the same group has equivalent fractions.

   Which is the largest group?

   Who has no one else in their group? What fractions could they have joined up with?

2. Now ask students to try to pair up with someone so that the total of the two fractions is 1.
   If anyone could not find a partner, ask what fraction they could have paired up with.

3. Ask students to stand up if their fraction has a denominator of 6.

   Next ask students to stand up their fraction has a numerator of 5. Then ask students to stand up if their fraction is greater than $\frac{1}{2}$. Discuss how students can tell.

   Get students to stand up if their fraction is equivalent to $\frac{9}{27}$.

- **Start point check: Target board**

  Choose from the board:

  - a number equivalent to $\frac{17}{5}$
  - a number equivalent to $4\frac{4}{5}$
  - a number equivalent to $\frac{54}{27}$
  - a number equivalent to $\frac{30}{54}$
  - a number equivalent to $\frac{1}{6} + \frac{1}{6}$
  - a number equivalent to $\frac{3}{8} + \frac{5}{8}$

$2\frac{1}{3}$	$\frac{13}{8}$	$\frac{1}{3}$	$2\frac{3}{5}$
$\frac{13}{5}$	$\frac{2}{12}$	$1\frac{3}{4}$	2
$1\frac{2}{3}$	1	$\frac{24}{5}$	$2\frac{1}{4}$
$\frac{5}{9}$	$3\frac{2}{5}$	$\frac{21}{8}$	$\frac{2}{9}$

Discussion ideas

Probing questions	Teacher prompts
Give me two fractions that add together to make $\frac{11}{12}$. And another pair…	Write the suggestions on the board. Encourage students to give fractions in their simplest form.
Explain why $\frac{1}{3} + \frac{1}{6}$ is not equal to $\frac{2}{9}$	Prompt students by asking what $\frac{1}{3}$ would be if expressed as ninths so that students can see that $\frac{2}{9}$ is smaller than $\frac{1}{3}$. Discuss the correct way to add fractions.

Probing questions	Teacher prompts
What is the next number in this sequence? $\dfrac{1}{8}, \dfrac{1}{2}, \dfrac{7}{8}, \dfrac{5}{4}, \dots$ Explain why.	Prompt students to write the fractions with a common denominator.
What is the same and what is different about these number calculations? $\dfrac{3}{4} \times 24$ $3 \times 24 \div 4$ $(\dfrac{1}{4}$ of 24$) \times 3$ 3×6	Guide students to identify that all these calculations relate to finding $\dfrac{3}{4}$ of 24.

Common errors/misconceptions

Misconception	Strategies to address
Students sometime believe that you add fractions by adding the numerators and adding the denominators, for example, thinking that $\dfrac{1}{2} + \dfrac{1}{4}$ is $\dfrac{2}{6}$	Show a cake divided into 4 sections. Shade $\dfrac{1}{2}$ and then shade a further $\dfrac{1}{4}$. Discuss what the correct fraction is for the total amount shaded.
When multiplying a fraction by an integer, students often try to multiply both the numerator and the denominator by the integer, for example giving $2 \times \dfrac{1}{3}$ as $\dfrac{2}{6}$	Discuss that $\dfrac{2}{6}$ is the same as $\dfrac{1}{3}$, so the size of the fraction has not changed. Relate multiplication to repeated addition, that is $2 \times \dfrac{1}{3} = \dfrac{1}{3} + \dfrac{1}{3}$.
Some students do not simplify their answers fully	Give students plenty of opportunities to practise questions related to this objective. Ensure that some questions have answers that cannot be simplified and some have answers that can be simplified so that students need to decide if it can be simplified or not.

Developing conceptual understanding

7Nf4 Add and subtract two simple fractions, for example, $\dfrac{1}{8} + \dfrac{9}{8}$, $\dfrac{11}{12} - \dfrac{5}{8}$; find fractions of quantities (whole number answers); multiply a fraction by an integer.

- FIX: Students may find it hard to conceptualise adding fractions when the answer is more than 1 (or subtracting fractions involving fractions greater than 1). Pictures may be helpful, for example:

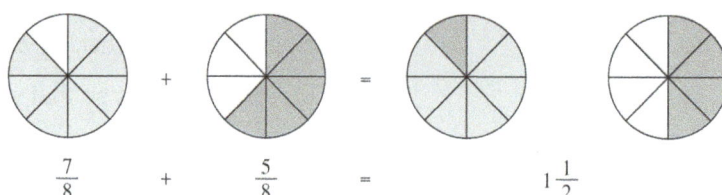

$$\dfrac{7}{8} \quad + \quad \dfrac{5}{8} \quad = \quad 1\dfrac{1}{2}$$

- FIX: Pupils could use fraction strips (see photocopiable resources online) as an alternative way to conceptualise equivalent fractions and their use in fraction addition for example:

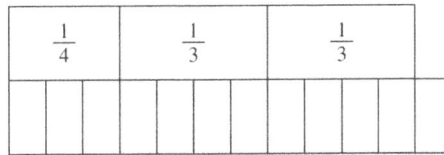

$$\frac{1}{4} + \frac{2}{3} = \frac{11}{12}$$

- FIX: Another way to think about the addition (or subtraction) of fractions (with unequal denominators) is to use grids:

$$\frac{3}{8} + \frac{1}{5} = \frac{23}{40}$$

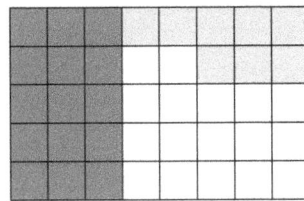

$\frac{1}{5}$ The size of the grid is decided by the denominators of the fractions.

$\frac{3}{8}$

- FIX: A simple way to think about multiplying a fraction by a whole number is to use repeated addition:

$3 \times \frac{5}{8}$

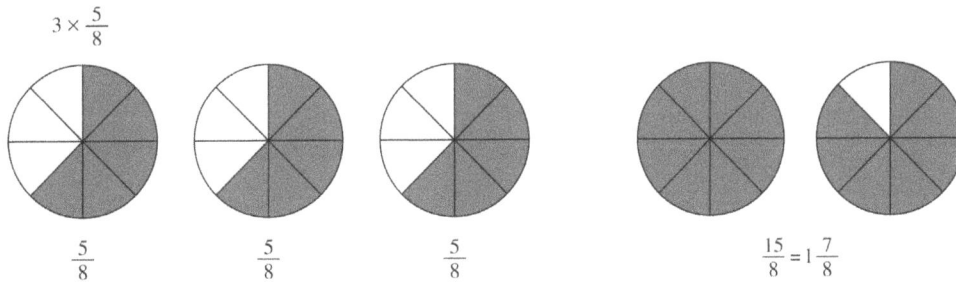

$\frac{5}{8}$ $\qquad$ $\frac{5}{8}$ $\qquad$ $\frac{5}{8}$ $\qquad$ $\frac{15}{8} = 1\frac{7}{8}$

STRETCH: Students who have mastered this objective could develop their knowledge by considering questions involving mixed numbers, for example, $\frac{2}{7} + 2\frac{3}{7}$, $\frac{4}{9} + 1\frac{1}{3}$, etc.

End of chapter mental maths exercise

1. I have $\frac{7}{10}$ of a litre of juice. I drink $\frac{3}{10}$ of a litre. What fraction of a litre is left?	4. Work out $\frac{1}{2} + \frac{2}{5}$.
2. Write $\frac{14}{3}$ as a mixed number.	5. Find $4 \times \frac{3}{8}$. Simplify your answer.
3. Here is a number statement. $\frac{3}{4} = \frac{?}{36}$. Find the missing numerator.	6. I eat $\frac{2}{5}$ of a bar of chocolate every day. How many bars of chocolate do I eat in 15 days?

Technology recommendations

- Students could explore how they can add and subtract fractions using their calculator (fraction button key).

- There are many websites available to aid the teaching and learning of fractions. Some websites that could be useful include:

  http://www.lancsngfl.ac.uk/curriculum/primarymaths/download/file/Fractions_2.swf

  https://streaming.discoveryeducation.com/braingames/iknowthat/Fractions/FractionGame.cfm? Topic=addfractions

  https://www.geogebra.org/m/BTCSvEDZ

Investigation/research tasks

- **Investigation: pizza shares**   *Problem solving*

  A pizza is cut into eight pieces. The whole pizza is shared between three people.

  Each person gets:

  > a whole number of pieces

  > a different amount to everyone else.

  Find all the ways that the pizza could be shared.

  For example, one person could get $\frac{1}{8}$, another could get $\frac{2}{8}$ and the third person could get $\frac{5}{8}$.

  Repeat the task but with the pizza cut into nine pieces and then ten pieces.

  > TIP: In this activity, sharing a pizza as one slice, two slices and five slices is considered the same division as one slice, five slices and two slices.

  > TIP: A sheet of pizzas divided into eight, nine and ten slices is provided in the photocopiable resources online.

- **Investigation: How I spend my day**   *Problem solving*

  Estimate (in whole hours) the amount of time you spend on different activities in a typical day (for example, sleeping, at school, eating, exercising, ….). Ensure your times add up to 24 hours.

  Write the time you spend on each activity as a fraction of the day.

  Then combine fractions together by finding, for example:

  > The fraction of the day spent sleeping or at school is …

  > The fraction of the day spent sleeping or eating is …

- **Investigation: fraction sequences**   *Problem solving*

  Jack has a series of cards:

Card 1	Card 2	Card 3	Card 4	Card 5
$\frac{1}{2} \times 2$	$\frac{2}{3} \times 6$	$\frac{3}{4} \times 12$	$\frac{4}{5} \times 20$	$\frac{5}{6} \times 30$

  What is printed on Cards 6 and 7?

  Find the answers to the calculations on the cards.

  What would be the answer to the calculation on card 12?

- **Investigation: strips** *Problem solving*

  Patrick has strips of wood measuring $\frac{1}{2}$ m, $\frac{1}{4}$ m, $\frac{1}{5}$ m, $\frac{1}{10}$ m and $\frac{1}{20}$ m.

  Show how Patrick can use two of his strips to make a length of $\frac{7}{10}$ m.

  Investigate what other lengths Patrick can make by using two or more strips of wood.

Percentages and fractions

Learning objectives

Learning objectives covered in this chapter:
7Nf5, 7Nc5

- Understand percentage as the number of parts in every 100; use fractions and percentages to describe parts of shapes, quantities and measures.
- Calculate simple fractions and percentages of quantities, for example, one quarter of 64, 20% of 50 kg.

Key term

- percentage

Prior knowledge assumptions

- Students should know how to find equivalent fractions.
- Students can simplify a fraction to its simplest form.
- They should be able to find a simple fraction of an amount.

The emphasis of the calculation work in this chapter is on developing efficient mental methods for calculating fractions and percentages of quantities.

Calculating percentages of quantities is developed further in Chapter 26.

Guidance on the hook

Film reviews

Purpose: This hook introduces students to finding simple percentages of quantities.

Use of the hook: Begin by leading a discussion with the class about different ways they could work out 40% of 180 in their heads. Possible methods might be:

- finding 10% by dividing by 10 and then multiplying by 4
- finding 10% by dividing by 10, doubling to get 20% and then doubling again
- finding 10% and finding 50% and then subtracting to get 40%
- finding 1% by dividing by 100 and then multiplying by 40
- changing 40% to $\frac{2}{5}$ and then dividing by 5 and multiplying by 2.

Discuss which methods students like.

Then ask students to work in a small group to answer the questions in the hook. Bring the class together after a few minutes and discuss their answers and the methods used.

TIP: In the discussion, you may wish to discuss aspects such as whether the people who rate the film will be representative of all people who have watched it.

Adaptation: The number of people could be shown pictorially. For example, the 250 people could be represented by this arrangement:

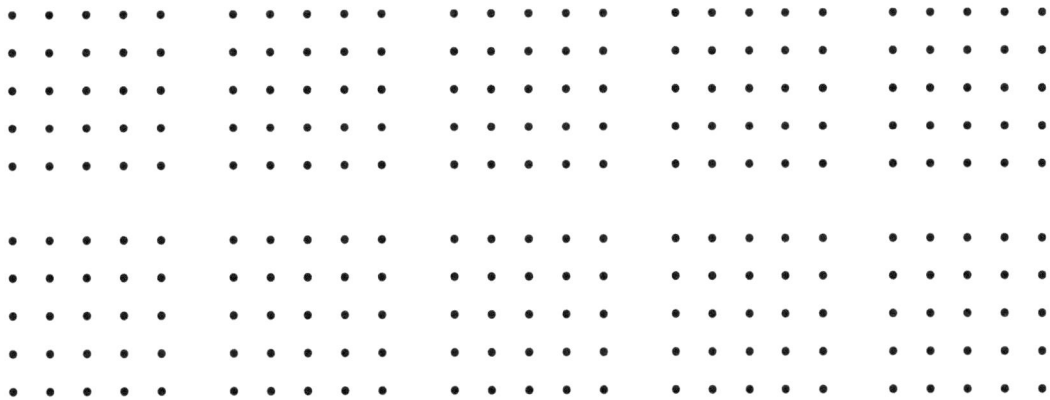

This may help students to find 80%.

Extension: The percentages or the number of reviews could be altered to make the calculations a little more challenging.

Starter ideas

Mental maths starter

$\frac{1}{3} = \frac{8}{?}$ Find the value of the missing denominator.	$\frac{2}{5} = \frac{?}{30}$ Find the value of the missing numerator.	$\frac{3}{4} = \frac{?}{28}$ Find the value of the missing numerator.	$\frac{2}{7} = \frac{10}{?}$ Find the value of the missing denominator.
Write $\frac{12}{15}$ in its simplest form.	Write $\frac{6}{18}$ in its simplest form.	Write $\frac{12}{16}$ in its simplest form.	Write $\frac{15}{35}$ in its simplest form.
Find $\frac{1}{3}$ of 15.	Find $\frac{1}{5}$ of 30.	Find $\frac{1}{4}$ of 28.	Find $\frac{1}{8}$ of 24.
Write 0.2 as a percentage.	Write 0.25 as a percentage.	Write 0.03 as a percentage.	Write 0.18 as a percentage.
Write 50% as a fraction in its simplest form.	Write 20% as a fraction in its simplest form.	Write 75% as a fraction in its simplest form.	Write 30% as a fraction in its simplest form.

Start point check: Follow-me game

Use the follow-me game relating to simplifying fractions (see photocopiable resouces online) to recap this prior knowledge.

Cut out the 32 cards along the solid lines and give out all the cards (one or more to each student).

The person with the START card begins the game.

TIP: You could time how long the game lasts and repeat the game at the start of several lessons to see if the class can complete the game more quickly.

- **Start point check: discussion**

  Give each student a mini-whiteboard and ask them the following questions:
  - Give me a fraction equivalent to 25%.
  - Can you find me a fraction equivalent to 25% that has numerator equal to 11?
  - Give me a fraction equivalent to 25% that has denominator equal to 60.
  - Give me a fraction equivalent to 20% where the numerator is a prime number.
  - Give me a fraction equivalent to 20% where the denominator is a prime number. (How many possible fractions are possible here?)

Discussion ideas

Probing questions	Teacher prompts
What fraction of 2 kg is 300 g? Explain how you know.	Encourage students to first change to a common unit and to simplify their fractions fully.
True or False? 10% of 80 = 8 so, dividing by 2 gives 5% of 40 = 4	Ask students how the second statement could be written correctly, for example: 10% of 40 = 4 or 5% of 80 = 4
Which is larger 20% of $50 or 50% of $20?	Encourage students to explain their answers. Is something similar true for similar situations (for example, 10% of 60 or 60% of 10).
Explain why one fifth of a number can be found by doubling the number and then dividing by 10.	First try out the method on some numbers, for example, use the method to find one fifth of 65 or one fifth of 130.
Sara says that 20% of an hour is 20 minutes. Is she correct? Explain your answer.	Remind students that percentages are parts per hundred. But is an hour equal to 100 minutes?
Can you have 200% of $30?	Discuss with students what percentages greater than 100% might mean... if 100% means the whole amount, what might 200% of an amount mean? Or 300%? Or 150%?

Common errors/misconceptions

Misconception	Strategies to address
Students do not always appreciate that a shape has to be divided into pieces of the same size in order to decide on what fraction is shaded For example, students may mistakenly think that $\frac{1}{4}$ of this shape is shaded: 	Ask students to shade one quarter of a 4 by 4 square by dividing the square into 4 congruent pieces in different ways. For example Ask students then to divide the square into 4 pieces with the same area. For example
To find 10% of a number you divide by 10, so some students think that to find 20% of a number you divide by 20	Relate percentages to equivalent fractions. Note that if you divide a number by 20, you are finding

Misconception	Strategies to address
	$\frac{1}{20}$ of it. But 20% is the same as $\frac{1}{5}$, so you should be dividing by 5. Note also that an easy way to find 20% would be to find 10% and then double the answer.
Students sometimes believe that one third is 30%	Examine what this would mean: 30% Three lots of 30% is only 90% not 100%.

Developing conceptual understanding

7Nf5 Understand percentage as the number of parts in every 100; use fractions and percentages to describe parts of shapes, quantities and measures.

- FIX: If students are struggling to shade different fractions of shapes, begin by first checking that they can shade $\frac{1}{2}$ of a shape (meaning that 1 out of each pair of squares needs shading) and $\frac{1}{4}$ of a shape (meaning that 1 out of every group of 4 squares needs shading).

- Ask students to sort the cards (see photocopiable resource online) into groups which illustrate the same proportion.

7Nc5 Calculate simple fractions and percentages of quantities, for example, one quarter of 64, 20% of 50 kg.

- FIX: Spider diagrams can help students to visualise connections between percentages of amounts:

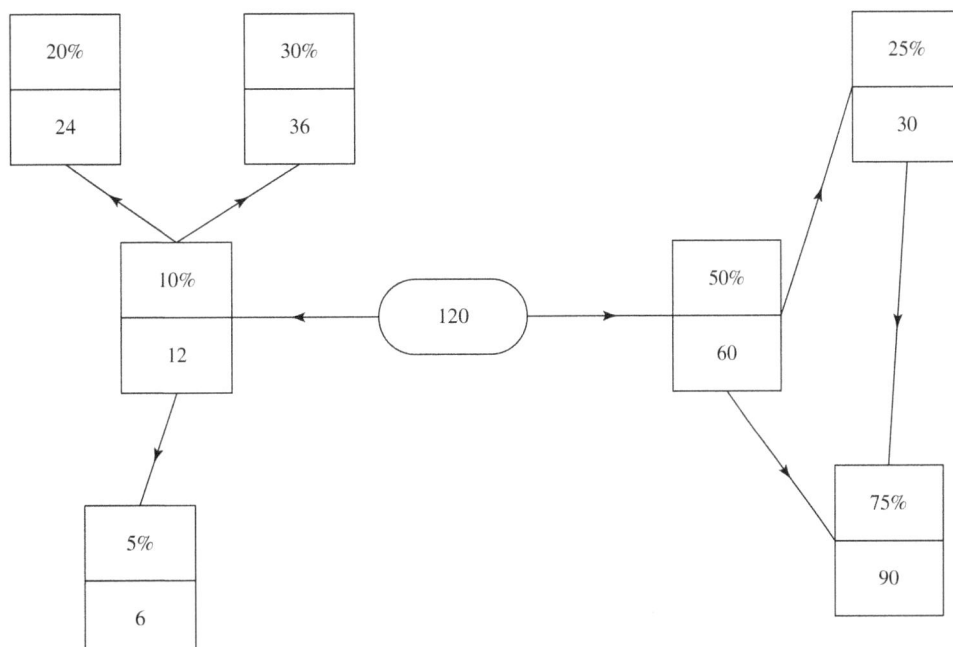

- Discuss the different ways to find 20% of an amount, for example:

    divide by 5

    find 10% and double

    divide by 100 and then multiply by 20….

STRETCH: Students that have mastered finding simple percentages of amounts mentally could start to explore finding other percentages of amounts, for example, 15%, 45%, 1%, etc.

End of Chapter Mental Maths Exercise

1. There are 24 coats on a rail. One third of the coats are blue. How many blue coats are there?	5. Find $\frac{1}{4}$ of 52.
	6. Find 10% of $140.
2. Simplify fully the fraction $\frac{18}{45}$.	7. Half of a square is shaded red. 20% of the square is shaded blue. The rest of the square is shaded green. What percentage of the square is shaded green?
3. 46% of the students in a class walk to school. What percentage do not walk to school?	
4. What percentage is equivalent to $\frac{4}{5}$?	8. Find $\frac{3}{10}$ of 40.

Technology recommendations

- Use the internet to research the art of Ellsworth Kelly. Some of his artwork was created using coloured squares – see for example the paintings 'Colors for a large wall' and 'Spectrum Colors Arranged by Chance'.

    Ask students to create their own piece of art work created by colouring in squares in a 10 by 10 square grid. Ask students to write down what percentage of their picture is each colour. Students could use a drawing package to create their design.

- Students could explore how they can find percentages and fractions of amounts using their calculator (fraction button key and percentage button key).

Investigation/research tasks

- **Investigation: packing pens** *Problem solving*

    A packet contains 24 pens.

    The packet contains at least one pen of each of these colours: red, blue, green and black.

    Find all the possible combination of colours in the packets if

    o one quarter of the pens in each packet must be black

    o each packet should have the same number of green pens as red pens

    o no more than 50% of the pens should be blue.

- **Investigation: shading 25%** *Problem solving*

    These diagrams show different ways of shading 25% of a 2 by 4 grid:

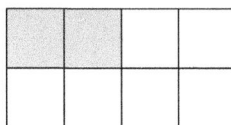

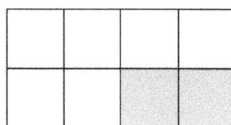

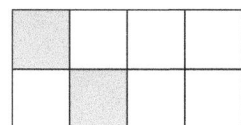

Find all the different ways of shading 25% of a 2 by 4 grid. Try to do this in a systematic way to make sure you have them all.

Extend the investigation by finding the number of ways of shading 25% of other size grids (for example 2 by 2 and 2 by 6). Can you predict the number of ways there would be for shading 25% of a 4 by 4 grid? Can you explain how you worked out your answer?

- **Investigation: Combining percentages and fractions**   *Problem solving*

Start with 600.

Work out $\frac{1}{3}$ of the start number.

Then find 50% of the new amount.

Then find 30% of that amount.

What is the overall answer?

Try other starting numbers, for example 150, or 3000 or 900.

How does the final answer relate to the starting number? Can you explain this?

Calculations

Learning objectives

Learning objectives covered in this chapter: 7Nc6, 7Nc11

- Use the laws of arithmetic and inverse operations to simplify calculations with whole numbers and decimals.
- Know when to round up or down after division when the context requires a whole-number answer.

Key term

- round

Prior knowledge assumptions

- Students should be able to add two numbers, for example, 173 + 249.
- Students should be able subtract two numbers, for example, 564 – 237.
- Students should be able to multiply a number by a single-digit number, for example 58 × 7.
- Students should be able to divide a number by a single-digit number, for example 63 ÷ 9.
- Students should be able to round to the nearest whole number, for example round 4.5 to the nearest whole number.

This work will be useful when students learn about Order of Operations.

Guidance on the hook

Usma's biscuits

Purpose: This hook introduces students to rounding up the answer to calculations in a real-life context.

Use of the hook: Display the recipe for 12 biscuits clearly to students. Discuss with the class how to scale the recipe ingredients to make 36 biscuits.

Next tell students the pack sizes that the ingredients can be bought in. Discuss with students how we can find how many packs of each type of ingredient are needed. Make sure that students are aware that two packs of butter will not be enough and that here we must round up all the answers to the nearest whole number.

Adaptation: Students could use wooden or plastic cubes to help them to find possible cuboids that can be made using exactly 72 cubes. To make it easier for some students, the number of cubes could be reduced to 36.

Extension: Could 48 biscuits be made from three packs of butter, one bag of caster sugar and two bags of flour? Could 60 biscuits be made from these same ingredients?

Starter ideas

Mental maths starter

Work out 46 + 37	Work out 81 − 28	Work out 540 + 280	Work out 630 − 390
Work out 40 × 30	Work out 0.9 × 3	Work out 80 × 40	Work out 0.6 × 6
Find 72 ÷ 8	Find 48 ÷ 6	Find 56 ÷ 8	Find 36 ÷ 9
Round 4.78 to the nearest whole number.	Round 3.32 to the nearest whole number.	Round 10.54 to the nearest whole number.	Round 7.47 to the nearest whole number.
Find 55 × 4	Find 34 × 6	Find 66 × 3	Find 74 × 5

Start point check: Class activity-target board

Ask students to work out the answers to these questions in their heads. The answers are in the target board.

340 + 270

820 − 350

5.1 × 100

60 × 7

65 × 4

85 ÷ 5

92 ÷ 4

42 000 ÷ 1000

11	17	19	23
42	56	260	270
420	470	480	510
520	550	610	620

- **Problem: Find the year**   *Problem solving*

  What is the year if:

  o when it is divided by 2, there is no remainder?

  o when it is divided by 25, the answer is greater than 81 but less than 82?

  o when it is divided by 52, the answer is greater than 38 but less than 39?

  Students could use calculators to help them. Ask students to explain how they arrived at their answer.

  (The answer is 2026.)

- **Game: Rounding down**

  The game involves two players.

  Player 1 chooses a starting number – this should be a whole number between 100 and 200.

  Player 2 chooses a digit card without looking (see photocopiable resources) and then divides the starting number by their digit card and rounds **down** the answer to the nearest whole number.

  Player 1 then chooses a digit card without looking and divides the new whole number by their digit card and rounds **down** the answer to the nearest whole number.

  The players alternate their turns.

The game finishes as soon as the number 0 is reached. The player who gets to 0 loses the game.

Example:

Player 1	chooses 145		
Player 2	Digit card picked 4	145 ÷ 4 = 36.25	rounds down to 36
Player 1	Digit card picked 2	36 ÷ 2 = 18	
Player 2	Digit card picked 5	18 ÷ 5 = 3.6	rounds down to 3
Player 1	Digit card picked 8	3 ÷ 8 = 0.375	rounds down to 0

Player 1 loses, so player 2 wins.

Discussion ideas

Probing questions	Teacher prompts
Tell me an easy way to work out mentally the answer to 177 + 148 + 23 + 352	Discuss whether the order in which the addition matters. Is there a way of adding the numbers that makes the calculation much easier to work out?
Apples cost $0.64 each. Bananas cost $0.36 each. How could we easily work out the cost of 7 apples and 6 bananas?	Encourage students to notice that the total cost of an apple and a banana is $1, so the total cost could be found by finding 6 × 1 + 0.64.
Show me that 26 × 17 + 74 × 17 and 112 × 17 − 12 × 17 have the same answer.	Encourage students not to work out all of the multiplications but to note that both calculations are equal to 100 × 17.
Give me an example of a number that gives a remainder of 2 when divided by 7. And another…. And another….	Ask students what all the numbers have in common? Determine that they are all 2 more than a multiple of 7.
Give me an example of a calculation that gives an answer of 6 when rounded to the nearest whole number. And another… And another…	Ask students to explain the strategies they used to think of a suitable calculation. TIP: If students find this hard, encourage them to work backwards. For example, 6.2 × 10 = 62 so 62 ÷ 10 would give an answer (6.2) which rounds to 6.

Common errors/misconceptions

Misconception	Strategies to address
Some students find mental calculations tricky. They can also sometimes struggle to work out answers to calculations efficiently	Give plenty of opportunities for students to practise skills such as complements to 100, multiplication tables and associated division facts. Emphasise that there are often many possible approaches that can be used to work out the answer to a mental calculation. Encourage students to reflect on their strategy and to think about whether there could be an easier way to work out the answer.

Misconception	Strategies to address
Some students think that a list of numbers has to be added in the order they are written	Encourage the students to think of the numbers as prices and get them to reflect on whether the total cost of the items depends on the order in which the items are bought.
Some students believe that each digit gets rounded For example, some students mistakenly believe 547 rounds to 600 to the nearest hundred (547 first rounds to 550 and then 550 rounds to 600).	Plot the number 547 on a number line showing numbers between 500 and 600. Look at how far 547 is from 500 and how far 547 is from 600.
When interpreting the value of a calculation that requires a whole number answer some students find it difficult to decide whether the answer should be rounded up or down	Give students access to a wide range of rounding problems. Encourage students to check their answers. For example, consider: How many coaches, that can each hold 42 children, are needed to transport 237 children? After working out that 237 ÷ 42 = 5.6…., encourage students to think about whether 5 coaches would be enough and whether 6 coaches would be enough.

Developing conceptual understanding

7Nc6 Use the laws of arithmetic and inverse operations to simplify calculations with whole numbers and decimals.

- FIX: Students need to be comfortable with addition and subtraction being inverse operations and multiplication and division being inverse operations. To reinforce this, you could practise reversing operations with students. For example:

  27 + 46 = 73 so 73 − 46 = 27

  6 × 14 = 84 so 84 ÷ 14 = 6

- FIX: In order to visualise the calculation 8 × 37 + 8 × 63, students could cut out the diagrams on the photocopiable resource. By fitting the pieces to together to form hundred grids, students should see that the answer is 800.

STRETCH: Students working at greater depth could begin to use laws of arithmetic to simplify calculations involving fractions, for example, $\frac{2}{5} \times 11 + \frac{3}{5} \times 11$ or $\frac{1}{7} \times 12 + \frac{1}{7} \times 58$

7Nc11 Know when to round up or down after division when the context requires a whole-number answer.

- FIX: If students find it hard deciding whether to round up or to round down an answer to a division problem, you could start by using the method of repeated subtraction.

  For example, consider this problem:

  A coach holds 42 children. How many coaches are needed to transport 237 children?

  A solution to this problem could be set out as follows.

Coaches	Number of children left

1 coach = 42 children	2 3 7 _ 4 2_ 1 9 5
2 coaches = 84 children	1 9 5 _ 4 2_ 1 5 3
3 coaches = 126 children	1 5 3 _ 4 2_ 1 1 1
4 coaches = 168 children	1 1 1 _ 4 2_ 0 6 9
5 coaches = 210 children	6 9 _ 4 2_ 2 7

At this point we can see that five coaches would not be enough, so six coaches would be needed.

End of chapter mental maths exercise

1. Work out 7.3×100.	5. Write down the missing number in this calculation: $112 + 65 + ? - 112 = 100$
2. Work out $54 + 67 + 46$.	
3. Round 10.34 up to the nearest whole number.	6. A booklet of stamps contains 8 stamps. Max needs 53 stamps. How many booklets of stamps does he need to buy?
4. Find $7 \times 16 + 3 \times 16$.	7. Work out $36 \times 4.5 \div 18$.
	8. Work out $4 \times 8.2 \times 5 \times 5$.

Technology recommendations

• Explore the following spreadsheet functions on a spreadsheet: **Round, Round down, Round up.**

Students could type the following spreadsheet formulae into Excel and consider the results.

	A	B	C
1	=ROUND(128/11,0)	=ROUNDDOWN(71/4,0)	=ROUNDUP(71/4, 0)
2	=ROUND(128/11,1)	=ROUNDDOWN(71/4,1)	=ROUNDUP(71/4, 1)
3			

Ask students to describe in their own words what the functions are doing.

- Students could use their calculators to help check their answers to questions. They should, however, take care not to prematurely round.

  For example, if they are asked to find 120 ÷ 13 × 13:

  If the calculation is typed into a calculator in one go, the answer will be 120.

  However, if a student first finds 120 ÷ 13 and records this as 9.23 and then multiplies 9.23 by 13 they will get 119.99.

Investigation/research tasks

- **Investigation: Making 1000**   *Problem solving*

  How many ways can you find to make 1000 by adding together numbers from this grid?

198	65	156	138
162	140	144	617
260	378	120	480
383	202	222	635

- **Problem: Rounding**   *Problem solving*

  When a number x is divided by 7 the answer is 11 when rounded down to the nearest whole number.

  When the number x is divided by 8, the answer is 11 when rounded up to the nearest whole number.

  What are the possible values for x if x is a whole number?

  (The solution here is that x could be 81 or 82 or 83.)

- **Investigation: Rounding**   *Problem solving*

  A whole number divided by 12 gives an answer of 7 when rounded down to the nearest whole number. What is the largest possible value for the original number?

  A whole number divided by 12 gives an answer of 20 when rounded down to the nearest whole number. What is the largest possible value for the original number?

  Describe how to find the largest possible whole number that, when divided by 12, gives an answer of a when rounded to the nearest whole number.

Area and perimeter

Learning objectives

Learning objectives covered in this chapter: 7MI2, 7Ma1, 7Ma2

- Know abbreviations for and relationships between metric units; convert between:
  - kilometres (km), metres (m), centimetres (cm), millimetres (mm)
  - tonnes (t), kilograms (kg) and grams (g)
  - litres (l) and millilitres (ml)
  - square metres (m^2), square centimetres (cm^2), square millimetres (mm^2).
- Derive and use formulae for the area and perimeter of a rectangle; calculate the perimeter and area of compound shapes made from rectangles.

Key terms

- perimeter
- length
- width
- height
- millimetre (mm); centimetre (cm); metre (m); kilometre (km)
- area
- square millimetres (mm^2); square centimetres (cm^2); square metres (m^2); square kilometres (km^2)
- compound shape
- units
- convert
- mass
- gram (g); kilogram (kg); tonne (t)
- capacity
- millilitre (ml); litre (l)
- metric (units)

Prior knowledge assumptions

- Students can multiply and divide whole and decimal numbers by 10, 100 and 1000.
- Students know the abbreviations for metric units, for example, cm for centimetres.
- Students can convert between metric units, such as converting 435 cm to 4.35 m.
- Students know how to construct simple algebraic expressions and how to multiple a constant over a bracket.
- Students can find perimeters of shapes given the lengths of all their sides.
- Students can find/estimate the area of a shape by counting squares.
- Students can calculate the area of a rectangle or square by calculation.

Guidance on the hook   *Problem solving*

Purpose: This task encourages students to investigate the different (rectilinear) shapes that can be made using a fixed perimeter and how the area of each shape varies. This should enable them to recap the concepts of perimeter and area as well as apply their problem solving skills.

Use of the hook: As suggested in the student book, give all students a piece of square dotty paper.

Model to the whole class how to produce a shape using 12 connecting horizontal or vertical lines, such as

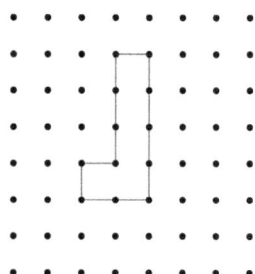

Now ask students to find as many shapes made of 12 connecting horizontal or vertical lines between two dots as they can and record them on their paper.

How do they know they have got them all?

Compile a whole class list.

Here are some examples:

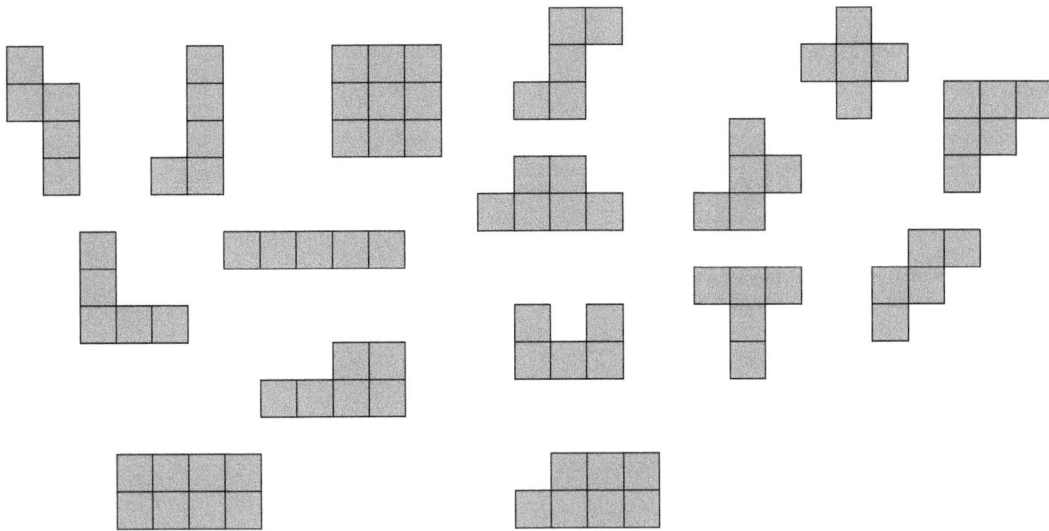

Discuss whether shapes that are the same but in a different orientation count as the same or different.

Similarly, are shapes that have sections that touch only at a vertex to be included? Such as

?

Discuss with the whole class that all these shapes have the same perimeter.

Ask students to find the area of each of their shapes.

Which shape has the largest area? Why is this?

Which shape has the smallest area? Why is this?

BEWARE: Students may try to position the lines diagonally. However, it is important that the students only position the lines vertically and horizontally on the grid to keep the perimeter fixed at 12.

Adaptation:

TIP: You could use matchsticks or straws to make this task practical first of all. Give each student 12 sticks and ask them to arrange them horizontally and vertically to form the outside of a shape.

Extension: Students working at greater depth can apply their learning to a different perimeter, for example, 16 cm. They could predict which shape will give the largest area and which the smallest area.

Starter ideas

Mental maths starter

Add 7, 8, 5 and 4	Add 8, 9, 4 and 11	Add 5, 9, 8 and 6	Add 9, 4, 6 and 12
Double 7.5	Double 3.6	Double 3.7	Double 7.8
Add and then double: 6 and 7	Add and then double: 4.5 and 6.5	Add and then double: 4.2 and 7.8	Add and then double: 3.1 and 8.4
Multiply 4 and 21	Multiply 3 and 17	Multiply 5 and 32	Multiply 6 and 43
Multiply 2.5 and 6	Multiply 3 and 3.5	Multiply 4.5 and 8	Multiply 7.5 and 8
Divide 36 by 4	Divide 46 by 4	Divide 33 by 6	Divide 52 by 8
Convert 3 m to cm	Convert 8 km to m	Convert 40 mm to cm	Convert 750 cm to m
Convert 4000 ml to l	Convert 2000 g to kg	Convert 5.5 litres to ml	Convert 2.3 kg to grams

Vocabulary feature

Find other words that start with the prefixes: kilo, cent or milli
For example:
Century, Centigrade, Millipede, Centipede, Centenary, Millibar, Kilowatt
(Try to link milli- as a prefix with 1000ths and 1000s, for example, milligram.)

Start point check: Perimeter and area

Give the students squared paper, for example, cm^2
Ask them to draw:

- a shape with an area of 5 square centimetres
- a shape with a perimeter of 6 centimetres
- a rectangle with an area of 12 square centimetres
- a rectangle with a perimeter of 12 centimetres
- an L-shape with an area of 12 square centimetres
- an L-shape with a perimeter of 12 centimetres.

You could also do this task on mini-whiteboards to see the range of answers question by question.

Start point check: Estimation challenge

Read each of these measurements aloud to the students.

They need to estimate the measurement, including a suitable unit.

Award 1 point for a suitable unit and 1 for a measurement that is close to the real answer.

Examples:

- the height of the door to the classroom (~2 m)
- the mass of an apple (~100 g)
- the capacity of a can of drink (~300 ml)
- the length of an eyelash (~8 mm)

- the capacity of an Olympic swimming pool (~2 500 000 litres)
- the mass of a car (~ 2 tonnes)
- the distance to the moon (~400 000 km)
- the height of a desk (~75 cm).
- the mass of a grain of rice (~25 mg)
- the capacity of a kettle (~2 litres).

Discussion ideas

Probing questions	Teacher prompts
How many different rectangles with integer sides are there with a perimeter of 20 cm? What if we allow non-integer sides?	Reinforce the point about the sides being whole numbers. Students should discover five: 9 × 1, 8 × 2, 7 × 3, 6 × 4 and 5 × 5. Prompt them to list these systematically if possible. When non-integers are allowed are there an infinite number? Encourage the students to realise that we are simply looking for two numbers with a sum of 10 – and there an infinite number of these!
Convince me that the perimeter of a rectangle is double the sum of the length and width.	The mental maths starters above ask students to add and then double the result. This question asks them to show that this is a shortcut to find the perimeter of a rectangle. Students could form an algebraic expression for the perimeter as $P = l + l + w + w$ and then show that this is equivalent to $P = 2 (l + w)$.
How can you find the width of a rectangle if you know its area and length?	Students may write this as a missing number problem, for example, length x ? = area, and then try to find the value of ? You could use a numerical example to help students get started. For example, area is 27 and length is 9, so what must width be? Encourage students to use division as the inverse of multiplication. They can also use this to check their answers afterwards. You could ask them to come up with a rule to find the width when given the perimeter and length also.
If you know the area of a square, how can you find its perimeter?	Discuss use of square root to 'unsquare' the area to find the side length and then multiply by 4 to find the perimeter. Try this the other way round too, from perimeter to area.
Show me how you would find the perimeter of this shape ... 7 cm	Encourage students to realise that the rectangle is three times as long as it is wide to help them get started. They can then mark the lengths of the sides on a copy of the diagram.

© HarperCollins*Publishers* 2018

Chapter 17: Area and perimeter   115

Common errors/misconceptions

Misconception	Strategies to address
Forgetting to include sides that are not labelled when calculating perimeter	Imitate drawing round (or even walking round) the shape to show that there are some missing lengths.
	Ask students to label all sides before calculating, using their knowledge of shape properties and of the equal length markings shown on the diagram.
Counting incorrectly at corners when finding the perimeter of a shape drawn on a squared grid	This is a good opportunity for some debate between students with different answers. Ask students to visually show how they arrived at their perimeter to spot the error and say whose method is right.
	Look out for students only counting the corner square once when finding the perimeter.
	Encourage them to count the lines around the edge rather than the squares themselves.
Multiplying all lengths shown when finding the area of a rectangle	Count the squares in the rectangle to see whether the answer is right and, when the student realises it isn't, ask them why they have too many squares.
	Add the small unit squares of size 1 onto the diagram to show why we only need to multiply the length and the width.
Missing out or using the incorrect units for perimeter or area	Deliberately mis-state the units of an answer and check whether this is reasonable with students.
	Model the inclusion of units in examples.
	Relate the concept of area to the number of squares to help recall that the units are squared.
Being unable to deduce the missing lengths on a compound shape	Highlight parallel sides in the same colour to show that they must have the same total length.
	Ask students, "How long must this edge be to give a total length of ... cm?"
Multiplying or dividing the wrong way when converting units. For example, saying that 400 metres = 4 cm because there are 100 cm in 1 m.	Encourage students to visualise 400 m and to ask how many centimetres fit inside this length. Can it really be only 4?

Developing conceptual understanding

7MI2 Know abbreviations for and relationships between metric units; convert between:

– kilometres (km), metres (m), centimetres (cm), millimetres (mm)

– tonnes (t), kilograms (kg) and grams (g)

– litres (l) and millilitres (ml)

* Students can use a range of measuring equipment to investigate the relative sizes of mm, cm, m, km, g, kg, ml and l. This helps them make sensible checks of their conversions and estimates.

7Ma1 Know the abbreviations for and relationships between square metres (m²), square centimetres (cm²), square millimetres (mm²).

- FIX: Show students a rectangle measured in metres and ask them to find its area in square metres. Then convert the lengths to centimetres and ask them to find the area in square centimetres. What is the relationship between square metres and square centimetres? Now continue to millimetres.

BEWARE: Students commonly assume there are 100 square centimetres in a square metre so it can be useful to make a practical square metre from metre rules and ask them how many square centimetres fit inside it to show it cannot be only 100.

7Ma2 Derive and use formulae for the area and perimeter of a rectangle; calculate the perimeter and area of compound shapes made from rectangles.

- Show students shapes drawn on a squared grid initially to help them realise and deduce the formulae for the perimeter and area as just efficient ways of counting.

- FIX: You could also give students a number of squares to arrange into different rectangles to help them find different rectangles with the same area.

  When finding the length from an area and a width, students can arrange the squares into a rectangle with a given width to help deduce the length.

TIP: You could use geoboards and elastic bands to create shapes with a given area or perimeter. There are some electronic simulations of this equipment available online also.

STRETCH Students working at greater depth can investigate the relationship between area and perimeter by looking at the different possible perimeters given the area (and vice versa).

STRETCH Students working at greater depth could explore finding the area of compound shapes by dividing them differently.

- They could also explore this when one of the sides is an unknown, x.

For example:

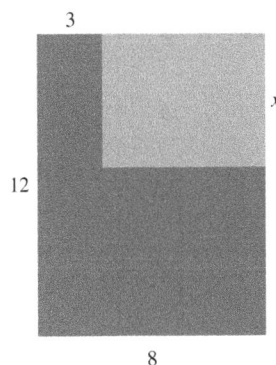

Students could try to show why the area of the dark grey shape here can be written as $96 - 5x$ or as $8(12 - x) + 3x$ or as $36 + 5(12 - x)$ - and then show that these are equivalent expressions.

End of chapter mental maths exercise

1. A rectangle has length 11.5 cm and width 5.5 cm. Find its perimeter.	6. A rectangle has an area of 12 000 cm^2. Its length is 400 cm. Calculate its width.
2. A square has a perimeter of 20 cm. Find its area.	7. A rectangle has an area of 30 cm^2 and a width of 1.5 cm. Calculate its length.
3. A rectangle has a length of 6 cm and a width of 3.5 cm. Find its area.	
4. A square has an area of 9 cm^2. Calculate its perimeter.	8. Convert 238 litres to millilitres.
	9. Convert 635 centimetres to metres.
5. A rectangle has a perimeter of 14 cm. Its length is 3.8 cm. Calculate its width.	10. Convert 4600 grams to kilograms.

Technology recommendations

- Use a spreadsheet to explore challenging maximum and minimum problems such as "A rectangle has an area of 30 cm^2 – what is the minimum and maximum value of its perimeter?"

  Students will need to create and use formulae to calculate the width from the chosen length and then the perimeter, before graphing their results to find the maximum and minimum values.

Perimeter	30	
Length	Width	Area
0.2	14.8	2.96
0.4	14.6	5.84
0.6	14.4	8.64
0.8	14.2	11.36
1	14	14
1.2	13.8	16.56
1.4	13.6	19.04
1.6	13.4	21.44
1.8	13.2	23.76
2	13	26
2.2	12.8	28.16
2.4	12.6	30.24
2.6	12.4	32.24
2.8	12.2	34.16
3	12	36

TIP: The formula $= \dfrac{(30 - 2*\text{'length'})}{2}$ will automatically calculate the width.

- Using dynamic geometry software to produce a compound shape (such as an L-shape) and calculate the area (or perimeter). This is best done with the background grid showing.

  You can then move the vertex of the cut-out section to see how the area or perimeter change in response.

Investigation/research tasks

- Is this statement true or false? Investigate.

  The perimeter of an L-shape is the same as the perimeter of the rectangle that surrounds it.

  You might want to encourage students to draw a selection of L-shapes and then complete the rectangle around it that has a length and width the same as the length and width of the L-shape.

  They should quickly realise that this statement is true.

  Students can try to show this more generally by starting with a rectangle of size $a \times b$ and cutting out a rectangle of size $c \times d$ and showing that this reduces the length of one side by c but adds an extra side of length c (and the same for d).

- **Area 36**   *Problem solving*

  How many different rectangles can you find with an area of 36 cm^2 with sides that are a whole number of centimetres?

  o What if you include decimals?

  o Which of your rectangles has the largest perimeter? Which has the smallest? Explain your answers.

  o Can you predict the smallest possible perimeter for a rectangle of area 16 cm^2?

  Students can relate this task to earlier work on factors when finding whole number pairs of sides.

> TIP: It is useful for students to draw their rectangles on squared paper initially to check they have got them all.

  Using decimals produces an infinite number of possible pairs because there are an infinite number of decimals between any two numbers.

  Encourage students to reason that the largest perimeter comes when the fewest edges of the 36 individual squares are inside the shape or when the squares are connected as little as possible i.e. a long rectangle.

  Similarly, the smallest perimeter comes when the edges are compacted together i.e. when the rectangle is as close to a square as is possible.

  BEWARE: This task is related to the hook task but reversed to have a fixed area rather than a fixed perimeter. Look out for students getting muddled and fixing the perimeter.

- Research the history of metric units such as the metre and the gram. You might like to investigate the work of Gabriel Mouton.

  You could also explore the SI units of today and why we use them.

  Encourage students to link their findings to our base 10 number system and the ease of calculating with it.

- Research the unit called a **ton**. How is this same as and different from a **tonne**?

Formulae

Learning objectives

Learning objectives covered in this chapter: 7Ae5, 7Ae6

- Derive and use simple formulae, for example, to change hours to minutes.
- Substitute positive integers into simple linear expressions/formulae.

Key terms

- unknown
- expression
- equation
- formula
- variable
- substitute

Prior knowledge assumptions

- Students understand that letters are used to represent unknown numbers.
- Students are familiar with algebraic notation including $3x$ representing $3 \times x$ and $x + x + x$.
- Students are familiar with terms, expressions and equations.
- Students know and can apply the correct order of operations to arithmetic calculations.

Guidance on the hook

Mobile phone charges   *Problem solving*

Purpose: this hook introduces students to the idea that relationships can be written as simple formulae.

Use of the hook: Start by asking students to explain how mobile phone companies calculate bills. Ask students to work in pairs or small groups to discuss the questions posed in the Student's book. Bring the whole class back together for a discussion of the questions. Give your students the worded formula and discuss how you can use letters to represent the unknowns to write an algebraic formula. In preparation for this you might ask students to research how mobile phone companies calculate bills.

BEWARE: At this stage students are not expected to write algebraic formulae of the form $a = bx + c$. This will be developed in Stage 8.

Adaptation: You could remove the fixed cost element and ask students to consider just the variable cost (which would be equivalent to pay as you go mobile phones).

Extension: You could give students other situations to write worded formulae for and ask them to write these using algebra.

TIP: Ensure that you reinforce the idea of writing down what the letters in the formula represent.

Starter ideas

Mental maths starter

Calculate $7 + 3 \times 4$	Calculate $20 - 16 \div 2$	Calculate $3 + 18 \times 4$	Calculate $15 - 2 \times 4$
Simplify $x + x + x + x$	Simplify $2 \times x \times 6$	Simplify $10x - x - x - x$	Simplify $6a + 3a$
Find the value of $3x - 1$ when $x = 15$	Find the value of $40 + 6x$ when $x = 7$	Find the value of $56 - 4x$ when $x = 7$	Find the value of $5x - 13$ when $x = 4$
Find the value of $5h$ when $h = 7$	Find the value of $f \div 8$ when $f = 96$	Find the value of $1000g$ when $g = 0.67$	Find the value of $x \div 7$ when $x = 56$
The fine for returning a library book late is $2 for each week that the book is late. Write a formula for the fine, F, in cents of returning a book w weeks late.	The cost of hiring a boat is $25 per hour. Write a formula for the cost, C, of hiring the boat for h hours.	The cost of delivering an order from a website is $5 for every kilogram that the parcel weighs. Write a formula for the total delivery cost, C, of sending a parcel of weight w kilograms.	The cost of hiring a plumber is $18 per hour. Write a formula for the cost, C, of hiring a plumber for h hours.

Start point check: Where did it come from?

Give students one of these terms/expressions and ask them each to suggest an expression that could be simplified to produce it.

> TIP: This could be run as a game with students playing in teams with 1 point being awarded for each unique solution.

- $3x$
- $2y$
- $10 + 7x$
- $x + y$
- $x - y$

Game/investigation

Like-term bingo

Ask students to draw a 3 by 3 grid in their book.

Write the following expressions on the board and ask students to put a different expression from the list into the grid.

a	$2a$	$3a$	$4a$	$5a$
b	$2b$	$3b$	$4b$	$5b$
$a + b$	$2a + b$	$a + 2b$	$2a + 2b$	$3a + 2b$

Read out expressions / write on the board expressions for students to simplify that give one of these terms. For example, $3a + a$ or $a + a + b$.

Students should cross out the simplified expression if they have it in their grid.

Students can aim for the first to a row or column completed and then can aim for the full grid completed.

Discussion ideas

Probing questions	Teacher prompts
Draw a shape whose perimeter, P, can be represented by the formula $P = 8a$. Make sure you show the lengths on your diagram. How many different shapes can you find with this perimeter?	Encourage students to think about different shapes. For example, you could prompt students to think about what side length a square with perimeter $8a$ would have. <table><tr><td>TIP: Some shapes may be impossible, for example, a triangle with side lengths a, $2a$ and $5a$ is not possible. Knowing that this triangle is not possible is Stage 8, but you might extend learning by suggesting students choose a value of a and try to draw the triangle.</td></tr></table>
For what value of x, does $3x$ have the value 39?	Look out for students stating that $x = 9$. This is a sign that they do not recognise $3x$ as $3 \times x$ and so are not including the multiplication sign when substituting.
Can a variable have a value that is not a whole number? Explain your answer.	Encourage students to think of examples where a variable might not be a whole number. For example, when measuring time in hours. Note that the pitch of this unit is for positive numbers only.

Common errors/misconceptions

Misconception	Strategies to address
Thinking that a letter is an object rather than a number	Ensure you define all variables, for example, let x be the weight of an apple in grams or let p be the number of pens rather than p = pens.
When writing a conversion formula multiplying the larger unit instead of the smaller one For example, expressing a formula to find the number of centimetres, a, in b metres as $100a = b$ rather than as it should be: $a = 100b$	Try getting students to write the relationship out in words first, before replacing the descriptions of the variables with letters. For example: the number of centimetres = the number of metres multiplied by 100 When a student has written an incorrect formula ask them to substitute some values and see if the answer to their conversion is reasonable. You could also ask students to think about which unit is larger and so which will be multiplied. <table><tr><td>TIP: Choose the variables carefully when dealing with lengths and weights. For example, m for metre and m as a variable can be confusing to students.</td></tr></table>

Misconception	Strategies to address
Believing that $6x$ means 6 tens and x units	Avoid using teaching resources that might lead to this misconception, for example problems where students have to find missing digits to make sums correct for example, $ab \times c = de$ where ab is being used to represent a two-digit number.
Not applying the order of operations to algebra	Give students numerical examples and then convert to an algebraic form. For example: $25 - 5 \times 4$ is the answer 5 or 80? Let $a = 4$, then we can write this as $25 - 5a$
Including units in a formula	Explain to students that a formula is a general instruction so Area = length × width is an instruction of how to calculate an area. The units will depend on the units of measurement that we are using.

Developing conceptual understanding

7Ae5 Derive and use simple formulae, for example, to change hours to minutes.

- Students could initially work on describing the relationships between variables in words, before replacing the descriptions with letters. For example, to write a formula for the number of days, d, in y years, students could write 'the number of days is the number of years multiplied by 365' before translating this to $d = 365y$.

- FIX: Give students two possible formulae for a situation and ask them to identify which is correct. For example, here are two possible formulae for converting the number of days, d, into a number of hours, h, $h = 24d$ and $d = 24h$. Which is correct?

  Students could consider this problem by trying to convert the formulae into words or by attempting a substitution and seeing which gives the correct answer.

  TIP: Emphasise with students the importance of checking if their answer makes sense.

STRETCH: Ask students to combine information in order to write a formula. For example, write a formula to convert weeks to hours.

STRETCH: Ask students to write formulae to convert between imperial units. For example, write a formula to convert feet to inches. Students could be given information about different imperial units to do this and could go on to formulate their own questions (with answers).

7Ae6 Substitute positive integers into simple linear expressions/formulae.

- You could use algebra tiles to represent a formula visually. When substituting, students can replace each element of the formula with its known value before calculating.

  For example, here is a representation of $A = 3x + 7$:

A			
x	x	x	7

- Students can practice substitution by playing the race track substitution game in the photocopiable online resources.

TIP: None of the answers to the substitution will give negatives.

STRETCH: Students could look at examples of formulae involving brackets or squaring.

STRETCH: Students could work backwards to find the input given the output value. It is best to start this in context.

For example, given the formula for the cost of hiring a house, C, in dollars for w weeks as $C = 250 + 500w$, students could find the number of weeks they could hire the house for with a budget of $4250.

End of chapter mental maths exercise

1. Calculate $39 + 7 \times 13$	5. Calculate the value of $3b + c$ when $b = 7$ and $c = 5$.
2. Simplify $3x + x + 5x + 2x$	6. The cost of travelling in a taxi is $2 per kilometre travelled.
3. Find the value of $3x + 2$ when $x = 8$.	Write a formula for the total cost, T, in terms of the number of kilometres travelled, d.
4. Find the value of $24d$ when $d = 5$.	

Technology recommendations

- Use a spreadsheet to list possible values of a variable and enter a simple formula to find the corresponding values. This could then be made into a graph.

- Use the internet research imperial units of measurement and write conversion formulae for these. This could be extended to look at other units of measurement and write conversion formulae for example cubits, palms and fingers (Egyptian measurements).

Investigation/research tasks

- **Pyramid numbers** *Problem solving*

Here is an example of a number pyramid:

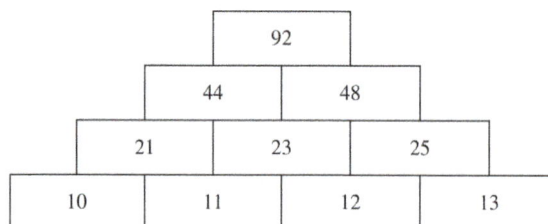

This particular type of number pyramid is formed by adding 1, then 2 and then 3 to the start number to create the numbers on the bottom row as shown in the diagram. Then adding two adjacent numbers together to form the number above.

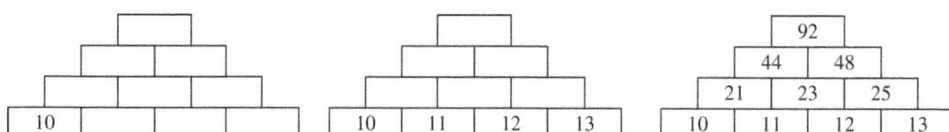

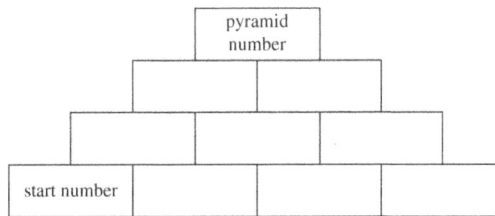

- If the start number is 20, what will the top (pyramid) number be?
- What if the start number is 50?
- If the pyramid (top) number is 340, can you find the start number?
- How could you find a formula for the pyramid number, P, in terms of the start number, n?

Solution:

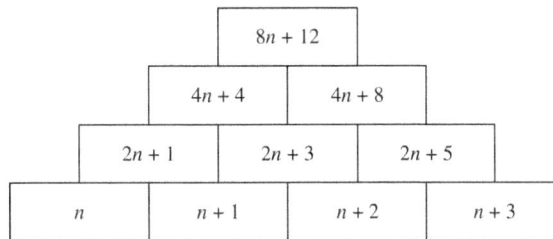

You could ask students working at greater depth to look at pyramids with an extra row (i.e. five boxes on the bottom row) or at pyramids where the numbers increase in 2s, 3s, ... on the bottom row.

- **Squares on number grids** *Problem solving*

1	2	3	4	5	6	7	8	9	10
11	12	13	14	15	16	17	18	19	20
21	22	23	24	25	26	27	28	29	30
31	32	33	34	35	36	37	38	39	40
41	42	43	44	45	46	47	48	49	50
51	52	53	54	55	56	57	58	59	60
61	62	63	64	65	66	67	68	69	70
71	72	73	74	75	76	77	78	79	80
81	82	83	84	85	86	87	88	89	90
91	92	93	94	95	96	97	98	99	100

The 10 by 10 number grid above has a 3 by 3 square drawn on it.

The numbers in opposite corners 3 by 3 square are subtracted from each other and the two answers are then added.

36 − 14 = 22 and 34 − 16 = 18

22 + 18 = 40

Ask students if they think the answer will be the same for a different 3 × 3 square.

Investigate this for the 3 by 3 grid drawn in different positions on the 10 by 10 grid.

Now look at the same calculation for a 4 × 4 square drawn on this grid.

Can you predict the answer for a 5 × 5 grid, a 6 × 6 grid, larger grids?

This can be extended to look different sizes of square or different sizes of grid.

> TIP: Get students to focus on trying out some squares on the 10 by 10 grid to start off with.

> TIP: Don't let students change the size of the square and the size of the grid at the same time.

Photocopiable grids are available in the online resources.

- **9s and 6s**   *Problem solving*

Consider the expression $9a + 6b$.

Can you find pairs of whole numbers for a and b which make this expression equal to 18? One example is $a = 2$ and $b = 0$. How many pairs of whole numbers can you find for which the value of $9a + 6b$ is 18?

Now find pairs of whole numbers for which the value of $9a + 6b$ is 27. How many pairs are there?

Now do the same for other multiples of 9, for example, 45, 54 etc.

Can you see a pattern for the number of pairs?

How many pairs of whole numbers can be found for which

$9a + 6b = 9000$?

Coordinates, functions, graphs and equations

Learning objectives

Learning objectives covered in this chapter: 7Gp1, 7As3, 7As4, 7Ae7

- Read and plot coordinates of points determined by geometric information in all four quadrants.
- Represent simple functions using words, symbols and mappings.
- Generate coordinate pairs that satisfy a linear equation, where y is given explicitly in terms of x; plot the corresponding graphs; recognise straight-line graphs parallel to the x- or y-axis.
- Construct and solve simple linear equations with integer coefficients (unknown on one side only), for example, $2x = 8$, $3x + 5 = 14$, $9 - 2x = 7$.

Key terms

- coordinate; x-coordinate; y-coordinate
- notation: (x, y)
- axes; x-axis, y-axis
- function
- notation: $\mapsto$
- function machine
- input
- output
- mapping diagram
- equation
- table
- plot
- graph
- line
- equation of a line
- unknown
- equation
- solve; solution

Prior knowledge assumptions

- Students can read and plot coordinates of points in the four quadrants (although this is recapped).
- Students are familiar with the x-axis and y-axis and the coordinate grid.
- Students can read and interpret a simple mathematical formula; they can substitute positive numbers into a simple formula.
- Students can solve calculation problems by using inverse operations

Guidance on the hook

Purpose: A game to revise coordinates and begin to notice the relationship between coordinates lying on the same horizontal or vertical line.

Use of the hook: Give each student a copy of the axes shown in the Student Book and available in the photocopiable resources online. Each pair of students also needs a set of number cards –5 to 5.

Allow students to play the game in pairs as described in the Student Book to try to get three points on a line. They should repeat the game two or three times to really begin to notice the connections.

Once they have finished, ask for one of the winners to come to show the whole class their line and the points they got on it.

BEWARE: Focus here on a horizontal or vertical line as the links between the coordinates on diagonal lines can be too complex for students.

Ask the students what they notice about all the coordinates on this line.

Can they think of any other coordinates that would lie on this line? What would all these coordinates be like?

Then pick a random card from the pack, for example, 4.
Ask students if they can predict the line that this point will lie on, even though they don't yet know the second (y) coordinate.

Adaptation: You could play this game with positive numbers only and focus on the first quadrant to discover the relationships between coordinates on horizontal and vertical lines. Alternatively, you could also play a 'battleships' type game with the axes to focus more on coordinate skills than on the next stage of equations of lines.

Extension: Students working at greater depth could explore the links between coordinates on diagonal lines, particularly $y = x$ or $y = -x$.

Starter ideas

Mental maths starter

Find the value of $3x$ when $x = 64$	Find the value of $2x - 1$ when $x = 27$	Find the value of $4x + 3$ when $x = 44$	Find the value of $3x - 5$ when $x = 31$
Find the value of $80 - 7x$ when $x = 3$	Find the value of $30 - 2x$ when $x = 8$	Find the value of $100 - 3x$ when $x = 19$	Find the value of $50 - 6x$ when $x = 2$
Give the equation of the horizontal line going through (0, 5)	Give the equation of the vertical line going through (7, 0)	Give the equation of the horizontal line going through (0, 3)	Give the equation of the vertical line going through (2, 0)
Solve the equation $2x = 36$	Solve the equation $4x = 68$	Solve the equation $3x = 81$	Solve the equation $6x = 92$
Solve the equation $13 - x = 9$	Solve the equation $7 - x = 5$	Solve the equation $4 - x = 1$	Solve the equation $23 - x = 16$

Start point check: Guess my number

Tell students the story of your number as a sequence of operations.

They must work backwards to find out the value of your number.

For example:

I am thinking of a number.

I double my number and then add 5.

I now have 17.

What was my number?

> TIP: Students may want to draw a function machine to represent the operations and then find the inverses.

Game: Substitution noughts and crosses

Give students a grid like this on the board:

$x + 1$	x^2	$3x - 1$
$2(x + 1)$	$2x$	$20 - x$
$\dfrac{x + 3}{2}$	$5 + x$	$\dfrac{x}{2}$

Split them into two teams.

Teams then take it in turns to roll a dice to determine the value of x and send a student to the board to substitute for one expression on the grid.

If they get it right, they claim that square with an O or an X.
Play then passes to the next team.
The winning team is the first to complete a line of 3.

Note: You could adapt the dice to generate more variety of numbers if desired.

Discussion ideas

Probing questions	Teacher prompts
Show me an example of a • term • equation • formula • expression	Note that some students do not realise that a term will also be an expression i.e. that terms are a subset of expressions. Check that students understand that equations and formulae require = signs.
What's the same and what's different? $3x + 1$ and 31	Ensure students realise that. $3x + 1$ is only worth 31 when $x = 10$.
Find a function machine that takes an input of 5 and produces an output of 10. And another … and another	Encourage students to find as many machines as possible using a range of operations For example, +5, ×2, −3 → × 5, +15 → /4
How many points do we need to plot to produce the graph of a function like $y = 2x + 5$?	You may want to allow students to try plotting this graph with 1 point, then 2 points and so on. This will help them realise that the minimum is 2, but 3 points allows them to check they are correct.
Convince me/a friend that the point (45, 17) will lie on the line $y = 17$ and on the line $x = 45$ Give the coordinates of a point that lies on the line $y = 32$ and on the line $x = 29$	Students should explain that every point on the line $y = 17$ has y-coordinate 17 and so on. You could relate this back to the Hook task. Initially students may think there are lots of answers to this but if you ask them to draw a sketch showing both lines they should realise there is only 1 point on both lines i.e. (29, 32)
Show me an equation with solution $x = 3$ And another … and another …	Encourage students to start with one equation such as $x + 4 = 7$ and then adjust it to create related equations. For example, $x + 5 = 8$ or $2x + 4 = 10$
What's the same and what's different? $x + 5 = 9$ $2x + 10 = 18,$ $x + 65 = 69$ $39 - 3x = 27$	Prompt students to solve the equations first They can then look at the structure of the equations to see which are alike. You could also ask them to find related equations by carrying out an operation to the original $x + 5 = 9$ themselves.

Common errors/misconceptions

Misconception	Strategies to address
Plotting or reading coordinates in the wrong order	Show both possible points and ask the students how we know which one is correct.
	Remind students to work horizontally first, then vertically.
Notating coordinates incorrectly using vector notation $\begin{pmatrix} a \\ b \end{pmatrix}$ or missing out the brackets	Emphasise that Cartesian coordinates should be separated by a comma and enclosed in brackets (x, y)
	Model this directly and explain that a vector means something different.
Confusing whether a letter is representing an unknown or a variable in a situation	Ask students whether a letter can take many different values or whether it can only have one value
	For example, $x + 3 = 7$, can x take lots of different values?
	But if $x + y = 7$, can x take lots of different values?
Substituting incorrectly to algebraic expressions, especially missing out necessary ×signs	Ask students whether $2x$ is 24 when $x = 4$. What if $x = 413$, would $2x$ be 2413?
	Emphasise that $2x = x + x = 2 \times x$
Struggling to relate an equation to a linear function	Show students a vertical or horizontal line and ask them to write down a selection of points on the line.
Specifically, students may find it hard to understand that the equation of a line describes the infinite set of all points that meet this rule.	Encourage them to do some points with decimal coordinates or those that are beyond the scale of the graph.
	This should help them see the connection between the coordinates and help them express this in words.
Thinking that an equation always has to be in the order $ax + b = c$	Ensure you show students equations in lots of formats so that they realise they can solve any of these types.
Believing that the solution to an equation has to be a whole, positive number	Ask students "what is the solution to $2x = 7$?" What could that mean in real life? For example, money or $3\frac{1}{2}$ pizzas
	Give students examples of equations where the solution is a decimal, for example, 2.5 or 0 (or a negative number) to show them that the solution can take any value.
Applying inverse operations to a function machine or to an equation in the wrong order.	Get students to check their answers by working back through the function machine from their answer to the given output.
For example, when working to find the input for an output of 24, with this machine, students may add 1 first and then divide by 3.	Draw arrows going back the other way from the output to the input to show that we should divide by 3 first and then add 1.
input → Subtract 1 → Multiply by 3 → output	Use a bar model to represent an equation.
For example, when solving $3x + 12 = 39$, dividing by 3 and then subtracting 12.	This helps students see that the first operation that needs to be 'undone' is the +12 and that this can be done by subtracting 12.
	$\begin{array}{\|c\|c\|c\|c\|} \hline x & x & x & 12 \\ \hline \multicolumn{4}{\|c\|}{39} \\ \hline \end{array}$
Struggling to solve an equation with a negative number of x	You could try covering up the $-2x$ term and asking students what the missing number must be to make this statement true $30 - \blacksquare = 22$ before using this to show that
For example, $30 - 2x = 22$	$2x = 4$ and so $x = 4$

Developing conceptual understanding

7Gp1 Read and plot coordinates of points determined by geometric information in all four quadrants.

- FIX: Students can revisit coordinates at the start of this chapter by using them to form shapes on blank axes. They could make letters or polygons and look at the relationship between coordinates on the same horizontal or vertical lines (when producing a letter E, for example)

7As3 Represent simple functions using words, symbols and mappings.

- FIX: When exploring function machines, it can help to have a blank function machine diagram for students to annotate as they calculate the outputs for given inputs. See the photocopiable resources online for some printable examples.

STRETCH: Students working at greater depth can begin to work backwards, to undo the steps with inverse operations to find the inputs given the outputs. They can also explore three step function machines.

7As4 Generate coordinate pairs that satisfy a linear equation, where y is given explicitly in terms of x; plot the corresponding graphs; recognise straight-line graphs parallel to the x- or y-axis.

- FIX: When plotting graphs, students could start by drawing a table of values and then plotting these points to produce a line. They may notice some connections between the points as they do this which can help them spot the links with y-intercept early!
- FIX: Show students horizontal and vertical lines and let them label a selection of points on each line to observe the rule of the coordinates

STRETCH: Students working at greater depth may be able to spot the connections between the coordinates on simple diagonal lines like $y = x$ or $y = 2x$.

7Ae7 Construct and solve simple linear equations with integer coefficients (unknown on one side only), for example, $2x = 8$, $3x + 5 = 14$, $9 - 2x = 7$

- FIX: Encourage students to represent equations using the bar model (or a function machine) to help them find the value of the unknown.

  For example, here is the image of the equation $2x + 3 = 17$

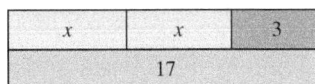

x	x	3
17		

  Students can then try to do this for equations with a subtraction. For example, here is the image of the equation $20 = 3x - 1$

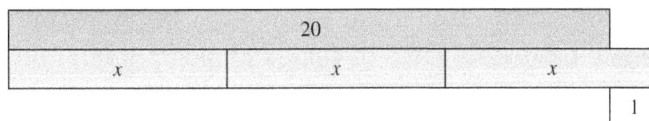

20		
x	x	x
		1

STRETCH: Students working at greater depth can also look at the (infinite) family of equivalent equations that can be found from one starting equation by carrying out the same operation to both sides.

For example, starting with the equation $2x + 7 = 23$, we can create these families of equations (and more!):

$2x + 8 = 24$	$2x + 6 = 22$	$4x + 14 = 46$	$3x + 7 = x + 23$
$2x + 9 = 25$	$2x + 5 = 21$	$6x + 21 = 69$	$4x + 7 = 2x + 23$
$2x + 10 = 26$	$2x + 4 = 20$	$8x + 28 = 92$	$x + 7 = 23 - x$

STRETCH: They can also explore examples where the solution is not a positive integer, such as, $3x + 10 = 4$ or $6x - 1 = 14$

End of chapter mental maths exercise

1. I think of a number.
   I triple it and then subtract 2.
   The result is 31
   What was my number?

2. Find the value of $3x$ when $x = 53$

3. Find the value of $60 - 2x$ when $x = 11.5$

4. Give the equation of the horizontal line going through (0, 1)

5. Name 2 lines that the point (3, 7) lies on

6. Solve the equation $2x + 3 = 37$

7. Solve the equation $16 - x = 13.1$

8. I think of a number, x.
   I multiply it by 4 and then subtract 3.
   The result is 13.
   Write an equation for x

Technology recommendations

- Use dynamic graphing software to explore lines connecting coordinates and their algebraic name.

  You could try plotting the line $y = x + a$ and using a slider to change the value of a so that students can see the effect on the graph.

  They should notice that the graph crosses the y-axis at the point $(0, a)$

  > TIP: Set the slider up to start with only whole number values of a from −10 to 10. You can then introduce decimals afterwards.

  You could also draw horizontal and vertical lines and ask students to label their coordinates to spot the rule connecting them.

  STRETCH: Students working at greater depth could explore how to solve an equation like $3x + 5 = 74$ graphically.

- Use a spreadsheet to produce a table of values to plot a graph from the equation.

  Students can use formulae to generate the y-coordinates automatically from the x-coordinates.

Investigation/research tasks

- Research the history of coordinates and particularly the work of the French mathematician Rene Descartes, who introduced Cartesian coordinates in the 17th century.

  Students could produce a poster or presentation to explain why and how coordinates were introduced.

They could also mention the other systems of coordinates that have been used alongside. Additionally, they could talk about the real life uses of coordinates such as in map reading and navigation.

- **Maths Magic Trick**   *Problem solving*

Think of a number.

Double it.

Add 10 to your answer.

Halve the result.

Subtract the original number.

What do you have?

Repeat this process.

What do you notice?

Will this always happen? Prove it!

Students should notice that they always get an answer of 5 and use algebra to prove this will always happen.

> TIP: Students can then try to make up their own maths trick and show why it works.

They can swap over and test out each other's tricks if they have time.

- **L-totals**   *Problem solving*

1	2	3	4	5	6	7	8	9	10
11	12	13	14	15	16	17	18	19	20
21	22	23	24	25	26	27	28	29	30
31	32	33	34	35	36	37	38	39	40
41	42	43	44	45	46	47	48	49	50
51	52	53	54	55	56	57	58	59	60
61	62	63	64	65	66	67	68	69	70
71	72	73	74	75	76	77	78	79	80
81	82	83	84	85	86	87	88	89	90
91	92	93	94	95	96	97	98	99	100

The 10 by 10 number grid has an L-shape (2 × 3) drawn on it.

The numbers inside the L are added together:

14 + 24 + 34 + 35 = 107.

We say that the L-total for this L, which we can call L_{14} is 107.

○   What will the L-total for L_{26} be?
○   What about L_{45}?

If we know the L-total of an L-shape, can we find the position of the L on the grid? For example, if the L-total is 263, where is the L positioned?

Investigate

Encourage students to represent their L-shape as

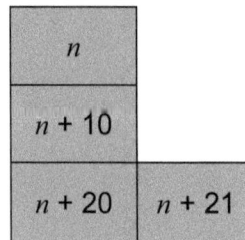

to help them write (and then solve) a suitable equation.

They can then draw a function machine to show what happens to the position number to arrive at the L-total (and then reverse this).

TIP: Students can then change the size of the L or of the grid to see how the equation will change. Don't allow them to change both at the same time though.

Angles

Learning objectives

Learning objectives covered in this chapter: 7Gs5, 7Gs6

- Start to recognise the angular connections between parallel lines, perpendicular lines and transversals.
- Calculate the sum of angles at a point, on a straight line and in a triangle, and prove that vertically opposite angles are equal; derive and use the property that the angle sum of a quadrilateral is 360°.

Key terms

- parallel
- perpendicular
- acute angle
- right angle
- obtuse angle
- alternate angles
- corresponding angles
- transversal
- vertically opposite angles
- angles on a straight line
- angles in a triangle
- angles in a quadrilateral
- angles around a point

Prior knowledge assumptions

- Students recognise and draw parallel lines.
- Students recognise and draw perpendicular lines.
- Students know the meaning of an acute angle.
- Students know the meaning of a right angle.
- Students know the meaning of an obtuse angle.
- Students know the side and angle properties of special triangles.
- Students know the side and angle properties of special quadrilaterals.

Guidance on the hook

Investigating quadrilaterals

Purpose: This hook encourages students to look for any patterns in the angle sum of quadrilaterals.

Use of the hook: Introduce Mia's example to the class. Ask students to draw a quadrilateral of their choosing, and then to measure its angles. They should compare with their neighbour, and then collect thoughts from the group as a whole.

BEWARE: Although the angle sum should be 360°, in reality a range of answers close to that value is to be expected. Students should draw diagrams using ruler and a sharp pencil, and large enough to enable the use of a protractor to measure angles. Even if this is successful, some students may have difficulty measuring angles that involve orienting the protractor in various ways, and they may have difficulty reading off the number of degrees in many cases. The class as a whole should be encouraged to see this as experimental evidence, which is subject to error.

Adaptation: Use dynamic geometry software to construct the shapes and measure the angles precisely.

Extension: Students could investigate for other polygons.

Starter ideas

London underground map

Put an image of the London underground map on the board and ask students to come up and draw over or show pairs of parallel lines. Ask them, for example, whether all parallel lines have to be horizontal or vertical? Can they see any pairs of perpendicular lines?

Mental maths starter

180 − 65	180 − 86	360 − 185	360 − 109
Find the number of degrees in three right angles.	Find the number of degrees in two right angles.	Find the number of degrees in three quarters of a turn.	Find the number of degrees in half a turn.
Subtract the sum of 26 and 54 from 180.	Subtract the sum of 67 and 16 from 180.	Subtract the sum of 43 and 189 from 360.	Subtract the sum of 56 and 147 from 360.
Two numbers have a total of 180. One of the numbers is 103. What is the second number?	Two numbers have a total of 180. One of the numbers is 143. What is the second number?	Three numbers have a total of 180. Two of the numbers are 65 and 94. Find the third number.	Four numbers have a sum of 180. Two of the numbers are 28 and 38. The other two numbers are equal. Find these numbers.
Three numbers have a total of 360. Two of the numbers are 60 and 130. Find the third number.	Three numbers have a total of 360. Two of the numbers are 70 and 120. Find the third number.	Four numbers have a total of 360. Three of the numbers are 30, 60 and 100. Find the fourth number.	Four numbers have a total of 360. Three of the numbers are 100, 49 and 81. Find the fourth number.

Start point check: Angles of a triangle

This start point check will give students the opportunity to see that all triangles have the same angle sum and that drawing and measuring isn't always exact.

Ask students to draw three different triangles, measure the three angles and add them up.

Before they start drawing, discuss whether the sharpness of the pencil matters (width of line) and how big the triangle should for them be to be able to measure the angles accurately.

Put their findings on the board and discuss, lead them to the conclusion that 180° is probably correct.

STRETCH: Do the same for quadrilaterals and ask them to make a conclusion suitable to the accuracy of the measurement.

Discussion ideas

Probing questions	Teacher prompts
How would you draw a pair of parallel lines on a piece of squared paper? How many different directions could you draw the lines in?	Start by asking them to draw 3 sets of parallel lines in different directions on squared paper. Remind them that lines do not just have to be horizontal or vertical.
A transversal is a line that crosses a pair of parallel lines. How many lines in this diagram, showing 2 pairs of parallel lines, could be called transversals? Explain your choice.	Students should recognise that any of the lines in the diagram could be a transversal.

Probing questions	Teacher prompts
Write the possible sizes of four angle that meet at a point. If someone else has chosen exactly the same 4 numbers you get 1 point. If someone else has 3 numbers the same you get 2 points. 2 numbers the same is 3 points, 1 number the same is 1 points and no numbers the same as anyone else in the class gets 10 points. Can you get 10 points for your 4 numbers?	Simple answers such as 90°, 90°, 90°, 90° are likely to get fewer points.

Common errors/misconceptions

Misconception	Strategies to address
Thinking that these two angles are the same: 	Ask students to identify whether the angles are acute or obtuse.
Thinking that these two angles are the same: 	Ask students which lines are parallel, so which must be transversals.
Thinking that perpendicular lines have to be horizontal or vertical	Ensure students are exposed to perpendicular lines in a range of orientations. Students can look for the notation and right angles to help them identify.
In an isosceles triangle, students choose the two angles nearest the 'base' (as defined by the orientation of the triangle) as equal, which is not always true	In the original Greek, *isos* means 'equal' and *skelos* means 'leg'. Isosceles means 'equal legs'. Ask students what they have at the bottom of their equal legs. The ideal answer is equal ankles! If they picture the triangle in an orientation with the equal sides being 'legs', then the equal angles are now at the base. Give students isosceles triangles in various orientations to demonstrate why this thinking can help them identify the equal angles.

Developing conceptual understanding

7Gs5 Start to recognise the angular connections between parallel lines, perpendicular lines and transversals.

Look for parallel/perpendicular lines in the environment. Challenge students to identify parallel lines and transversals, and vertically opposite angles, in the environment.

Students may benefit from seeing a dynamic image of geometrical situations. In particular, dynamic geometry software, can be used to set up a simple diagram with parallel lines and a moving transversal. The angle can be measured and compared. They can either observe, or move themselves, the transversal and observe that certain angles are always equal even though they constantly vary.

Ask students to create a diagram with a pair of parallel lines and a transversal (diagram 1 below). On tracing paper, an identical copy of this diagram should then be created and overlaid. (diagram 2). Students can then establish equal angles in the corresponding position: the tracing paper should be translated into a position such that the 'corresponding angles' match up (diagram 3).
If instead the top diagram is rotated, then the 'alternate angles' can be observed to be equal in a similar way. Students do not need to know the terms 'corresponding' and 'alternate' at this stage.

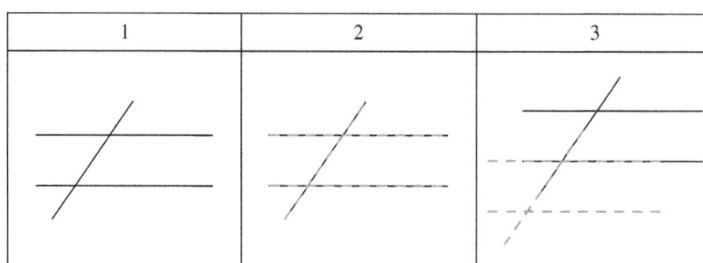

TIP: Alternatively, this can be presented to students using images created in a presentation package. The three lines will need to be grouped to enable this demonstration to work.

7Gs6 Calculate the sum of angles at a point, on a straight line and in a triangle, and prove that vertically opposite angles are equal; derive and use the property that the angle sum of a quadrilateral is 360°.

FIX: Some students will struggle with multi-step missing angle problems if they need to find angles that are not labelled with arcs as part of the process. Provide students with diagrams such as that in question 5 of section 1, but with no arcs labelled on unknown angles. Challenge them to find every angle they can. It doesn't need to be labeled with an arc to be an angle!

Problem solving

When helping students to correctly identify the equal angles in isosceles triangles, set them this problem which combines knowledge of parallel lines, isosceles triangles and angles on a straight line. Students should discuss strategies and be encouraged to share their thinking with the class.

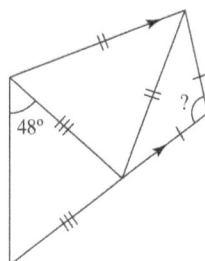

© HarperCollins*Publishers* 2018

STRETCH: For those students who are particularly fluent at solving missing angle problems, set them a challenge combining different areas of mathematics, such as:

Create a missing angle at a point problem such that:

- The solution is 71°.
- There are four angles.
- The number of degrees at each angle is a prime number.

How many different solutions can you find?

End of chapter mental maths exercise

1. Two angles form a straight line. One angle is 40° what is the size of the other angle?	5. Three angles form a straight line. Two of the angles are 61° and 29°. Find the third angle.
2. Two of the angles of a triangle are both 30°. What is the size of the third angle?	6. Two angles of a triangle are 40° and 70°, what is the size of the third angle of the triangle?
3. Two angles form a straight line. One of the angles is 47°. Find the other angle.	7. Two of the angles in a quadrilateral are 60° and 100°. The other two angles are equal. Find the size of these angles.
4. Three angles meet at a point. Two of the angles are 102° and 178°. Find the third angle.	

Technology recommendations

- Dynamic geometry software is particularly useful for displaying dynamic images of the angle connections with parallel lines and transversals. It can also be used to measure angles and calculate sums, and therefore dynamic images can be created for all the required angle facts. Students can also be challenged to create their own versions of these images.

- The free 'Pythagorea' app (square grid version) is excellent for developing students' ability to visualise and solve geometrical problems.

Investigation/research tasks

- **Triangles at a point**

  Pupils will need to work in small groups.

  Resources – sheets of equilateral, isosceles and scalene triangles

  Start with equilateral triangles which will need to be cut out. How many of these fit together around a single point? Students should get the answer 6. Now give out the isosceles triangles and ask if six can fit together around a point without leaving spaces. What about the scalene triangles? Can exactly 6 fit around a point?

  Ask pupils for applications of this – for example, tiled floors. Get them to find examples on the internet.

  STRETCH: Can any triangle be used as a pattern to tile a floor without leaving spaces?

- **Buildings and bridges**

  Ask pupils to research parallel and perpendicular lines in construction by finding pictures on the internet of buildings, bridges, etc. showing examples of parallel and perpendicular lines and get them to highlight the lines.

  Then ask them to research triangles in constructions and frameworks.

STRETCH: Ask pupils to classify the triangles that they find – equilateral, isosceles, scalene.

STRETCH: Ask pupils to find out why triangles are used so much in frameworks such as cranes and bridges.

- **Measuring angles**

  Some students may already have noticed that their scientific calculator can be in degrees mode, or one of two other methods of measuring angles (radians and gradians). They may be interested in researching units for measuring angles.

  Ask them to research the reasons for there being 360° in a full turn.

  > TIP: Although it is now known for certain, there are a number of competing theories behind this fact. For example, 360 has many factors and is therefore a 'nice' number to calculate with.

STRETCH: Students who are particularly keen can be encouraged to find out about radians and gradians, and also any other units. Wikipedia lists 16 different units, ranging from the 'turn' and 'quadrant', to the 'Mil' and the 'Second of an arc'. Some students may even have encountered a compass with mils on it.

Symmetry

Learning objectives

Learning objectives covered in this chapter: 7Gs9

* Recognise line and rotation symmetry in 2D shapes and patterns; draw lines of symmetry and complete patterns with two lines of symmetry; identify the order of rotation symmetry.

Key terms

* line symmetry
* line of symmetry
* rotational symmetry
* order (of rotational symmetry)
* centre

Prior knowledge assumptions

* Students are familiar with the names of special triangles and quadrilaterals.
* Students are familiar with the simple properties of special triangles and quadrilaterals.
* Students understand language such as full turn, quarter turn, etc.

The work in this chapter will be developed when students learn about transformations and constructions.

Guidance on the hook

Butterflies and cats and dogs

Purpose: This hook reminds students of some of the ideas of reflection symmetry that were developed during the primary framework.

Use of the hook: Demonstrate to the whole class the steps that are discussed in the Student's Book:

1. Folding a piece of A5 or A4 paper in half vertically
2. Drawing half a butterfly adjacent to the fold line
3. Cutting out the half butterfly
4. Opening up the cut-out design to reveal the whole butterfly.

Then get students in the class to each produce their own butterfly designs and then to colour these so that the two halves of the butterfly remain symmetrical.

Students can then try making their own symmetrical animal design.

TIP: Using A5 paper will mean that less time is needed for colouring.

TIP: The completed animals would make a colourful classroom display.

BEWARE: When some students colour in their shapes they may not colour them in to preserve the symmetry.

Adaptation: Students could use paint to colour the butterfly. Paint one side of the butterfly, fold in half, press down hard and then open up.

Extension: Students could make some snowflake patterns by folding a piece of square paper in half vertically, then horizontally and then diagonally.

They should then snip some small triangular pieces out along the folds.

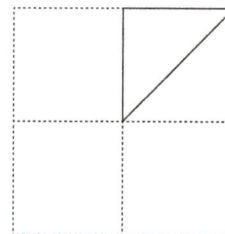

Starter ideas

Mental maths starter

Write the name of a polygon with 0 sides.	Write the name of a polygon with 10 sides.	Write the name of a polygon with 4 sides	Write the name of a polygon with 5 sides.
Write the number of lines of symmetry in a square.	Write the number of lines of symmetry in a regular hexagon.	Write the number of lines of symmetry in a regular pentagon.	Write the number of lines of symmetry in a rectangle.
How many degrees are there in one full turn?	How many degrees are there in a quarter turn?	How many degrees are there in half a turn?	How many degrees are there in two full-turns?
An equilateral triangle is folded exactly in half. Write down the name of the shape that is formed.	A square is cut in half along a line connecting the midpoint of one side and the midpoint of the opposite side. Write down the name of each of the shapes formed.	A regular hexagon is folded in half along a diagonal. Write down the name of the shape that is formed.	Two equilateral triangles are joined together edge to edge. Write down the name of the shape that is formed.
I am facing due North. I turn through a quarter of a turn in a clockwise direction. What direction am I now facing?	I am facing due East. I turn through half of a turn. What direction am I now facing?	I am facing due West. I turn through a quarter of a turn in an anticlockwise direction. What direction am I now facing?	I am facing due South. I turn through a quarter of a turn in a clockwise direction. What direction am I now facing?

Start point check: Quadrilaterals

Ask each student in the class to draw a quadrilateral on a mini-whiteboard. They should keep their shape to themselves.

Get all the students to stand up.

Ask students to remain standing if their quadrilateral:
- has at least one angle that is smaller than a right angle
- has at least two sides that have the same length
- has a line of symmetry.

Discuss the types of quadrilateral that those standing have drawn.

TIP: If you don't have mini-whiteboards, you can get students to drawn their shape on a piece of A4 paper.

- **Real-life symmetry: flags**

  Show students the flags of some countries, for example:

Bangladesh

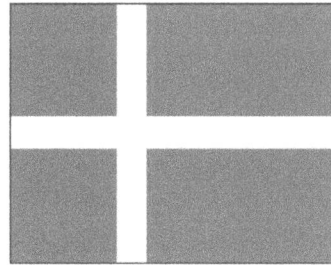
Denmark

Dominican Republic

Tanzania

Discuss the properties of these flags. Which have line symmetry? Are the lines of symmetry vertical or horizontal? Which flags would look the same if turned upside down?

TIP: Show large versions of these flags in colour to your class using an interactive whiteboard or projector. Alternatively show them A4 or A3 sized print outs of the flags.

Discussion ideas

Probing questions	Teacher prompts
Show me an example of a right-angled triangle that has a line of symmetry. Can a right-angled triangle have rotational symmetry?	Students should realise that a right-angled triangle can be isosceles but it cannot be equilateral.
Pose the following challenges. 1. Draw a quadrilateral that has rotational symmetry but no line symmetry. 2. Draw a quadrilateral that has line symmetry but no rotational symmetry.	1. Establish that the only such quadrilateral is a parallelogram. 2. Ask students if there is more than one possible quadrilateral with these properties. Establish that the quadrilateral could be any of these: kite　　　delta　　　isosceles trapezium
Can a triangle ever have rotational symmetry of order 2? Can you explain why?	Encourage students to try drawing a range of triangles and decide what orders of rotational symmetry are possible.
True or False? The number of lines of symmetry for a polygon is equal to the number of sides. If a pentagon has rotational symmetry of order 5, the pentagon must be regular.	How could the first statement be altered to make it always true? Encourage students to suggest different ways of changing it to make it true.

Common errors/misconceptions

Misconception	Strategies to address
Thinking that the diagonals of a rectangle are lines of symmetry	Fold a rectangular piece of paper (such as A4) first along its two lines of symmetry to show how the piece of paper folds in half. Then try folding the rectangle along one of the diagonals.
Reflecting incorrectly in a diagonal mirror line, for example	Encourage use of a mirror or tracing paper to reflect shapes correctly.
Thinking that a shape with no lines of symmetry must have no rotational symmetry	Show an example of a shape that has no lines of symmetry but does have rotational symmetry, for example:
When using tracing paper to find the order of rotational symmetry of a shape, not counting the tracing paper in its original position	Model carefully using tracing paper to find the order of rotational symmetry of a shape.
Believing that a shape has rotational symmetry if it is described as having rotational symmetry of order 1	Ensure students are familiar with both ways of describing a shape without rotational symmetry.
Ignoring shading on a shape when describing its symmetry	Use a mirror to check lines of symmetry. When using tracing paper to find rotational symmetry, ensure any shading is also marked onto the tracing paper.

Developing conceptual understanding

7Gs9 Recognise line and rotation symmetry in 2D shapes and patterns; draw lines of symmetry and complete patterns with two lines of symmetry; identify the order of rotation symmetry.

* Cut out the shapes provided as a photocopiable resource online and sort them according to their symmetry properties.
* FIX: Allow students to check for lines of symmetry by either allowing them to cut out shapes or by providing them with a mirror or tracing paper.
* FIX: Encourage students to check the order of rotational symmetry of a shape by using tracing paper.

STRETCH: Students working at greater depth could explore shading triangles in a regular hexagon to create shapes with different symmetry properties. A sheet of hexagons is provided as a photocopiable resource online.   *Problem solving*

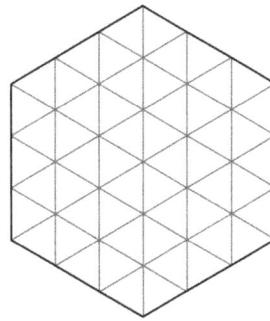

For example, students could try to shade six triangles to produce a design with

1. 6 lines of symmetry
2. 2 lines of symmetry
3. rotational symmetry of order 2 but no line symmetry
4. 1 line of symmetry but no rotational symmetry
5. rotational symmetry of order 6 but no line symmetry
6. rotational symmetry of order 3 and 3 lines of symmetry.

End of chapter mental maths exercise

1. Write the order of rotational symmetry for the letter **Z**.

2. Draw a quadrilateral with exactly one line of symmetry.

3. What is the smallest number of additional squares that would need to be shaded so that this pattern has rotational symmetry of order 4?

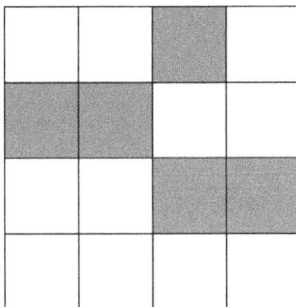

4. Write the sum of the number of lines of symmetry in an equilateral triangle and the order of rotational symmetry for a regular pentagon.

5. Two of the angles in a triangle are 70° and 40°. Write down the number of lines of symmetry this triangle has.

Technology recommendations

- Drawing packages could be used to create patterns with given symmetry properties. For example, students could find different ways of shading eight squares in a 4 by 6 grid to produce a shape with two lines of symmetry.   *Problem solving*

- Students could use a drawing package to design a flag with given symmetry properties (such as rotational symmetry of order 2).

Note also that interactive whiteboards are a powerful tool for teaching line and rotational symmetry.

Investigation/research tasks

- **Rangoli patterns:**

  Ask students to research Rangoli patterns.

  Ask students to create their own Rangoli pattern with two lines of symmetry:

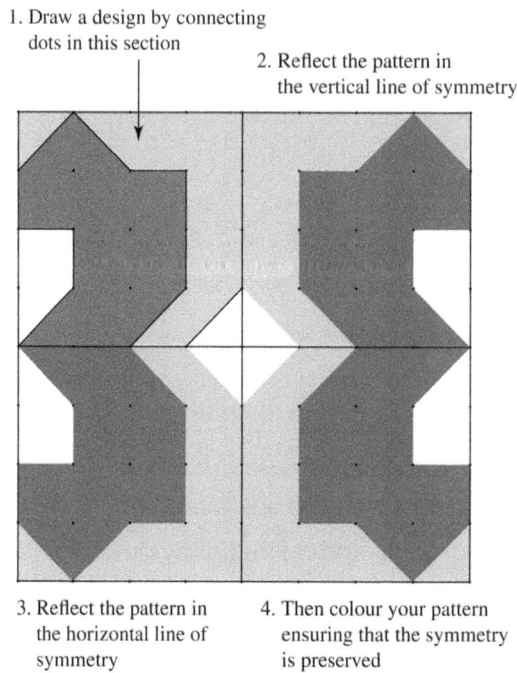

  1. Draw a design by connecting dots in this section

  2. Reflect the pattern in the vertical line of symmetry

  3. Reflect the pattern in the horizontal line of symmetry

  4. Then colour your pattern ensuring that the symmetry is preserved

- **Dotty quadrilaterals:**   *Problem solving*

  By joining dots on a 3 by 3 dotty grid, draw as many different quadrilaterals as possible. Mark the lines of symmetry on each shape and write down the order of symmetry.

  TIP: A sheet of 3 by 3 dotty grids is given in the photocopiable resources online.

- **Pentominoes:**   *Problem solving*

  A pentomino is a shape made by connecting five squares together edge to edge.

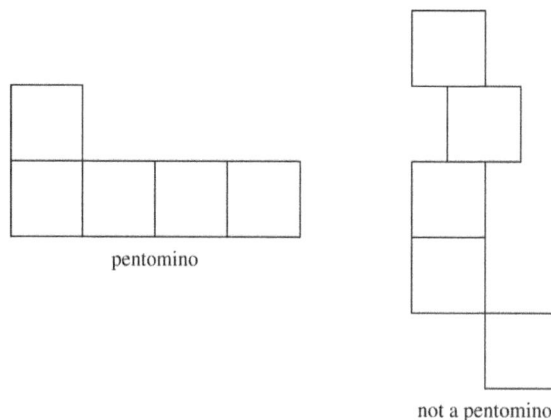

  pentomino

  not a pentomino

  How many different pentominoes are there? Find the number of lines of symmetry and the order of symmetry for each pentomino.

- **Snowflakes:**

  Snowflakes all have rotational symmetry of order 6. Ask students to use triangular dotty paper to create their own mathematical snowflakes.

  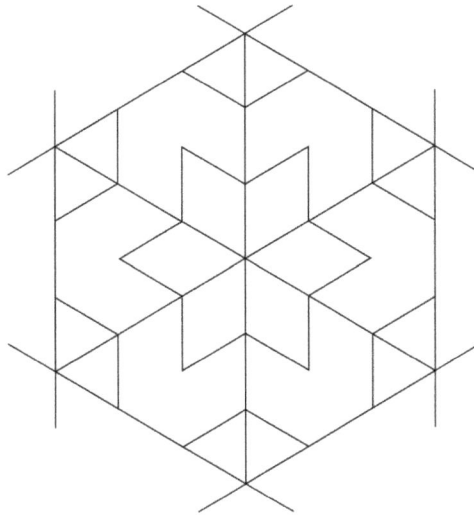

- **Internet research: symmetry in buildings**

  Use the internet to research symmetry in architecture.

  Ask students to find examples of buildings that have line or rotational symmetry. Students could make a poster to illustrate their work.

Averages

Learning objectives

Learning objectives covered in this chapter: 7Dp1, 7Dp2

- Find the mode (or modal class for grouped data), median and range.
- Calculate the mean, including from a simple frequency table.

Key terms

- average
- spread
- mode
- median
- mean
- range
- modal class
- bimodal

Prior knowledge assumptions

- Students can find the mode and range from a list of data in a relevant situation, for example, scientific experiment.
- Students can complete and read simple frequency tables. For example, they can find a value from the table or a total or difference.

Guidance on the hook

Purpose: To give students a real context in which averages (and spreads) are used that helps them realise why we need these statistics.

Use of the hook: Show students the table of data in the Student's Book.

Ask them to give their instinctive (gut) reaction as to which skater did better.

Ask students to suggest ways to decide for sure which skater did better.

Students may suggest finding a total score, finding an average of some type (mode or mean most likely) or using a calculation of their own choosing.

Follow through on these suggestions to see what it shows about who did better. If no one has suggested finding the total, ask students to calculate this.

As in the Student's Book, Student 3 was awarded a total score of 784 with the same score from each judge. Ask students what Skater 3's scores must have been? How did they calculate this?

Then explore the spread of the scores to see who got the most consistent scores and who had the largest spread. Ask students what could account for differences in the scores like this.

Adaptation: You could carry out this task as a primary data collection task by creating a judging panel from students and asking them to rate different performances (live or from video!).

Extension: Students working at greater depth may be able to calculate the median and/or the mean of the data and use this to help decide who did better.

They may also be able to comment on whether the range is a good measure of the spread, especially where there is one outlying piece of data.

These students could consider the merits of scoring systems which discount the highest and lowest score first, for example.

Starter ideas

Mental maths starter

Find the sum of 7, 11 and 12.	Find the sum of 17, 21 and 15.	Find the sum of 16, 26 and 23.	Find the sum of 27, 14 and 22.
What number is halfway between 17 and 20	What number is halfway between 23 and 37	What number is halfway between 90 and 104	What number is halfway between 14 and 19
Calculate $91 \div 7$	Calculate $85 \div 5$	Calculate $78 \div 6$	Calculate $92 \div 4$
Find the difference between 319 and 284	Find the difference between 175 and 332	Find the difference between 59 and 213	Find the difference between -3 and 24
Find the sum of 2 multiplied by 7 and 9 multiplied by 3.	Find the sum of 3 multiplied by 5 and 8 multiplied by 4.	Find the sum of 4 multiplied by 6 and 8 multiplied by 5.	Find the sum of 6 multiplied by 8 and 9 multiplied by 4.

Start point check: Class survey

Complete a survey of the class to find out the number of hours of television they watched yesterday.

Design a suitable data collection sheet for this (i.e. a table).

Record the results as a list and using a frequency table.

Ask students to find the mode, mean, median and range from the list.

Be prepared that they may only know the mode and range.

Ask them how they could find the mode directly from the table (category with the highest frequency). Then find the range directly from the table.

Game: Claim that square!

Players work in groups of two to four.

Give the students a copy of this square and three dice.

2	3	4	3	3
3	4	$2\frac{2}{3}$	$3\frac{2}{3}$	5
6	2	3	$1\frac{1}{3}$	$3\frac{1}{3}$
5	$1\frac{2}{3}$	3	4	2
3	2	2	$2\frac{2}{3}$	4

Players take it in turns to throw three dice. The player then chooses either the mean, median, mode or range of the scores and claims a square (if that value is available).

The first player to claim four squares, arranged together as a larger square, is the winner. (You could adapt as needed to, for example, four touching squares if the groups are larger.)

See photocopiable resources online for this grid and a recording table.

Discussion ideas

Probing questions	Teacher prompts
Show me a set of data with • a mode of 5 • a median of 8 • a mode of 5 and a median of 8 • a range of 10 • a range of 10 and a mode of 5 • a range of 10, a mode of 5 and a median of 7	This is a good activity to do on mini-whiteboards so that you can see each student's response. You can also then progress a question by asking for a set of data with a mode of 3 first, before then asking students to refine that data so the median is 4. Ask students how they know that the median is 8 and the mode is 5, for example. Also prompt students to consider if there are other possible solutions (and if so, how many).
Convince me/a friend that a set of data can have more than one mode.	Students may give an example, such as 2, 2, 2, 5, 6, 6, 6, 7, 10 Discuss term 'bimodal'.
True or False? The median will be a number in the data set.	Encourage students to give an example when it is true and one where it is false, such as: True Example: 1, 2, 3 – median = 2 False Example: 1, 2, 3, 4 – median = 2.5 Help students to notice that whenever there are an even number of pieces of data, the median will be an average of the middle two pieces (which will not be in the list unless they are the same).
Convince me/a friend that I can find a missing piece of data in a list if I know all the others and the mean.	Encourage students to represent this problem as a list of data with one piece missing. If they know the mean and the number of pieces of data, then *total = mean × number of pieces of data*
How does the data in a frequency table relate to the list of data it represents? For example, what is the list of data represented by this table? <table><tr><td>**Score**</td><td>**Frequency**</td></tr><tr><td>7</td><td>1</td></tr><tr><td>8</td><td>6</td></tr><tr><td>9</td><td>3</td></tr><tr><td>10</td><td>2</td></tr></table>	Students can write out each score the number of times it came up, that is 7 8 8 8 8 8 8 9 9 9 10 10 A nice activity here is to represent the table using students. Give a student a mini-whiteboard saying '7' and then given 6 more students whiteboards saying '8' and so on to help students see what the table means.
What is the same and what is different? Mode; Median; Mean; Range	Possible answers: Same: All measures to help describe a data set Different: Mode, Median and Mean are averages but Range is a spread Mode, Median and Mean lie within the bounds of the data list but range does not (you may need to support students in understanding what is meant by 'bounds of data'). Mode is a value in the data list, but the others do not

Probing questions	Teacher prompts
	have to be.
	If students have not identified these characteristics themselves, give them some prompts. Ask: Does the mean lie within the bounds of the data? Is this true/false for median/mode/range. Can you add this to your same/different lists.
Always, Sometimes, Never? The mean is greater than the median.	Encourage students to give an example when it is true and one where it is false, such as: True Example: 1, 2, 9 (Median = 2, Mean = $\frac{12}{3}$ = 4) False Example: 1, 8, 9 (Median = 9, Mean = $\frac{18}{3}$ = 6) You could ask about the mean versus the mode. You could also ask students to create their own examples.

Common errors/misconceptions

Misconception	Strategies to address
Not realising that there can be more than one mode	Show students examples of data sets where there are 2 or more modes and ask them what the mode is. When they give two answers, ask them what that means. For example: 6, 7, 7, 7, 8, 9, 10, 11, 11, 11, 12, 16
Mistakenly thinking that there can be 2 medians (when there are an even number of pieces of data)	Treat the 2 cases separately: 1. If there are an odd number of pieces of data, then find the middle one. 2. If there are an even number of pieces of data, then find the middle two and find the value exactly halfway between them.
Alternatively, struggling to find the middle value between 2 numbers	Use a number line to help students find the halfway value.
Forgetting to order the data before finding the median	Initially you could show that this gives a different answer to help students realise that this is a problem. For example, say that the median of this data is 3, right?! 4, 1, 5, 3, 7, 9, 6 If more depth is needed, ask students to reflect on whether the order the data is presented in is significant. Give students a set of data and tell them that it has a mean/mode/median of for example,3, 5, 4. Tell students, 'now I'm going to rearrange the data' Does the mean/median/mode change? Ensure that students understand that the average of a set of data is the same regardless of the order it is presented in. This will help when calculating the median. Demonstrate to students that rearranging the order of

Misconception	Strategies to address
	data changes the number written in the middle. Be clear to differentiate between the middle value (which might be in the, for example, 2nd position) to the number written in the middle. Explain that the quickest and most reliable way to find the middle value is to write the numbers in order.
Believing that the range is an average	Give an example of a data set where the range is a totally different number to the data.

For example, what is the range of ages of students in Year 7? This will usually be small such as 1 or 2 as the students are very close in age. This number bears no relation to the actual age of Year 7 students of 11 12.

Help students to see the meaning of the range visually by placing the data on a number line and looking at the spread of the data.

Discuss how a set of data can have the same average but a different range. |
| Incorrectly calculating the mean on a calculator by omitting the brackets

For example, to calculate the mean of 1, 2, 3, typing $1 + 2 + 3 \div 3$ rather than $(1 + 2 + 3) \div 3$ | Ask students to sense check their answer to see if it makes sense. This will help them realise that the value cannot be correct.

Remind students about the order of calculation (multiplication prior to addition) and the need to use brackets to break this order.

Encourage students to write down each individual step of working. |
| When calculating a mode from a frequency table, giving the frequency as the mode. | Ask students to write out the data in a list to help their understanding between data and its frequencies.

This will help them see the actual value that is most common (or the minimum and maximum values). |
| Dividing the total by the number of rows in the table rather than the total frequency (when finding the mean from a table) | Again, ask students to write out the original list of data to see how many pieces there are. This shows them that they need to add the frequencies together. |

Developing conceptual understanding

7Dp1 Find the mode (or modal class for grouped data), median and range.

- Give students opportunities to work with real data at every point. Give them opportunities to collect their own data. Encourage them to create hypotheses and then use their understanding of mean/median/mode/range to answer questions.

- Some ideas for real-life data they could collect are:
  - house prices in a town compared to 20 years ago
  - populations of countries compared to 50 years ago
  - the number of hours' exercise undertaken each week by different ages/genders.

  This will also provide opportunity to discuss which averages are good measures.

- FIX: Help students understand why averages are a useful tool by asking them to reflect on large sets of raw data, where there is too much data to interpret it effectively.

- FIX: Discuss the strengths and weakness of each measure to understand why there isn't just one measure of average. It is also worth explaining to students that there are many ways to find an average; the mode, median and mean are just three well-known ways but any form of summing up the typical value of a data set with a single value is an average.

- FIX: The range is best introduced by comparing two data sets to see what the effect of having a larger range is.

For example, you could share the number of goals scored by two football teams to discuss the consistency and reliability of their scoring.

Team A	1	2	1	1	2	2	3
Team B	5	0	0	0	1	6	0

- FIX: When learning about the mean, emphasise that the total of the data is a crucial value and can be found directly by multiplying the mean and the number of pieces of data. Try to focus on what the sum of the data means, asking the students to explain what this value means in a real context.

STRETCH: Students working at greater depth can work backwards to find a missing value given the rest of the values and the mean.

7Dp2 Calculate the mean, including from a simple frequency table.

- FIX: Show students how a list of data and a frequency table relate by collecting data in a list and then putting it in a table. Relate the product of the value and the frequency to the efficient totalling of the repeated data in the list.

TIP: Give students the opportunity to read the data from a bar chart as well as a table to help them relate these ideas to a visual image of the data. For example, they can see the range as an interval more clearly than from a frequency table. Similarly, they can see the mode visually as the highest bar.

STRETCH: Students working at greater depth could look at the effect of including a negative number in a data set on the mean particularly.

STRETCH: Students working at greater depth could also begin to think about why we cannot simply calculate the mean from a grouped frequency table (or the median or the range).

End of chapter mental maths exercise

1. Find the mean of 7, 11 and 12.
2. Find the median of 2, 5, 8 and 11
3. Find the mode of 2, 2, 5, 8, 8, 9
4. Find the range of 7, 11 and 22
5. 6 numbers have a mean of 12.
What is the sum of the 6 numbers?
6. I have 5, 7 and one other number.
The mean of the numbers is 8.
What is the third number?
7. A data set has 67 pieces of data. Which data point will be the median?

Technology recommendations

- Use a spreadsheet and the formulae to calculate the averages and spreads of the data listed.

You can then amend the data values to see the effect on the averages and range.

You could challenge students to try to achieve a specific range or mean by adjusting one piece of data.

- Use a spreadsheet to produce a frequency table from the raw data using the *countif* function.

   This table can then be used to produce a bar chart. A chart like this will then show how the mode and range particularly relate to the shape of the bar chart.

Investigation/research tasks

- **Investigation: Five digits**   *Problem solving*

   Each of these five cards must show a single-digit number.

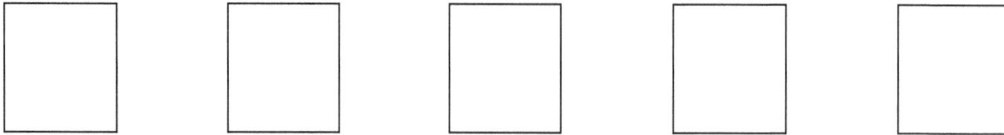

   The mode of the numbers = mean of the numbers = median of the numbers = range of the numbers.

   What are the numbers?

   Is there only one solution?

   Let students experiment with sets of numbers to see if they can adjust them to make the mode = mean = median = range.

   Some examples of solutions focused on 5:

   - 3, 4, 5, 5, 8
   - 2.5, 5, 5, 5, 7.5

   You could share these solutions and ask students to find one with an answer of 4 (for example, 2, 4, 4, 4, 6) and so on.

   BEWARE: You may need to prompt students to work out what the total of the numbers will need to be to create a mean of 4, for example.

   TIP: You could use a spreadsheet to help speed up the calculation processes here.

- **Investigate the mean of sets of consecutive numbers.**   *Problem solving*

   Think of a set of three consecutive numbers.

   Calculate the mean of your numbers.

   What do you notice?

   Is this always true? Check with another example.

   Can you prove it?

   Students should realise that the mean is the median (i.e. it is the middle number when there is an odd number of consecutive numbers and halfway between the middle two numbers when there are an even number of consecutive numbers).

   Students could show this using algebra, although this may be challenging for some given they have only just encountered algebra this year.

For example, for three numbers:

$$\text{Mean} = \frac{n + n + 1 + n + 2}{3} = \frac{3n + 3}{3} = n + 1$$

- **Investigation: How many sweets in a packet?**

  Each group has a sample of sweet packets of the same type.

  Open each packet and record the number of sweets inside.

  Produce a frequency table for your results.

  Share your results with other groups to increase your sample size.

  Now calculate the mean, mode, median and range of your data.

  What does this tell you about the number of sweets in a packet?

  > TIP: This activity can be very independent and provides a useful opportunity for students to carry out some simple real data collection and then analysis. Allow them to explore the best way to record and share the data themselves.

  You will need to bring the group back together at the end to share and interpret their findings. Ask students what the implications of their findings are for people buying these sweets in the future.

Displaying data

Learning objectives

Learning objectives covered in this chapter: 7Dp3

- Draw and interpret bar-line graphs and bar charts, frequency diagrams for grouped discrete data and pictograms.
- Draw and interpret simple pie charts.

Key terms

- pictogram
- frequency
- bar chart
- bar-line graph
- discrete data
- pie chart
- sector

Prior knowledge assumptions

- Draw and interpret pictograms (symbol representing 1, 2, 5, 10 or 20 units).
- Draw and interpret bar charts (intervals labelled in ones, twos, fives, tens or twenties).
- Solve a problem by representing, extracting and interpreting data in frequency tables and bar charts with grouped discrete data.
- Draw and interpret bar line charts (vertical axis labelled for example in twos, fives, tens, twenties or hundreds).

Guidance on the hook

Errors

Purpose: this hook asks students to identify errors in pictograms and bar charts.

Use of the hook: Give students a copy of the pictogram. Ask them to find three errors, working individually. For example:

- The symbols are not a consistent shape.
- The symbols are not a consistent size.
- There is no key.
- The final group is not labelled.
- There is no title.

Survey the students to find out what they identified. Give students a set of data and ask them to create a bar chart with deliberate errors. They should then swap with a partner and attempt to identify the errors in the bar charts.

Starter ideas

Start point check

The lady with the lamp

Share the following fact with students in order to help them appreciate some of the history of statistics.

Florence Nightingale is well known as a nurse. But it was her work as a statistician that was most significant. She was concerned about the mortality rates in her hospital, and started to use statistics to argue for health reform. Florence Nightingale was the first female member of the Royal Statistical Society. She also invented a type of diagram based on the pie chart that had been introduced by William Playfair about 50 years earlier.

Discussion ideas

Probing questions	Teacher prompts
What is the same: bar chart/bar-line graph? What is different: bar chart / bar-line graph? Explain any advantages of a bar chart over a bar-line graph. Explain any advantages of a bar-line graph over a bar chart.	For example, in any of these charts, the bars are equal width and the lines are an equal width. Some student may even claim that there are no real differences as the lines are just very thin bars. For example, one uses rectangles and the other uses lines. Encourage students to consider the visual impact and the ease of construction.
Show me a bar chart that could be constructed using the same data as this pie chart. And another, and another … 	Encourage students to be ever-more creative with their responses to this question and the re-asking of it. If students are sketching graphs on a mini-whiteboard, they should ensure that the axes are labelled in a way that makes their frequencies clear. On the third occasion, rephrase the question as 'show me an example that you think no one else in the class will think of'. Some students may benefit from being told that the angles are 180°, 120° and 60° degrees.

Common errors/misconceptions

Misconception	Strategies to address
Not leaving gaps between the bars in a bar chart	Discrete data is described as having clearly separate values, so the bars have to be clearly separate. In stage 8 students will explore continuous data (data that can take any value in a range). A 'bar chart' for this type of data will have bars that touch.
Drawing a half pictogram symbol regardless of the actual fraction required	Give students a key and a half pictogram symbol – ask them how many the symbol represents. Then give a different fraction of the symbol and ask what this represents. This can be repeated using different examples to build understanding of use of part symbols in pictograms. Then begin to ask students to draw the fraction of the symbol to represent different numbers. Extend this to examples where they are drawing a number of whole symbols and a fractional part of a symbol. You may find it helpful to discuss the suitability of symbols. For example, if a symbol represents 5, then it is helpful to choose a symbol that can easily and identifiably be split into fifths. Show an irregular symbol on the board, and ask students to draw $\frac{1}{5}$ of the symbol in their books/mini-whiteboard. Did they all draw a symbol the same size?
Interchanging percentages and degrees when interpreting a pie chart. For example, thinking that 25% of the pie chart is 25°.	Emphasise the number of degrees in a full turn (pie chart) and the percentage that represents the total amount. Allow students who are making this error to complete their chart and ask them about the unused section –

Misconception	Strategies to address
	why has this happened? Can they identify their own error.
	Another possible strategy to assess this would be to include it in a piece of 'work' for the students to mark and identify the errors in. Can the students see the errors in the piece and explain how the pie chart should have been drawn?
Measuring each fraction from a vertical radius, resulting in overlapping sectors	Demonstrate how to measure a sector in a range of positions in the circle, not always from the vertical radius.
	Where students have made this error ask them to consider the unused section of the pie chart – why has this happened? What mistake have they made? This is potentially an opportunity for students to work with their peers to identify the error that has been made.

Developing conceptual understanding

7Dp3 Draw and interpret bar-line graphs and bar charts, frequency diagrams for grouped discrete data and pictograms. Draw and interpret simple pie charts.

Ensure students see a range of different bar charts, both horizontal and vertical. Ask them to find an example of a bar chart in the media or on the internet. Students can discuss the similarities and differences of their bar charts – what do they each show? Are there any that are incorrect or misleading?

FIX: Some students may struggle to interpret a scale when each square represents an amount other than one unit. Show a scale as shown below:

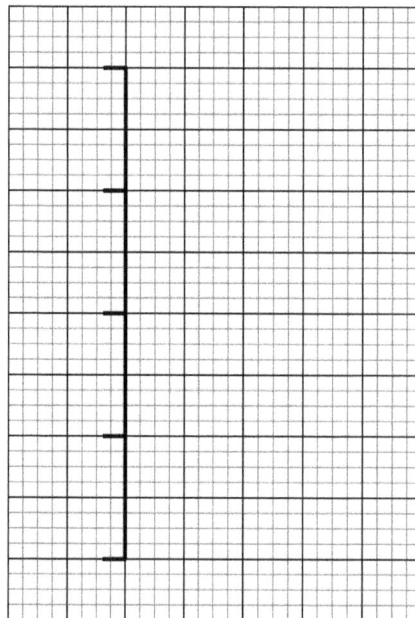

Label the 5 points 0, 20, 40, 60, ... Ask students to identify what one small square represents, and to justify their decision.

Repeat for 0, 50, 100, 150, ...

Repeat for 0, 1, 2, 3, ...

Repeat for 0, 2, 4, 6, ...

TIP: Ask students to comment on the final two options if used for a bar chart. They should recognise that consideration of the small squares is unnecessary when interpreting the frequencies.

Use pie chart templates (see photocopiable resources online) to help students who are struggling to use compasses efficiently. While it would be good if students could measure the fractions of a pie chart themselves, at this stage students should be provided with versions with marks around the outside that divide the circumference into fractional sections.

FIX: Some students will try to measure each fraction of a pie chart from the starting radius. Model the correct way of measuring each fraction from the radius that completes the previous slice.

STRETCH: Students working at a greater depth with pie charts could explore sets of data where the sum of the frequencies is not a convenient factor of 360; i.e. one that means the sectors are not quarters, eighths, tenths or twelfths. In these cases, they will need to calculate the angle for each sector and measure them using a protractor. A useful approach is to calculate the angle for each item by dividing 360° by the total frequency. The size of each slice is then this number multiplied by the frequency for the slice. If necessary, does rounding to one decimal place, or the nearest whole number, for each sector make a difference? For example, the data here gives a total of 359°.

Food	Frequency
Indian	46
Chinese	31
Turkish	23
Italian	37

End of chapter mental maths exercise

1. The symbol for a pictogram represents 8 items. The pictogram includes 6 whole symbols and $\frac{3}{4}$ of a symbol. How many items are there in total?

2. The symbol for a pictogram represents 10 items. The pictogram includes 8 whole symbols and $\frac{2}{5}$ of a symbol. How many items are there in total?

3. A bar chart gives information about the preferred hot drinks of 30 people. There are four bars. 10 people choose tea. 2 people choose chai. Twice as many people choose hot chocolate as coffee. How many people choose coffee?

4. A bar chart gives information about the preferred subject of 60 students. There are four bars. 15 people choose Maths. 9 people choose Science. Three times as many students chose Geography as History. How many students chose Geography?

5. A pie chart gives information about the preferred car colour of 30 people. 10 people choose silver. What fraction is the slice for silver?

6. A pie chart gives information about the preferred food of a group of people. There are four sectors. The slice for 'Indian' is $\frac{1}{3}$. The slice for 'Chinese' is $\frac{1}{4}$. The slice for 'Mexican' is $\frac{1}{8}$. The final slice is for 'Italian'. What is the fraction of people that prefer Italian food?

Technology

- Give students the opportunity to use graphing tools in a spreadsheet, but discuss the suitability of the graphs afterwards, and encourage caution where necessary. Spreadsheets do have the ability to create bar charts and pie charts. However, there are a large number of misleading charts available, and it is often not easy to adapt the axes as required.

- An internet search of images for bar charts is likely to reveal a large number of bar charts with errors. It is interesting for students to explore this and identify the errors.

Investigation/research task

Real data

Give students a real-life question to research, some ideas are:

- Number of World Heritage Sites in the different continents of the world

- Circulation figures for different local and national newspapers

- Opportunities for cross-curricular work within your own school

Ask them to create a variety of different charts and graphs – what are the strengths and weaknesses of each graph?

William Playfair

Ask students to research the Scottish engineer and economist, William Playfair. In particular, they should look for information connected to this topic. Students should bring their findings to a future lesson to share.

Playfair (born 1759) invented both the bar chart and the pie chart, among other statistical representations. Images of these diagrams are readily available online.

> BEWARE: William Playfair should not be confused with his nephew, the architect William Henry Playfair (born 1790).

Bad statistics

Challenge students to research examples of 'bad statistics' and create a presentation of their findings for the class. In particular, they should search for examples of pictograms, bar charts and pie charts that are misleading or incorrect. They should justify their choices and comment on whether they think their examples are either deliberately misleading or due to other's misunderstanding of correct statistical diagrams.

Probability 2

Learning objectives

Learning objectives covered in this chapter: 7Db4, 7Db5, 7Db6

- Identify all the possible mutually exclusive outcomes of a single event.
- Use experimental data to estimate probabilities.
- Compare experimental and theoretical probabilities in simple contexts.

Key terms

- outcomes
- event
- mutually exclusive
- theoretical probability
- experimental probability

Prior knowledge assumptions

- Students should be familiar with how to find a simple probability (using the idea of equally likely outcomes).
- Students should know how to convert common fractions to decimals or percentages.

The work in this chapter will be helpful in later work when students learn more about listing outcomes of events to find probabilities.

Guidance on the hook

Insurance claims

Purpose: This hook introduces students to the idea that events are not always equally likely and that sometimes probabilities need to be estimated.

Use of the hook: Before discussing the scenario of travel insurance claims, begin by discussing the possible outcomes for a football team's next match. Ask students what the possible outcomes are for the match (win, lose, draw). Discuss whether the probability of winning the match is $\frac{1}{3}$.

Ask for suggestions about how the probability of winning the next match could be estimated.

Now turn to the scenario discussed in the hook. As the four types of insurance claim are not equally likely, discuss how it is important to have data in order to be able calculate the probability of each type of claim. Discuss the answers of the two questions posed in the Student's Book. Ask other similar questions, such as:

- What percentage of claims are for medical expenses or cancellations?
- What percentage of claims were not for medical expenses?
- What is the probability that the next person claiming on their holiday insurance will do so for lost baggage or money?

Discuss how the data explains why Sanjay finds that the cost of insurance for a skiing trip is more than for a beach trip.

Discuss further how better estimates of probabilities in this context could be found.

Extension: A different insurance company's claims are distributed as follows:

Half as many claims were for Other as were for Baggage and money.

Six times as many claims were for Medical as were for Baggage and money.

Five times as many claims were for Cancellations as were for Other.

For this insurance company, find the percentage of claims that are of each type.

> TIP: Students could adopt a numerical method of solving this, by first guessing the proportion of claims that were for Baggage and money and then seeing whether the percentages add to 100 or not.

Starter ideas

Mental maths starter

1. Simplify fully the fraction $\frac{8}{24}$	1. Simplify fully the fraction $\frac{10}{25}$	1. Simplify fully the fraction $\frac{32}{40}$	1. Simplify fully the fraction $\frac{12}{18}$
2. Give the decimal that is equivalent to $\frac{1}{10}$	2. Give the decimal that is equivalent to $\frac{3}{5}$	2. Give the decimal that is equivalent to $\frac{3}{4}$	2. Give the decimal that is equivalent to $\frac{7}{100}$
3. What percentage is equivalent to $\frac{1}{4}$?	3. What percentage is equivalent to $\frac{9}{10}$?	3. What percentage is equivalent to $\frac{1}{5}$?	3. What percentage is equivalent to $\frac{19}{100}$?
4. I roll an ordinary dice. Write down the probability that I roll the number 5.	4. I roll an ordinary dice. Write down the probability that I roll an even number.	4. I roll an ordinary dice. Write down the probability that I roll a number less than 3.	4. I roll an ordinary dice. Write down the probability that I roll a multiple of 3.
5. A letter from the word YELLOW is picked at random. Write down the probability that the letter picked is L.	5. A letter from the word BLUE is picked at random. Write down the probability that the letter picked is B.	5. A letter from the word GREEN is picked at random. Write down the probability that the letter picked is E.	5. A letter from the word PAINTING is picked at random. Write down the probability that the letter picked is N.

- **Start point check: Probability**

  Give each student a set of probability cards numbered from 0 to 1 going up in tenths (see photocopiable resources online).

  A number is picked at random from the numbers 1, 2, 3, 4, … , 10.

  Ask students to choose the correct probability cards for each of these situations:

  - The number picked is 4.
  - The number picked is an odd number.
  - The number picked is less than 5.
  - The number picked is more than 5.
  - The number picked is a multiple of 3.
  - The number picked is positive.

> TIP: As an alternative you could place the probability cards at different places around the classroom or school hall. You could then ask students to go to stand by the correct probability.

- **Probability activity**

  Put ten coloured cubes into a bag or box (ensure the contents cannot be seen by the class) – the bag could for example contain five blue and five red cubes.

  Take a cube from the box, show the colour and then replace it.

  Repeat this for a total of eight times.

  Ask students to predict the colours of the ten cubes in the bag and the number of each. See how many students predicted correctly.

  Repeat the activity several times.

  Discuss the results with students (for example, even if half of the cubes in the bag are blue, it will not mean that you will get a blue counter exactly half of the time).

- **Interesting context: Murphy's law**

  Murphy's law states that if something can go wrong, it will go wrong! One context where this law has been explored relates to dropping toast off a table. Scientists have explored the question as to whether a piece of buttered toast dropped off a table always lands with the butter side down. A team of scientists from Manchester MET University tested this by dropping 100 buttered pieces of toast off a table. They found that it landed butter side down on 81% of occasions.

  Here are some relevant websites

  https://www.physics.org/facts/toast-toast.asp

  http://www.bbc.co.uk/news/blogs-magazine-monitor-23957303

  http://www.manchestereveningnews.co.uk/news/greater-manchester-news/-rav--r-manchester-boffins-5842879

Discussion ideas

Probing questions	Teacher prompts
When a dice is rolled … Think of a pair of outcomes that are mutually exclusive. Think of a pair of outcomes that are not mutually exclusive.	For outcomes that are mutually exclusive, answers like getting a 4 and getting a 5 are likely to be common. Encourage students to give more complex answers too, such as getting an even number and getting a factor of 5. Encourage students to give reasons for their answers.
Think of a situation when a probability would need to be found by experiment.	Establish that suitable situations would be those where the probability could not be found using the method of equally likely outcomes. Possible scenarios could be: • finding the probability that someone could catch a ball thrown directly towards them • finding the probability of having to wait at a particular set of traffic lights.
What is the event if the outcomes are: • 1, 2, 3, 4, 5, 6 • Win, lose, draw	Lead the discussion to get suggestions for possible situations that have these outcomes.

Probing questions	Teacher prompts
• 28, 30, 31 • D E R • A H P Y	Possible answers are • Throwing a dice • the result of a football match • choosing a month at random and recording the number of days in it (in a normal year of 365 days) • choosing a letter at random from the word RED • choosing a letter at random from the word HAPPY.
Unlikely/impossible: There are 2 bags: Bag 1 contains 1 red and 4 blue balls Bag 2 contains 4 red balls I do an experiment by choosing a bag and then picking a ball from my chosen bag 10 times (putting the ball back each time before picking the next). • I get 10 red balls. Is the bag more likely to be Bag 1 or Bag 2? Is it possible for the bag to be Bag 1? • I get 5 red and 5 blue balls? Is it possible for me to have picked either bag this time?	Use these questions to discuss the distinction between situations that may be very unlikely and those that are impossible.
How could you convince me that a dice is biased?	Encourage students to decide how many throws of the dice may be needed to be convincing.
An ordinary dice is thrown 300 times. How many times would you expect to score a 2? Would you be surprised if you got a 2 52 times? 60 times? 25 times? 300 times?	Establish that although getting a 2 on 50 occasions is the most likely result, getting exactly 50 2's on 300 throws is not that likely. However, we would expect to get fairly close to 50 2's. So only 25 2's would be surprising. Getting 300 2's would be exceptionally suspicious!

Common errors/misconceptions

Misconception	Strategies to address
When listing outcomes, missing some outcomes out or repeating outcomes For example, when listing the outcomes when picking a letter from the word APPLE, listing the letter P twice.	Encourage students to list the outcomes in a sensible order, such as numerical order or the order they occur.
When trying to estimate a probability from an experiment, failing to repeat the experiment enough times	Get all students to estimate the probability of getting Heads on a coin by throwing it 10 times. Discuss the range of theoretical probabilities that students in the class have obtained and establish that throwing 10 times will not be enough to get a reliable estimate.
Thinking that if a normal dice is thrown 60 times, you must get a 6 on exactly $\frac{1}{6}$ of the throws	Perform the experiment as a class and see how many sixes are obtained.

Developing conceptual understanding

7Db4 Identify all the possible mutually exclusive outcomes of a single event.

* Give each student a set of 12 letter and numbers cards and a set of outcome cards (see the photocopiable resources online). Use the cards to help develop understanding of mutually exclusive events.

  Students could, for example, pick a pair of outcome cards and then decide whether their pair of outcomes are mutually exclusive or not. Encourage them to explain their answer.

STRETCH: Those students working at a greater depth could explore the outcomes when two successive events are combined (for example, when two dice are rolled and the total score is found). Students could list the outcomes and decide if the outcomes are equally likely. Encourage students to explain their answers.

7Db5 Use experimental data to estimate probabilities.

* FIX: Give students plenty of opportunities for carrying out practical experiments to estimate probabilities. These practical experiments help to give students a feeling for the randomness of the results. Experiments could involve throwing coins, rolling dice or spinning spinners.

STRETCH: To extend understanding further, students could explore how the experimental probability of an outcome changes the more times the experiment is repeated.

7Db6 Compare experimental and theoretical probabilities in simple contexts.

* Students may find it easier to decide if a set of experimental probabilities are roughly similar to what is expected if they show the experimental probabilities on a bar chart.

* FIX: Students often benefit from practical activities. Give students a dice and get them to bias it by putting a few sticky labels on one of the sides. Ask students to throw the dice 60 times and then to compare their outcomes with those that would be expected if the dice were fair.

End of chapter mental maths exercise

1. Simplify fully the fraction $\frac{27}{45}$.	5. A bag contains 2 red balls and 3 white balls. If a ball is taken at random from the bag, find the probability that the ball is white.
2. Give the decimal that is equivalent to $\frac{1}{4}$.	6. An ordinary dice is rolled 120 times. How many sixes would you expect to roll?
3. What percentage is equivalent to $\frac{7}{10}$?	7. A spinner is spun 50 times. It lands on the number 1 on 31 of the spins. Estimate the probability that the spinner lands on the number 1.
4. I choose a letter at random from the word BOOKMARK. Write a list of all the possible outcomes.	

Technology recommendations

* There are many websites that can be used to simulate spins of a spinner or throws of a dice (search for experimental probability simulation). These could be used to compare the simulated results with the theoretical probabilities.

- The **randbetween(,)** function can be used in a spreadsheet to generate random whole numbers within an interval. For example, randbetween(1,6) generates whole numbers between 1 and 6. Students could compare the frequency that each number occurs with what would be expected.

Investigation/research tasks

- **Practical investigation: coin game**   *Problem solving*

  Split the class in groups of three and give each group two coins.

  On each turn of the game, the two coins are spun.

  – Player 1 wins if the coins show two heads.
  – Player 2 wins if the coins show a head and a tail.
  – Player 3 wins if the coins show two tails.

  Spin the coins a total of 30 times and record who won each time.

  Ask students if the game is fair. Estimate the probability of each player winning. Can students explain the results?

  TIP: Encourage students to record who won each game using tallies.

- **Practical investigation: throwing a pair of dice**   *Problem solving*

  Split the class in groups of three and give each group two ordinary dice.

  On each turn of the game, the two dice are rolled.

  – Player 1 wins if the total score on the two dice is 1, 2, 3 or 4.
  – Player 2 wins if the total score on the two dice is 5, 6, 7 or 8.
  – Player 3 wins if the total score on the two dice is 9, 10, 11 or 12.

  Roll the pair of dice a total of 30 times and record who won each time.

  Ask students if the game is fair. Estimate the probability of each player winning. Can students explain the results?

- **Practical activity**   *Problem solving*

  Ask students to make their own dice.

  Students should perform an experiment to estimate the probability of getting each score on their dice. Do they think that their dice is fair?

  TIP: A possible net of a dice is given in the photocopiable resources online.

Calculation

Learning objectives

Learning objectives covered in this chapter: 7Nc7, 7Nc8, 7Nc9, 7Nc10

- Use the order of operations, including brackets, to work out simple calculations.
- Add and subtract integers and decimals, including numbers with different numbers of decimal places.
- Multiply and divide decimals with one and/or two places by single-digit numbers, for example, 13.7 x 8, 4.35 ÷ 5.
- Know that in any division where the dividend is not a multiple of the divisor there will be a remainder, for example, 157 ÷ 25 = 6 remainder 7. The remainder can be expressed as a fraction of the divisor, for example,

$$157 \div 25 = 6 \frac{7}{25}$$

Key terms

- order of operations
- brackets
- indices
- multiplication; division
- addition; subtraction

Prior knowledge assumptions

- Students know that multiplication and division should happen prior to addition and subtraction in calculations.
- Students can add and subtract whole-numbers of up to three digits mentally.
- Students can multiply a two-digit number by a single digit mentally.
- Students can divide a two-digit number a single digit (no remainder) mentally.
- Students can add and subtract whole numbers of up to six digits, including numbers with a different number of digits, using a written method.
- Students can multiply a whole number by a single digit using a written method.
- Students can divide a whole number by a single digit (no remainder) using a written method.

Guidance on the hook   *Problem solving*

Purpose: Task is a problem based on calculation that enables students to (re)discover the importance of using the correct order of operations.

Use of the hook: Ask students if they can make the number 20 using up to four 4s. They may suggest 4 × 4 + 4. Ask students if there is a way using all of the 4s (such as $4 \times \left(4 + \frac{4}{4}\right)$).

Now ask students to write the numbers 1–20 on their page and to try to find at least one way to make each of these numbers. (They can find multiple ways where appropriate too.)

Some possible solutions:

$1 = \frac{4}{4}$	$11 =$
$2 = \frac{(4 + 4)}{4}$	$12 = 4 + 4 + 4$
$3 = \frac{(4 + 4 + 4)}{4}$	$13 =$
$4 = 4$	$14 =$

$5 = 4 + \dfrac{4}{4}$	$15 = 4 \times 4 - \dfrac{4}{4}$
$6 = 4 + \dfrac{(4 + 4)}{4}$	$16 = 4 \times 4$
$7 = 4 + 4 - \dfrac{4}{4}$	$17 = 4 \times 4 + \dfrac{4}{4}$
$8 = 4 + 4$	$18 =$
$9 = 4 + 4 + \dfrac{4}{4}$	$19 =$
$10 =$	$20 = 4 \times 4 + 4$

Bring the whole class back together and share answers.

Discuss how best to record the calculations so that the order is correct – see if students can recall that multiplication and division should happen before addition and subtraction from earlier work.

Support students in positioning brackets where necessary to ensure that their calculations are carried out in the correct order.

Which numbers were not possible – why are these difficult?
Could you do it if you had five 4s?

Draw students' attention to the use of the $\dfrac{4}{4}$ term as a tool for going 1 above and 1 below a given number.

Adaptation: You could give students these 4s as number cards and provide them with operation cards (including brackets) to arrange in different ways and see what they come up with.

Extension: Students could explore which other numbers greater than 20 could be produced.
Are there any negative numbers that are possible?
What about fractions (or decimals)?
Students working at greater depth could consider using indices too, such as 4^4.

Starter ideas

Mental maths starter

Calculate $3 \times (2 + 7)$	Calculate $20 - 6 \div 2$	Calculate $(15 - 2) \times 3$	Calculate $(30 - 3) \div (2 + 7)$
Find the sum of 2.3 and 5.9	Add 4.7 to 9.4	Find the sum of 0.67 and 1.8	Add 16.7 and 5.8
Subtract 1.7 from 11	Find the difference between 0.72 and 0.4	Subtract 1.23 from 5	What number is 0.81 less than 2.5?
Multiply 2.3 by 4	Find the product of 12.7 by 3	Multiply 1.6 by 8	Find the product of 11.6 and 4
Divide 6.08 by 2	Divide 4.8 by 8	Find the quotient of 0.45 and 5	Divide 0.51 by 3
Divide 67 by 8	Find the quotient of 85 and 7	Divide 88 by 6	Find the quotient of 93 and 5

Vocabulary challenge

Ask students to come up with as many words as they can that represent the four main operations of addition, subtraction, multiplication and division.

Possible solutions:

- o Addition: Add, Plus, More; Total; Sum; And; Increase
- o Subtraction: Subtract, Take Away, Remove, Less, Difference, Minus, Below, Deduct
- o Multiplication: Multiply, Times, Lots Of, Groups Of, Product, By
- o Division: Divide, Shared Between, Grouped Into, How many ... go into..., Quotient.

Start point check: How did you do it?

a) Read these questions aloud for students to complete mentally (using mini-whiteboards if available)

1. Calculate: 346 add 291.
2. Calculate: 675 subtract 256.
3. Multiply 26 by 7.
4. Divide 87 by 3.

Follow up this task with a discussion in class about how students completed their calculations. Ask a student to explain their method. Ask if anyone had a different strategy. What are the pros and cons of each?

b) Write these questions on the board for students to complete with a written method (using mini-whiteboards if available)

1. Calculate 5 + 7 × 2.
2. Calculate 57 895 + 4291.
3. Calculate 6273 − 256.
4. Multiply 562 by 8.
5. Divide 7156 by 4.

Follow up this task with a discussion in class about how students completed their calculations. Ask a student to explain their method. Ask if anyone had a different strategy. What are the pros and cons of each?

What's the question?

Ask the students to write a unique question with a given answer.

Give each student a mini-whiteboard to put their response on.

For example:

Write an addition sentence that has the answer 293.

Write a division calculation that has an answer of 143.

Then ask students to hold up their boards and see who has a unique question. Award these students 1 point.

> TIP: Draw students' attention to the structure and pattern of possible answers.

For example, if you know that 200 + 93 = 293, then you can find another equivalent sum by increasing the first number by x and decreasing the second number by x, such as 231 + 62 (change of 31 to each number).

Continue with a further question for a given answer.

The winner is the student with the most points at the end.

Estimators vs calculators

Assign half the class as 'estimators' and half the class as 'calculators'. Write a calculation on the board and ask the estimators to estimate the answer.

Say: If you think the answer is going to be greater than 500 then stand on this side of the classroom. If you think the answer is going to be the less than 500 then stand on this side of the classroom.

Ask the calculators to find the answer. Award 1 point for the calculators who were correct in their answer, and 1 point to all estimators who were correct in their answer.

Discussion ideas

Probing questions	Teacher prompts
Is there a time that you do the additions before the other operations?	Ask students when the additions happen in these calculations: $$7 + 2 \times 4$$ $$20 \times (3 + 2)$$ Prompt students to consider additions in brackets if required. Remind them that this is the purpose of a bracket (to change the standard order and make an addition, for example, happen earlier than it should).
What is the largest value you can make using the single-digit numbers 3, 4, 5 and 6 and any combination of the operations $+, -, \times, \div$?	Try to focus on the structural things here, i.e. that without combining digits, the highest value is achieved by finding the product, i.e. $3 \times 4 \times 5 \times 6 = 360$. Similarly, the lowest value is achieved by subtracting, i.e. $3 - 4 - 5 - 6 = -12$. You could give students other answers to try to make, such as 0. Alternatively, you could allow students to include brackets and hence find lower numbers for example, $(4 \times 6) \times (3-5) = -48$.
If I know that $34 \times 8 = 272$, what else do I know?	Students may give answers relating to place value changes, for example: $3.4 \times 8 = 27.2$ $0.34 \times 8 = 2.72$ $34 \times 0.8 = 27.2$ $340 \times 80 = 27\ 200$ They may also look at doubling relationships and so on, for example: $34 \times 16 = 548$ $34 \times 4 = 136$ $17 \times 8 = 136$
How many pairs of positive decimals with one decimal place are there that sum to 3?	For instance: 3.0 and 0.0; 2.9 and 0.1, 2.8 and 0.2, ..., 1.6 and 1.4, 1.5 and 1.5. So, assuming order does not matter, there are 16 pairs. You could ask students how many pairs there are that sum to 2, 5, 9 and so on to see if they can generalise this.

Probing questions	Teacher prompts
How can you predict whether a division will leave a remainder? Can you predict what that remainder will be?	Encourage students to refer back to tests of divisibility (see Chapter 3). For example, 4567 ÷ 5: We know that this calculation will have a remainder because 4567 is not a multiple of 5 (as it does not end in 5 or 0). In fact, it is two higher than the previous multiple of 5 (4565) so the remainder will be 2 or $\frac{2}{5}$ when expressed as a fraction of the divisor.
How can you check an addition calculation to see if your answer is right? A subtraction? Multiplication? Division?	Look for students using the inverse operation and applying it to the answer or using estimation rather than simply repeating a calculation.

Common errors/misconceptions

Misconception	Strategies to address
Calculating in the wrong order, usually from left to right, rather than prioritising brackets, then multiplication and division, then addition and subtraction	Asking students use a scientific calculator to check their answers to calculations will help them realise they are making an error, for example, for 2 + 3 × 5. Ensure students know the order of operations and search for any brackets first, then for any multiplications and divisions. Encourage students to rewrite the calculation, replacing the pieces they have already worked out.
Believing that division always precedes multiplication (and addition always precedes subtraction)	Get students to test whether the order matters on a statement such as 24 × 20 ÷ 5 × 2 This should help them realise that it does! Then you can revisit the conventions and ensure students are fully aware that division and multiplication have the same position in the order of operations and so should be carried out from left to right when two or more of them appear. (They need to be aware that the same is true for addition and subtraction.)
Adding or subtracting by combining values with different place values	Checking answers with a calculator will flag up that the student's answers are incorrect. Encourage students to line decimals up so that their decimal points are positioned directly above one another. They can use placeholder 0s to fill any gaps that confuse them (to make the numbers the same length).
Making errors in exchanging when adding and subtracting using a written method That is, not correctly carrying digits forward to the next stage of calculation.	Encourage students to check their answer using the inverse operation to spot these errors. Try using place value counters to show what happens when you add two digits and the result is more than 9. Similarly, show how you need to exchange a larger counter for 10 smaller counters when subtracting a larger digit from a smaller one.
Making errors of place value when multiplying or dividing decimals by an integer. This may appear as positioning the decimal point in the wrong place.	Ask students to round their decimal to find the approximate size of their answer and check that their answer is reasonable

Misconception	Strategies to address
	For example, 2.81 × 3 is roughly 3 × 3 and so we expect an answer of approximately 9. This should help them realise that an answer of, for example, 84.3, cannot be right! They can then use this rounding to help them decide where to position the decimal point. Since 281 × 3 = 843, we need to position the decimal point between the 8 and the 4 to give 8.43 to get an answer near 9.
Writing the remainder from a division calculation as a fraction of the original number (and not the divisor)	Use the bar model to represent the calculation. This will help students to see the remainder and compare it to the divisor.

Developing conceptual understanding

7Nc7 Use the order of operations, including brackets, to work out simple calculations.

- It is important that students realise that, while <u>an</u> order of operations is necessary to help us all agree on how to calculate, the specific order we have today is just a <u>convention</u>. Therefore, we have decided that this will be the order we use internationally so we can all understand each other.

- FIX: You could use number cards to represent a calculation and then replace sections of the calculation with their new values as you calculate each operation.

- For example, 2 + 3 × 7 − 4 could start as separate cards before replacing the 3 × 7 cards with a 21 card and so on.

STRETCH: Students working at greater depth could begin to find all the possible answers to a given calculation depending on where a set of brackets were placed. For example: 2 + 3 × 7 − 4, the brackets could be positioned like 2 + 3 × 7 − 4 or 2 + 3 × (7 − 4) or 2 + (3 × 7 − 4) or (2 + 3 × 7) − 4 or 2 + (3 × 7) − 4 or (2 + 3 × 7 − 4). However, not all of these create a new answer. The students can investigate this further.

7Nc8 Add and subtract integers and decimals, including numbers with different numbers of decimal places.

- FIX: When teaching mental methods for addition and subtraction with decimals, encourage students to use number facts to partition a calculation using the nearest whole. For example, to calculate 1.47 + 0.92 a student might consider that 0.53 is needed to reach 2. Therefore, there is 0.39 of the original 0.92 remaining to be added. So the answer is 2.39.

- FIX: When teaching written methods of calculation, place value counters can provide a useful concrete (and visual) representation of the processes.

Addition and subtraction

For example, to show 3.82 − 1.56

Build 3.82 using place value counters:

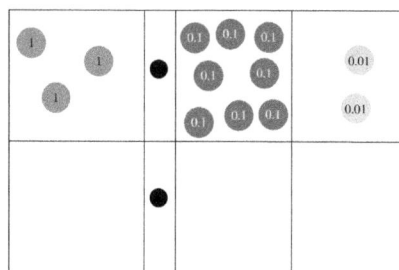

Then try to remove 6 hundredths or six yellow (light grey) counters – this is impossible, so you will need to exchange 1 tenth (red/dark grey) for 10/light grey hundredths (yellow/light grey):

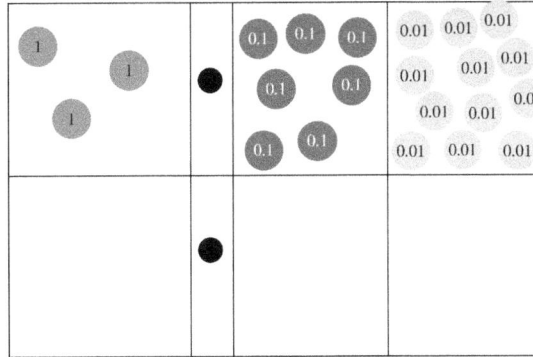

Now you can remove 1 one (green/mid-grey), 5 tenths (red/dark grey/light grey) and 6 hundredths (yellow/light grey) to the row below, leaving the answer in the top row – 2.26:

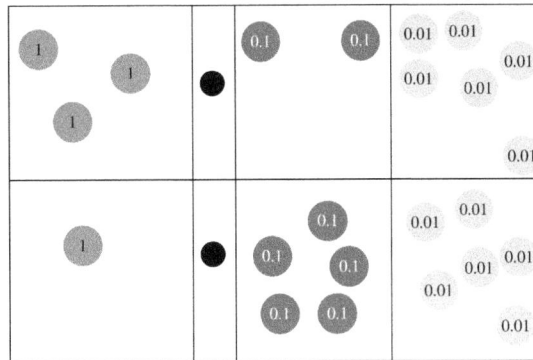

STRETCH: Students working at greater depth could try to find multiple pairs of numbers with a given sum or difference.

7Nc9 Multiply and divide decimals with one and/or two places by single-digit numbers, for example, 13.7 × 8, 4.35 ÷ 5.

- FIX: When teaching mental methods for multiplication and division, you could get students to check their answers by looking at the equivalent whole number calculation and then considering where to position the decimal point using estimation.

- For instance, to calculate 3.84 ÷ 3, begin by calculating 384 ÷ 3, which has an answer of 128. Then estimate the answer to 3.84 ÷ 3 ≈ 1 and then position the decimal point to create an answer close to 1, that is 1.28.

- FIX: When teaching written methods of calculation, place value counters can provide a useful concrete (and visual) representation of the processes.

Multiplication

For example, to show 2.13 × 4

Produce 2.13 using place value counters:

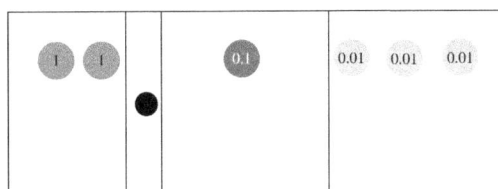

Then copy this row a further three times so you have four lots of this image:

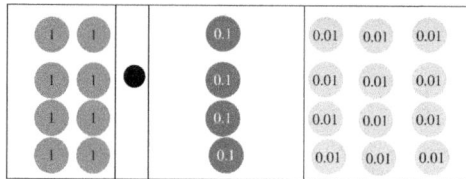

Then, since the hundredths column has more than nine counters, exchange 10 hundredths (yellow/light grey/dark grey) for 1 tenth (red):

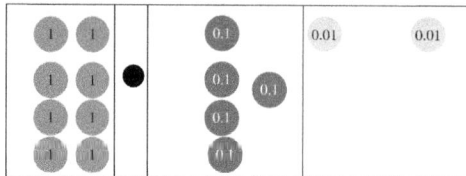

This leaves an answer of 8.52.

Division

For example, to calculate 5.24 ÷ 4

Build 5.24 using place value counters:

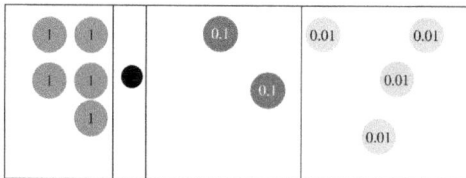

Then group the ones (green/mid-grey) into 4s:

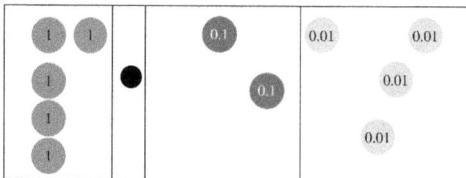

Exchange the remaining, ungrouped one counter (green/mid-grey) for 10 tenths (red/dark grey).

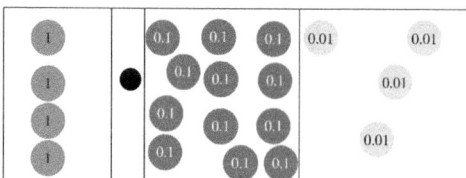

Then group the tenths (red/dark grey) into 4s:

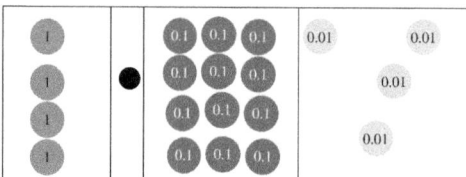

Then group the hundredths into 4s:

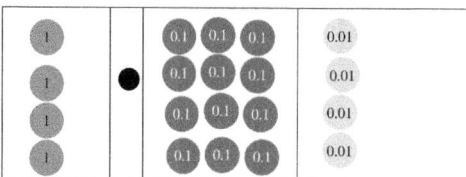

This leaves the answer as the top row of the array you have made – that is 1.31.

STRETCH: Students working at greater depth could begin to investigate calculations that combine two or more operations (and hence the order of operations also).

STRETCH: Students working at greater depth could try to find multiple pairs of numbers with a given product or quotient.

7Nc10 Know that in any division where the dividend is not a multiple of the divisor there will be a remainder, for example, 157 ÷ 25 = 6 remainder 7. The remainder can be expressed as a fraction of the divisor, for example 157 ÷ 25 = 6 $\frac{7}{25}$.

- FIX: You can show students why remainders can be written as fractions of the divisor using the bar model

  For example, to show 7 ÷ 5 you could show 13 wholes, grouped into 5s.

  This leaves three ungrouped – which compared to a whole 5 is $\frac{3}{5}$.

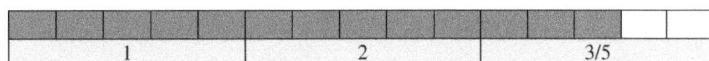

End of chapter mental maths exercise

1. Calculate 54 ÷ (2 + 7).	7. Find the sum of 3.87 and 2.4.
2. Add 9.5 and 3.7.	8. Find the quotient of 89 and 3.
3. What number is 1.23 less than 4?	9. Mary has a piece of ribbon measuring 3.13 m. She wants to cut a piece measuring 1.8 m off. Will she have enough for a further 1.3 m piece?
4. Find the product of 9.3 and 7.	
5. Divide 0.84 by 7.	10. Noah and his three friends are sharing a bill of $85 equally. How much will they need to pay each?
6. Find the difference between 7.8 and 10.5.	

Technology recommendations

- *Problem solving*

  Use scientific and basic calculators to experience the effects of calculating in the wrong order.

  Give half the class a standard, basic calculator and the other half the class a scientific calculator.

  Ask them to all quickly calculate the answers to these calculations to check they can use a calculator correctly:

  1. 20 × 6 – 9   2. 14 + 2 × 3   3. 58 ÷ 2 + 7   4. 28 – 12 ÷ 4

  Then go through the answers really quickly (111, 20, 26, 25) and ask the students to mark theirs.

  The students using the basic calculators will quickly cry out because they have the wrong answers to Q2 and Q4 (they will have 48 and 4 respectively).

  This should then lead to a good exploration of why they all have the wrong answer.

- Using calculators to carry out inverse operations to check answers to mental or written calculations.

Investigation/research tasks

- **Remainder challenge**   *Problem solving*

  The calculations 94 ÷ x and 143 ÷ x both leave a remainder of 3.

  What is the value of x?

  STRETCH: Can you make up your own problem like this for a friend to solve?

Solution:

We need to subtract 3 from both numbers to find two multiples of x.

$94 - 3 = 91$ and $143 - 3 = 140$, so x is a factor of both 91 and 140.

The only factors of 91 are 1, 7, 13, 91.

The factors of 140 are 1, 2, 4, 5, 7, 10, 14, 20, 28, 35, 70, 140.

So, the only shared factors are 1 and 7. 1 cannot be a solution since it is less than 3 (the remainder) Therefore, x has to be 7.

- **Brackets to 100**   *Problem solving*

Show students the digits 1 2 3 4 5 6 7 8 9.

Ask them to insert brackets and operations +, −, ×, ÷ to make a calculation with an answer of 100. They can use any or all of the signs and repeat them as they wish.

You could allow students to combine digits together to make $\frac{2}{3}$-digit numbers and to reorder the digits if you wish.

Possible solutions:

- ○ $1 + 2 + 3 + 4 + 5 + 6 + 7 + 8 \times 9$
- ○ $(1 + 2 + 3 + 4 + 5) \times 6 - 7 + 8 + 9$
- ○ $(1 \times 2 + 3) \times 4 \times 5 + 6 - 7 - 8 + 9$

> TIP: You could use number digit cards for this activity with operations on cards.

- Research the method of multiplication called Napier's Bones for whole numbers and decimals using the internet.

  Show how you can use this method to calculate 5.67 × 8.

  Compare this method to another written method that you know. What are the advantages and disadvantages of each?

- **Missing numbers task**   *Problem solving*

  Give students a copy of the calculations with missing numbers in the online photocopiable resources for this chapter. Ask them to try to work out the value of the missing digits using their understanding of written calculation.

  You may need to prompt students to think about what the range of possible values could be each time to help them to eliminate the digits that cannot be correct.

  [Beware] Students may try to use the first digit they think of that is correct and not consider whether it works with other parts of the calculation. Prompt them to check their answers carefully by carrying out the calculation to see if they get the same answer.

Percentages

<table>
<tr><td>

Learning objectives

Learning objectives covered in this chapter: 7Nf6, 7Nf7

- Calculate simple percentages of quantities (whole number answers).
- Express a smaller quantity as a fraction or percentage of a larger one.
- Use percentages to represent and compare different quantities.

</td><td>

Key terms

- percentage; %
- whole
- part(s)
- numerator
- denominator
- simplify
- equivalent fraction

</td></tr>
</table>

Prior knowledge assumptions

- Students understand percentage as parts in every 100.
- Students can express these fractions as percentages: $\frac{1}{2}, \frac{1}{4}, \frac{1}{3}, \frac{1}{10}, \frac{1}{100}$.
- Students can find simple percentages of a shape or (whole number) quantity.

Guidance on the hook

Purpose: This task helps students to see the use of fractions and percentages in the real world and to consider how to use mathematics to solve best value problems.

Use of the hook: Using the diagram in the Student's Book, ask students to work in pairs to calculate how much a 200 g packet of biscuits would actually cost using each of the four offers. Then bring the group back together to compare their methods and answers.
You may need to explain the meaning of 'extra free' as getting extra biscuits in the packet.

TIP: You could use bar models to represent (and then calculate) the costs.

For example:

Original Pack	50% extra free	20% off
$1.50	$1.50	80% of 0 to $1.5 = $1.20 / free
200g	200g / 100g	200g

3 packs for the price of 2		Save 1/4	
2 × $1.50 = $3.00		3/4 of $1.50 = $1.13	free 1/4
200g	200g / 200g	200g	

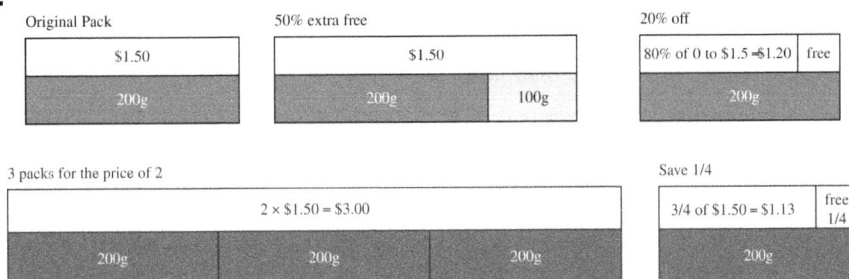

Ask the students what practical things they should also consider. For example, it may be cheaper to buy lots of biscuits but do you have enough storage for all of them? Do you want to limit the number of biscuits you buy for other reasons?

Adaptation: You could get students to investigate other supermarket offers for similar products to see which examples of discounts using fractions and percentages they can find. They can then work out which is the best value item.

Extension: Students could design their own offers that use different fractions and percentages as problems for others to solve. They could use more complex fractions and percentages if appropriate. They could also produce an answer guide to their problem that others can use to check their calculations afterwards.

Starter ideas

Mental maths starter

Find 50% of 126	Find 10% of 2300	Find 20% of 380	Find 30% of 710
Find 10% of 34 000	Find 1% of 28 000	Find 5% of 220	Find 2% of 315 000
Find 20% of 480	Find 60% of 480	Find 80% of 430	Find 15% of 320
25% of a number is 17. What is the number?	20% of a number is 31. What is the number?	5% of a number is 16. What is the number?	40% of a number is 28. What is the number?
Write $\frac{1}{3}$ as a percentage	Write $\frac{3}{4}$ as a percentage	Write $\frac{1}{5}$ as a percentage	Write $\frac{1}{20}$ as a percentage
Which is greater? 10% of 60 or 25% of 20?	Which is greater? 50% of 360 or 20% of 950?	Which is greater? 10% of 130 or 75% of 16?	Which is greater? 3% of 6000 or 90% of 200?

Start point check: Representing percentages

1. Give students some squares divided into 100 equal squares (see resources section) and ask them to colour in 1%, 10%, 50%, 23% and so on.

   Now do the same with decimals such as 0.1, 0.2, 0.5, 0.03, 0.24 and so on.

   Share the answers as a larger group and discuss which percentages and decimals are equivalent.

   See if students can begin to think about how to convert between these.

   Ask the students "If I made my 100 square larger/smaller (enlarged) what would happen?".

2. Draw a range of shapes on the board for example, circle, rectangle, square, triangle, shapes made of smaller squares.

   Ask students to discuss in pairs how they would shade 10% of the each of the shapes.

   Then bring different students to the board to share their solutions.

   Emphasise the importance of there being ten equally sized parts, one of which is shaded (to link to earlier fractions work).

   Repeat for other percentages, for example, 25%, 1%, 5%.

English language leading into vocab feature

Ask students to work in pairs to come up with other words that involve 'cent' and have a link with 100.

Possible answers: century, centipede, centurion, centimetre, Centigrade, cent, centennial (also, non-English words meaning 100 such as cento in Italian or cent in French).

Paper strip and paperclip

Give each student a strip of paper and a paperclip.
Tell the students the paper strip represents a number line from 0% to 100%.
Ask them to position their paper clip at 50% and then hold their strip up for you to see

Then try these percentages:

- 25%
- 75%
- 10%
- 20%
- 30%

- 90%
- 1%
- 3%
- 51%
- 33% etc.

The aim of this activity is to develop students' number sense and proportional reasoning to help them use the bar model confidently.

You should be able to see which students are confident in doing this by both the accuracy and speed of their responses.

Discussion ideas

Probing questions	Teacher prompts
Amy has been offered either 90% of one packet of sweets or 20% of another packet of sweets. Amy wants the most sweets possible. Which deal should Amy pick?	Encourage students to explain that even though 90% sounds better than 20%, it depends on how big the packets of sweets are. Give students examples of different size packets to help them unpick this further and conclude that more information is needed to make a decision.
Can you have a percentage greater than 100%?	Prompt students to give possible examples – e.g. the price of something could rise by more than the original amount so this would be a price rise of over 100% Ask students when a percentage of over 100% would not make sense. For example, 120% of the class are on a school trip.
True or False? 15% of 80 = 80% of 15	Students could represent this as a bar model and actually calculate the answers. However, encourage them to think more generally if possible and give students the opportunity to investigate with other numbers. Ask students to think of the calculation for 15% of 80 as $\frac{15}{100} \times 80$, which could be rearranged to $\frac{80}{100} \times 15$ since multiplication is commutative.
The value of two houses goes up by $10 000. One was worth $200 000 originally but the other was worth $250 000. Which house has gone up by a higher percentage? Will this always be true?	Again, students can actually work this out for the example given (increases of 5% and 4%) and then think about the more general case. Encourage them to explain that the lower valued item will always have increased by a higher percentage because you are always comparing to a smaller original value.
Can you have a decimal percentage? For example, 2.5%? What would this mean?	Prompt students to give examples involving decimals (and to explain 2.5% is exactly half of 5%). For example, interest rates, pay rise, proportion of people who are colour blind in the world.
True or false? $\frac{1}{3} = 33\%$	You might like to use a calculator to investigate this. Alternatively, students could use a bar model to show that $\frac{1}{3}$ is equal to 100% ÷ 3 which is 33.333333.... % or $33.\dot{3}$% .

Probing questions	Teacher prompts
	(and that this is slightly more than the exact 33%). Students could think of other fractions with a recurring decimal percentage equivalent, for example, $\frac{1}{6}$.

Common errors/misconceptions

Misconception	Strategies to address
Not realising that a percentage is simply a different way of describing the proportion of the whole and so seeing fractions and percentages as unrelated	Show students that 'per hundred' directly related to a fraction with denominator 100. Write percentages as fractions out of 100, e.g. 23% means 23 parts per hundred or 23 out of 100 or $\frac{23}{100}$.
Believing that you can find x% of a quantity by dividing it by x (based on the logic that you can find 10% by dividing by 10)	Ask students to test whether this works for example, can you find 20% by dividing by 20? (For example, of 600). To see what you need to divide by, they could try representing the percentage on a bar model or paper strip (to show that 20% = $\frac{1}{5}$). Students could explore whether there are any other percentages like 10% that this works for (and discover that there are not!).
Believing that x% is equivalent to $\frac{1}{x}$ For example, thinking that $5\% = \frac{1}{5}$	Use a bar model or paper strip to represent the fraction and the percentage to show they are not equivalent.
Not realising that the percentage relates to a whole and so the value of that percentage cannot be determined until the whole value is known For example, thinking that 75% is automatically better than 60% without knowing the values of the whole	Give all the students two different length paper strips (from a mixture of many different lengths in the class) and ask them to find 75% of one and 60% of the other. See which paper strip students think is bigger and point out that everyone thinks differently because they have different wholes.

Developing conceptual understanding

7Nf6 Calculate simple percentages of quantities (whole number answers) and express a smaller quantity as a fraction or percentage of a larger one.

- FIX: Students who are struggling with the meaning of percentages can colour in a 10 by 10 square to show percentages (and tenths and hundredths), as well as the equivalence of, for example, 40% and 4 tenths or $\frac{4}{10}$.

  For example, here is 71%.

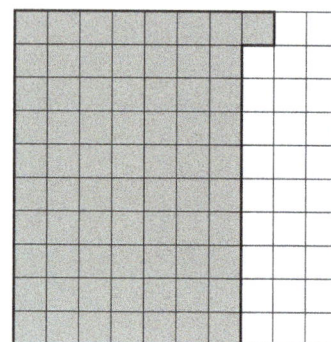

- FIX: Also, using a number line representation (visual or washing line/paper strips) to represent 0-100 and to position percentages correctly, linking this to the position of fractions can help students develop a sense of percentage values.

> TIP: All students would benefit from folding paper strips to represent percentages from 0% to 100% by making the whole worth 100%.

They can then find the equivalent fractions to different percentages by counting the parts in the whole and the parts used for the percentage.

STRETCH: Students working at greater depth could also find percentage equivalents for common fractions that involve decimals, for example, $\frac{1}{8}$ or $\frac{1}{40}$.

7Nf7 Use percentages to represent and compare different quantities.

- FIX: Use the bar model to represent percentage problems.

For example: Here we are showing 30% of 70:

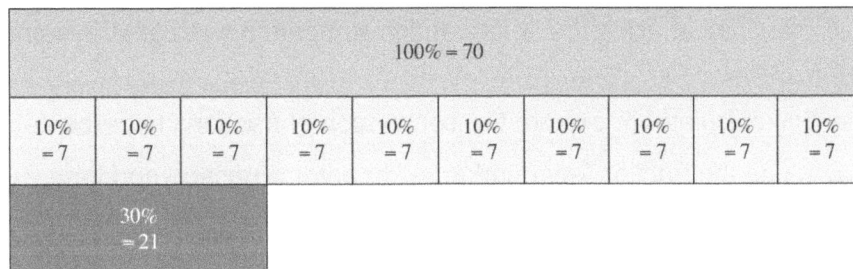

> TIP: Try also showing students a percentage as a bar and asking them what the whole amount was.

For example, here is a bar worth 20% – what was the whole amount?

Solution:

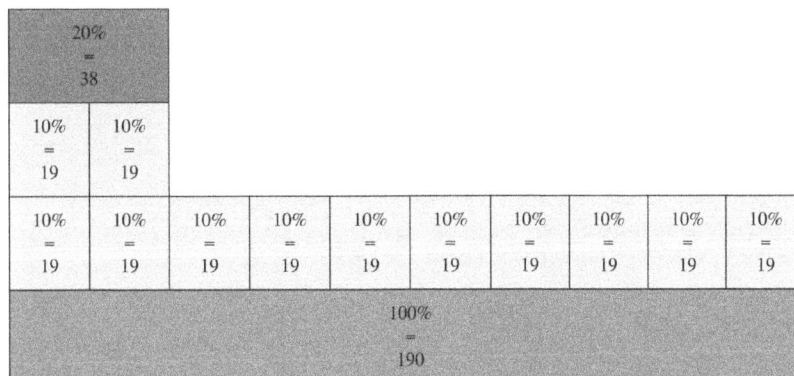

STRETCH: Students working at greater depth could try to devise problems to compare percentages of amounts using a 'would you rather' template.

For example:

Would you rather be bitten by 5% of 1200 ants or 11% of 500 ants?

End of chapter mental maths exercise

1. Find 30% of 810.	6. Write $\frac{2}{5}$ as a percentage
2. Find 3% of 28 000	7. Write 29% as a fraction
3. Find 90% of 460	8. Which is greater? 10% of $5 or 70% of 80 cents?
4. 20% of a number is 56. What is the number?	9. Would you rather sit in a traffic jam for 44% of 1 hour and 40 minutes or $\frac{1}{3}$ of 2 hours?
5. 3% of a number is 21. What is the number?	

Technology recommendations

* Using the % key on a scientific calculator to calculate percentages by multiplying.

  Students could start by calculating percentages by multiplying by the percentage and dividing by 100. For example, to find 23% of 462 they would type 462 × 23 ÷ 100.

  They could then investigate using the fraction key (marked ─) for this i.e. $462 \times \frac{23}{100}$.

  They could then look at using the % key and investigate how to get the same answer (by typing 462 × 23%).

* Use a scientific calculator to explore the conversion of fractions to percentages.

  Students can use the fraction key (marked ─) to enter a fraction and then explore the answer to see how to convert it to a percentage (by multiplying by 100).

Investigation/research tasks

* **Challenge:** Calculate 20% of 30% of 40% of 6000.

  Can you make up a similar problem with a whole number answer?

  What sort of number do you need to make sure that 20% of it is a whole number?

  What sort of number do you need to make sure that 30% of it is a whole number?

  So what kind of number do you need to make sure that the answer will be a whole number when you have three percentages of 20%, 30% and 40%?

  Students should get an answer of 144.

  Prompt students to think about the type of number needed at each stage to get a whole number answer. They can then work backwards to find that the original number must be a multiple of 125.

  They could explore why this must be.

  One possible explanation:

  20% x 30% x 40% = 0.024 = $\frac{24}{1000} = \frac{12}{500} = \frac{6}{250} = \frac{3}{125}$

  So we are finding $\frac{3}{125}$ of the original number.

  Therefore, the original number must be divisible by 125.

STRETCH: How would this change with different percentages (that are not multiples of 10)?

* Find some examples of percentages being used in real life.

  You could look at newspaper articles, product packaging, financial information and much more.

Produce a collage of your findings and label it to explain how the percentages are used in each example.

- **Population Explosion**   *Problem solving*   *Tech*

The population of the world is currently rising at approximately 1.1% per year.

The world population in 2017 is approximately 7.5 billion.

- o How many extra people are there in the world each year at this rate of growth?
- o Using this rate, how many people will there be in 2018? 2019? 2020?
- o Use a spreadsheet to work out how many people there will be by 2030.
- o By what year will the population reach 10 billion?

Students can begin this task using a calculator to find 1.1% of 7.5 billion.

BEWARE: You may need to help students enter 7.5 billion correctly on a calculator. Alternatively, you could encourage them not to work in billions and use just 7.5.

Students can repeat their earlier process to find the population in 2018, 2019 and 2020 by adding on the extra people each time.

However, to carry out these calculations beyond the first few years, you should encourage students to use a spreadsheet to automatically calculate the additional people and add this to the existing population.

For example:

	A	B	C
2			
3	Year	Population	Increase
4	2017	7,500,000,000	82,500,000
5	2018	7,582,500,000	83,407,500
6	2019	7,665,907,500	84,324,983
7	2020	7,750,232,483	85,252,557
8	2021	7,835,485,040	86,190,335
9	2022	7,921,675,375	87,138,429
10	2023	8,008,813,804	88,096,952
11	2024	8,096,910,756	89,066,018
12	2025	8,185,976,775	90,045,745
13	2026	8,276,058,519	91,036,248
14	2027	8,367,058,767	92,037,646
15	2028	8,459,096,413	93,050,061
16	2029	8,552,146,474	94,073,611
17	2030	8,646,220,085	95,108,421
18	2031		
19	2032		
20	2033		
21	2034		
22	2035		
23	2036		

which comes from these formulae:

	A	B	C
2			
3	Year	Population	Increase
4	2017	75000000000	=1.1%*B4
5	=A4+1	=B4+C4	=1.1%*B5
6	=A5+1	=B5+C5	=1.1%*B6
7	=A6+1	=B6+C6	=1.1%*B7
8	=A7+1	=B7+C7	=1.1%*B8
9	=A8+1	=B8+C8	=1.1%*B9
10	=A9+1	=B9+C9	=1.1%*B10
11	=A10+1	=B10+C10	=1.1%*B11
12	=A11+1	=B11+C11	=1.1%*B12
13	=A12+1	=B12+C12	=1.1%*B13
14	=A13+1	=B13+C13	=1.1%*B14
15	=A14+1	=B14+C14	=1.1%*B15
16	=A15+1	=B15+C15	=1.1%*B16
17	=A16+1	=B16+C16	=1.1%*B17
18	=A17+1		
19	=A18+1		
20	=A19+1		
21	=A20+1		
22			

Ratio and proportion

Learning objectives	Key terms
Learning objectives covered in this chapter: 7Nf8, 7Nf9, 7Nf10	• ratio
• Use ratio notation, simplify ratios and divide a quantity into two parts in a given ratio.	• colon (:) • simplify • common factor • proportion
• Recognise the relationship between ratio and proportion.	
• Use direct proportion in context: solve simple problems involving ratio and direct proportion.	

Prior knowledge assumptions

- Students can use ratio implicitly to solve a proportion or scaling problem, for example, to adapt a recipe for 6 people to one for 12 people or 3 people.
- Students can recognise and find a simple proportion of a set of objects; they can state the proportion of the set with a given feature.

Guidance on the hook

Paint cans special offer

Purpose: The purpose of this task is to introduce learners to ratio and proportion in a way that they are familiar with.

Use of the hook: Start by asking learners to think about the two questions posed in the hook, this could be done very effectively as a think, pair, share activity (individual learners should think about their answers, then discuss as a pair with another student and then ideas can be shared as a class). When learners are giving their answers ensure that you ask them to explain their method. At this point one option would be to introduce ratio notation and discuss with the group how their methods could be shown working with ratio notation (see below for example).

Question 1	Question 2
Buy : Free 2 : 1 14 : __	Buy : Free 2 : 1
Discuss what operation is needed to move from 2 to 14. Learners should identify multiply by 7, however they may suggest add 12 – this can be addressed by returning to the context and asking learners to think about if this would make sense in context.	Each 'group' of paint cans bought using the offer has 2 bought and 1 free so 3 cans altogether. How many lots of 3 cans are there in 12 cans? $12 \div 3 = 4$ Buy : Free 2 : 1 ×4 8 : 4 ×4

Alternatively, the use of more formal ratio notation can be left until later and students can just explore their own questions relating to the ratio/proportion in context given here.

If learners are setting their own problems then they can ask these of others within the class or be asked to give model answers.

Adaptation: This could be made easier by starting with a buy one, get one free offer.

Additional practice could be included by giving other offers for paint or for other contexts. A good extension activity is to look at mixing paints in a ratio and there are some internet resources that can be found to support this.

Extension: In addition to creating their own questions related to this context, learners can also research other offers where a number of items are bought and a number of items are obtained for free.

Starter ideas

Mental maths starter

Find $\frac{1}{5}$ of 45	Find $\frac{1}{6}$ of 78	Find $\frac{1}{8}$ of 120	Find $\frac{1}{7}$ of 147
Find $\frac{2}{3}$ of 66	Find $\frac{2}{9}$ of 180	Find $\frac{3}{4}$ of 144	Find $\frac{5}{6}$ of 84
Find the fraction that sums to 1 with $\frac{7}{12}$	Find the fraction that sums to 1 with $\frac{5}{13}$	Find the fraction that sums to 1 with $\frac{11}{20}$	Find the fraction that sums to 1 with $\frac{3}{15}$
Simplify $\frac{24}{30}$	Simplify $\frac{15}{25}$	Simplify $\frac{11}{33}$	Simplify $\frac{28}{35}$
Simplify 7 : 28	Simplify 24 : 12	Simplify 16 : 40	Simplify 42 : 48
Divide 18 in the ratio 2 : 1	Divide 28 in the ratio 5 : 2	Divide 36 in the ratio 2 : 7	Divide 40 in the ratio 3 : 5

Start point check: Scaling

1.   Write this recipe on the board:

> **Pancakes**
> **(Recipe makes 12 pancakes)**
> 120 g flour
> 2 large eggs
> 300 ml milk
> 30 ml of vegetable oil

Ask students to work in pairs scale this recipe up and down for 24 pancakes and 6 pancakes respectively.

Students working confidently could try to produce the recipe for 18 and 3 pancakes also.

Start point check: Ratio

Show students this image (see photocopiable resources online):

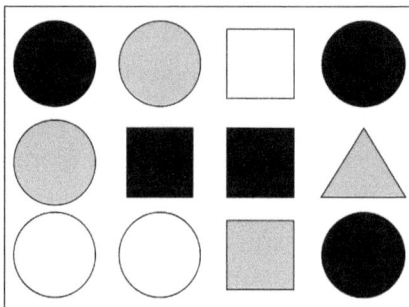

Verbally ask them questions about the image to work on in pairs. Students could then share their answers using mini-whiteboards.

Feedback their answers to a whole class discussion.

For example:

- What proportion of the shapes are triangles? squares? circles?
- What proportion of the shapes are black? white? grey?
- What is the ratio of squares to triangles? triangles to squares?
- What is the ratio of grey circles to white circles?
- If there were 24 shapes in the box and the proportions and ratios of this set were the same, how many grey triangles would there be? black circles? squares?

Game: Simplifying ratios shoot out

Two students stand facing each other and put their hands behind their backs.

They are going to make a ratio together, with one student nominated as the first number in the ratio.

Each student decides on a number between 1 and 10 and, after a countdown of "ready, steady, go", holds their hands up in front of them showing the number they have chosen with their fingers.

The students need to simplify the ratio they have made and say it aloud.

The first student to say it correctly wins 1 point.

They then repeat.

Discussion ideas

Probing questions	Teacher prompts
Draw a set of objects where the ratio of shaded to unshaded is 1 : 4. How many objects did you draw? Now draw another (different set) of objects with the same ratio. How many objects did you draw this time? What do you notice?	Encourage students to realise that the number of objects they draw will need to be a multiple of 5 because there are 5 parts in the ratio. Try to get them to see that, in any of their drawings, the proportion shaded is always $\frac{1}{5}$ (and the proportion unshaded is always $\frac{4}{5}$). You could prompt them to systematically come up with similar diagrams (of 10, 15, 20 objects and so on).

Probing questions	Teacher prompts
Convince me/a friend that if the ratio of adults to children in a group is 4 : 5, then the proportion of adults is $\frac{4}{9}$ and the proportion of children is $\frac{5}{9}$.	You could encourage students to use a bar model to help show the whole divided in the ratio 4 : 5 and hence why there are 9 parts altogether i.e.
Change one thing about this image so that: a) the ratio of triangles to squares is 1 : 5 b) the proportion of circles is greater than $\frac{1}{2}$ c) the proportion of hexagons is $\frac{1}{13}$ d) the proportion of hexagons is $\frac{1}{12}$ e) the ratio of black shapes to white shapes is 1 : 1 f) the ratio of red shapes to white shapes is 1 : 2 g) the proportion of squares = $\frac{1}{4}$	Try to force students to only alter one item of the image each time. They could: – remove a shape – add a shape – change a shape – change the colour of a shape. You could also encourage students to come up with their own 'change one thing...' questions for others to try.
True or False? If two people divide some money in the ratio 5 : 7 the first person will get $\frac{5}{7}$ of the money:	You could get students to draw a bar model to represent this problem to show that the number of parts in the whole is 12 (and not 7) and hence the first person receives $\frac{5}{12}$ of the money:
What happens if you mix two quantities in different ratios? For example, you can make soda by mixing syrup and water. If you combine two different batches of soda, what happens to the ratio of syrup to water?	Encourage students to see that the resulting soda will have a concentrate to water ratio that lies between the 2 original ratios, depending on the volume of each one included in the mix. You could try this practically with water and food colouring.

Common errors/misconceptions

Misconception	Strategies to address
Interchanging fractions and ratios incorrectly For example, writing 2 : 3 as $\frac{2}{3}$ and not identifying that each part of the ratio 2 : 3 will be $\frac{2}{5}$ and $\frac{3}{5}$ of the whole.	Give students an example with objects such as 15 sweets. Ask them to divide them in the ratio 2 : 3. If they put $\frac{2}{3}$ of the sweets in one pile and $\frac{1}{3}$ in the other, ask them whether one person has 2 sweets for every 3 of the other's.

Misconception	Strategies to address
	You could arrange objects in groups of 2s and 3s to check and show that this is not true. Alternatively, use a bar model to represent the ratio as 2 boxes and 3 boxes to show the 5 parts in the whole: whole This will show them that neither share is $\frac{2}{3}$. Recap that the denominator tells us the number of parts in the whole also.
Believing that the smaller number comes first in every ratio	Give an example that can be reversed and act this out practically for example, you share some sweets with your friend in the ratio 2 : 1. How can we explain a ratio where your friend gets twice as many sweets as you?
Simplifying a ratio without ensuring that the units of each part are the same (or carrying the units forward)	You could show this practically using, for example, sugar and water. You could show (and taste!) the difference between a ratio of 2 : 1 and a ratio of 2 teaspoons: 1 litre.
Not understanding how a ratio can be simplified because the smaller numbers don't seem to reflect the whole population	Divide the whole group into smaller groups of the size of the simplified ratio to show why this ratio is equivalent For example to show that 8 : 12 is the same as 2 : 3 represent 8 : 12 as an array: The whole image shows a ratio of 8 : 12 but within each row the ratio is 2 : 3.
Believing that a ratio always shows the relationship between 2 parts (and not realising that one of the quantities can be the whole if you want)	Expose students to problems of this type so they can see that a ratio can represent any quantities as long as they are defined. For example, the ratio of teachers to people in the school is 1 : 30. If the only people in the school are teachers and pupils, what is the ratio of teachers to pupils?
Not realising that the relationships between quantities in proportion are multiplicative and so trying to use an additive relationship instead. For example, when trying to adjust a recipe for 10 to one for 15, adding 5 instead of multiplying by 1.5	Explore the recipe example in more detail. If we only add 5 g of flour, will this be enough for an extra 5 people? What if we add an extra 5 eggs?!
Struggling to divide an amount in a given ratio because they cannot easily identify the total number of parts (the whole)	Use a bar model to help visualise and quickly recognise the total number of parts as above.

Developing conceptual understanding

7Nf8 Use ratio notation, simplify ratios and divide a quantity into two parts in a given ratio.

- FIX: You can help students to understand ratio and proportion by giving them sets of double-sided counters and asking them to build sets of objects with a specific ratio/proportion. Alternatively, you could get them to draw/colour in a set of shapes and shaded them (in) a given ratio/proportion.

  For example, make/draw a set of counters where:

  o the ratio of red to yellow is 3 : 1

  o the proportion of red is $\frac{1}{3}$

  o the proportion of yellow is $\frac{1}{4}$

  o the ratio of yellow to red is 1 : 2.

7Nf9 Recognise the relationship between ratio and proportion.

> TIP: It is helpful if students arrange the objects into an array structure like this to help them see the ratios/proportions.

This also links ratio and proportion to multiplication, which is a useful connection.

For example, these arrays all show groups of objects where the ratio of yellow (light grey) to red (dark grey) is 3 : 1 (and hence why the number of objects must be a multiple of 4).

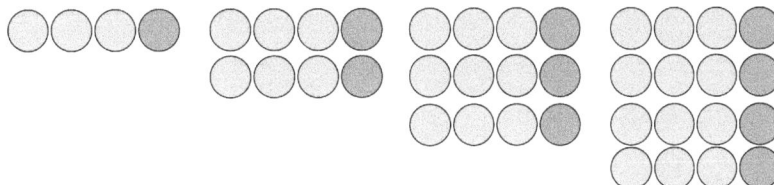

7Nf10 Use direct proportion in context; solve simple problems involving ratio and direct proportion.

- Encourage all students, but especially those who need to develop their conceptual understanding, to use the bar model to represent a ratio or proportion problem.

  This will help them to visualise the problem and decide which calculations to carry out.

  For example, the problem "The ratio of juice to water in a recipe is 2 : 5. Joanna has 300 ml of water, how much juice is needed?" can be represented like this:

juice	juice	water	water	water	water	water
?		300 ml				

This makes it easy to see that we can find one part of the ratio by calculating 300 ÷ 5 = 60 ml.

juice	juice	water	water	water	water	water
60 ml	60 ml	60 ml	60 ml	60 ml	60 ml	60 ml
	120 ml					

Hence the solution is that 60 × 2 = 120 ml of juice is required.

* All students can apply these concepts just to numbers but then also to measures to provide broader context and interpretation.

STRETCH: Students working at greater depth can look at problems combining proportion and ratio. For example, Amy and Bob share some sweets. They are both going to eat and save their sweets in the ratio 3 : 4. Amy gets $\frac{5}{11}$ of the sweets while Bob receives 84 sweets. How many sweets do they save?

STRETCH: Students working at greater depth can also begin to consider the effect of merging two quantities in a given ratio. For example, if a 1-litre jug of flavoured water has a ratio flavouring to water of 1 : 10 and another has a ratio of flavouring to water of 1 : 8, what is the ratio of flavouring to drink if these two jugs of drink are mixed together?

End of chapter mental maths exercise

1. Find $\frac{1}{7}$ of 91.

2. Find $\frac{4}{5}$ of 135.

3. Find the fraction that sums to 1 with $\frac{9}{11}$.

4. Simplify the fraction $\frac{18}{54}$.

5. Simplify the ratio 48 : 72.

6. Divide 49 in the ratio 1 : 6.

7. Divide 120 in the ratio 5 : 3.

8. Ratio of red to blue paint in a purple paint tin is 4 : 3.
   There are 200 ml of red paint. How much blue paint is needed?

9. The ratio of flour to sugar in a recipe is 2 : 3. There are 87 g of sugar in a recipe. How much flour is needed?

Technology recommendations

* Use a spreadsheet to record results in a proportion calculation and then plot these as a graph to observe that the graph is linear and goes through the origin.

   For example, if we know that 8 cupcakes cost $6, then we can find the cost of 16 cupcakes, 4 cupcakes, 2 cupcakes and so on. We can record these in a table (on a spreadsheet) and then produce a graph.

* Use a drawing package to look at the ratio of the length and width of the diagram and how these change as the image is resized.

Investigation/research tasks

* **Rectangle proportion**   *Problem solving*

   A rectangle has an area of 126 cm^2.

   The sides of the rectangle are in the ratio 2 : 7.

   What is the perimeter of the rectangle?

   Students could represent this problem algebraically.

For example, as a rectangle of length $7x$, width $2x$ and so area of $2x \times 7x = 14x^2$:

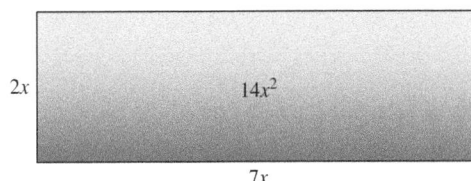

By setting this equal to the area of 135 cm^2, i.e. $14x^2 = 126$, students can find that x must be 3 cm.

They can then substitute to find that the perimeter is 54 cm.

> TIP: Students can then try to produce their own problem like this before swapping and trying each other's out.

BEWARE: Students need to ensure that the total number of parts in the ratio is a factor of the area. If they want a whole number answer, they should make sure that its factor pair is a square number.

- **Coin ratios**   *Problem solving*

  Take a coin.

  How many of these coins fit on a piece of A5 paper?

  What is the ratio of coins: pieces of A5 paper?

  How can you calculate an estimate the number of coins that would fit on the bottom of an Olympic Swimming Pool?

  What is the ratio of pieces of A5 paper: area of swimming pool?

  Students could estimate the number of coins first and then test it out practically using a piece of A5 paper and drawing round the coins.

> TIP: Students could use different coins in different groups to allow comparison between them.

You may want to help students use the links between different paper sizes for example, the fact that there are 16 A5 pieces of paper within a single A1 sheet.

They can then use the paper links to bridge from coins to the swimming pool!

Information: An Olympic swimming pool usually measures 50 m by 25 m.

- Investigate the role of ratio in music, particularly in chords and harmony. You might like to start with a stringed instrument such as a guitar or piano or violin.

  Why is ratio important to achieving a pleasant sound?

Fractions and decimals

Learning objectives

Learning objectives covered in this chapter: 7Nf3

- Compare two fractions by using diagrams.
- Compare two fractions by using a calculator to convert

  the fractions to decimals, for example, $\frac{3}{5}$ and $\frac{13}{20}$.

Key terms

- numerator
- denominator
- fraction button

Prior knowledge assumptions

- Students should be aware about how to change a fraction to a decimal by division.
- They should be familiar with the signs <, > and = when comparing whole numbers and decimals.

The work in this chapter will be helpful in Stage 8 when students learn more about comparing fractions and converting between fractions, decimals and percentages.

Guidance on the hook

Comparing fractions

Purpose: This hook introduces a method for comparing two fractions using diagrams.

Use of the hook: Start by demonstrating to students Artem's method for comparing fractions.

TIP: You may want to get two large square pieces of paper and visually show each being split into three columns and five rows. Discuss with students how to shade $\frac{4}{5}$ of the first and $\frac{2}{3}$ of the other.

Then split the class into pairs in order to play the game. Each pair of students will need two dice and some paper to record their work.

TIP: Get player 1 to form the first fraction by rolling the dice first. Then get player 2 to form the second fraction by rolling second. The player with the larger fraction wins.

Adaptation: If students find it difficult to compare the fractions, give students a copy of the photocopiable resource sheet (online) showing some prepared squares.

Extension: Instead of using dice to generate the numerator and denominator, students could draw cards out of a set numbered from 1 to 10.

Starter ideas

Mental maths starter

Write $\frac{1}{4}$ as a decimal.	Write $\frac{41}{100}$ as a decimal.	Write $\frac{3}{10}$ as a decimal.	Write $\frac{2}{5}$ as a decimal.
Find $17 \div 100$	Find $3 \div 5$	Find $11 \div 100$	Find $9 \div 100$
Simplify $\frac{40}{60}$	Simplify $\frac{36}{48}$	Simplify $\frac{22}{55}$	Simplify $\frac{27}{63}$
Here are two fractions $\frac{7}{12} \cdots\cdots \frac{1}{2}$. Which sign should connect these fractions, <, = or >?	Here are two fractions $\frac{5}{12} \cdots\cdots \frac{1}{3}$. Which sign should connect these fractions, <, = or >?	Here are two fractions $\frac{1}{4} \cdots\cdots \frac{5}{20}$. Which sign should connect these fractions, <, = or >?	Here are two fractions $\frac{7}{16} \cdots\cdots \frac{1}{2}$. Which sign should connect these fractions, <, = or >?
What fraction is shaded?	What fraction is shaded?	What fraction is shaded?	What fraction is shaded?

- **Start point check: Pairs**

  Students work in pairs. Give each pair a set of fraction and decimal cards (see photocopiable resources online).

  Lay out the cards in a 4 by 4 grid, with each card face down.

  Player 1 begins first. They turn up two cards – if the cards match, the player wins the cards, otherwise they are turned face down again.

  Then it is player 2's turn to turn up two cards.

  Play alternates between the players until there are no more cards to win.

  The winning player is the one with most cards.

- **Start point check: Show me**

  Give each student a mini-whiteboard.

  Ask the students to show you, for example:

  - a fraction equivalent to $\frac{3}{5}$
  - a fraction with a denominator of 12
  - a fraction that has a numerator less than 4
  - the decimal equivalent to $\frac{3}{100}$
  - a fraction smaller than $\frac{1}{4}$
  - a fraction between 0.2 and 0.3.

> TIP: If you don't have mini-whiteboards, you could give students a sheet of paper to write their answers on.

Discussion ideas

Probing questions	Teacher prompts
Convince me that $\frac{2}{3}$ is smaller than $\frac{7}{10}$.	Encourage students to think of different ways to explain this. Try to encourage students to mention methods such as converting to decimals as well as diagrammatic approaches.
Always, sometimes, never…. $\frac{1}{a}$ is larger than $\frac{1}{b}$ if $a > b$. Explain your answer.	Encourage students to think about dividing a shape into a equal sections and then into b equal sections.
Think of a fraction that is between $\frac{1}{4}$ and $\frac{3}{10}$. And another…. And another…. Is there a fraction with numerator 1 that lies between $\frac{1}{4}$ and $\frac{3}{10}$? How do you know?	Encourage students to explain how they know their suggested fraction is between $\frac{1}{4}$ and $\frac{3}{10}$.
Using a number grid method, what size grid could I use to compare the sizes of $\frac{5}{9}$ and $\frac{6}{11}$? How many squares would be shaded if I was shading $\frac{5}{9}$? …. $\frac{6}{11}$?	Encourage students to draw a grid based on the values of the denominator.
Use a fraction wall to explain why $\frac{1}{2}$ of $\frac{3}{4}$ is $\frac{3}{8}$. What is $\frac{1}{3}$ of $\frac{2}{3}$?	How many eighths is $\frac{3}{4}$ equivalent to?

Common Errors/Misconceptions

Misconception	Strategies to address
Students sometimes think that a fraction such as $\frac{2}{3}$ means 2 parts out of 3 without appreciating that the parts need to be equal size 	Show students how the diagram could be divided into equal parts: Discuss what fraction is actually shaded.
Students sometimes think that $\frac{1}{9}$ is larger than $\frac{1}{8}$ because 9 > 8	Encourage students to think about fractions in the context of sharing. For example, if one bar of chocolate is shared between 9 people, and another bar is shared between 8 people, which person would receive a larger amount of chocolate?
Students sometimes look purely at the numerator when comparing fractions, for example believing $\frac{5}{12}$ is larger than $\frac{3}{4}$ because 5 > 3	Encourage students to appreciate that $\frac{5}{12}$ is smaller than $\frac{1}{2}$ whereas $\frac{3}{4}$ is more than $\frac{1}{2}$. Fraction walls could also be used to compare the sizes.
Students sometimes think of the decimal 0.58 and 'nought point fifty-eight' rather than 'nought point five eight'. This then leads them to believe that 0.58 is greater than say 0.8.	Plot the decimals on a number line. Encourage students to pronounce decimals correctly.

© HarperCollins*Publishers* 2018

Developing conceptual understanding

7Nf3 Compare two fractions by using diagrams. Compare two fractions by using a calculator to convert the fractions to decimals, for example, $\frac{3}{5}$ and $\frac{13}{20}$.

- FIX: A good way to explore the effect of increasing the denominator of a fraction is by shading parts of a circle:

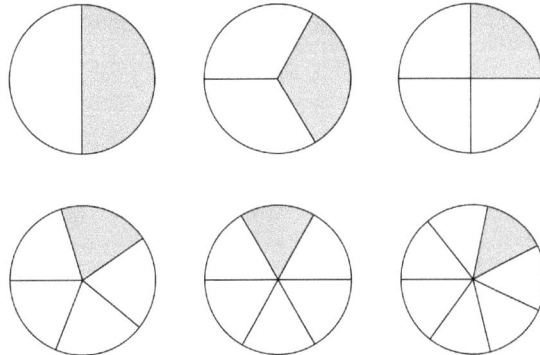

  Likewise, the effect of increasing the numerator can also be seen by shading parts of a circle.

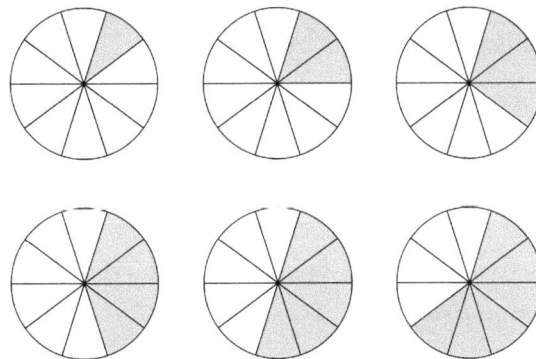

- Fraction walls (see photocopiable resources online) are an excellent way to visually compare the size of two or more fractions with different denominators.

  Students could for example compare a list of fractions (for example $\frac{1}{2}, \frac{1}{4}, \frac{2}{5}, \frac{2}{7}, \frac{3}{8}, \frac{2}{11}$ ...) with $\frac{1}{3}$. Which of the fractions are greater than $\frac{1}{3}$ and which are small than $\frac{1}{3}$?

  Students could for example use a fraction wall to put a set of fractions (like $\frac{5}{8}, \frac{3}{6}, \frac{5}{9}$) in order of size.

  > TIP: Students could also make their own number wall using coloured strips of paper.

- A fraction $\frac{4}{5}$ can also be related to division. For example, 4 metres of cloth is shared equally between five people. Each person will receive $\frac{1}{5}$ of the cloth, i.e. a length of $\frac{1}{5} \times 4$ m = $\frac{4}{5}$ m. The amount that each person receives can also be found by division i.e. as 4 ÷ 5. So the fraction $\frac{4}{5}$ can be interpreted as the division 4 ÷ 5.

- The rectangular grid method provides another way to compare two fractions:

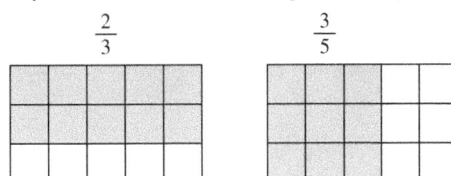

  $\frac{2}{3}$ $\frac{3}{5}$

STRETCH: Students who have mastered the key ideas of this objective could begin to compare fractions numerically by converting to a common denominator.

End of chapter mental maths exercise

1. Write $\frac{3}{20}$ as a decimal.	4. Simplify $\frac{18}{42}$.
2. $\frac{2}{3} = \frac{?}{24}$. Write down the value of the missing numerator.	5. Write down the smaller of these decimals: 0.27 or 0.3
3. A grid measures 3 squares by 5 squares. $\frac{2}{5}$ of the grid is shaded. How many squares are shaded?	6. Which is larger, $\frac{1}{2}$ or $\frac{1}{3}$?

Technology recommendations

- Interactive fraction walls can be found on the internet: see for example:
  http://www.visnos.com/demos/fraction-wall or
  http://www.transum.org/Software/sw/Starter_of_the_day/Students/Fraction_line/Fraction_Wall.asp
  Teachers could use these interactive fraction walls to demonstrate their use to compare fractions (such as to compare $\frac{3}{5}$ and $\frac{4}{7}$).

- You can use scientific calculators (– key) or a spreadsheet package to convert fractions to decimals).

Investigation/research tasks

- **Fraction walls**   *Problem solving*

Use fraction walls to find a fraction with a denominator up to 12 that:

   (1) is as close as possible to $\frac{2}{5}$ without being equal to it

   (2) is greater than $\frac{1}{4}$ and is as small as possible

   (3) has a numerator of 4 and is between $\frac{3}{7}$ and $\frac{1}{2}$.

TIP: It helps if the fraction wall is cut into strips so that specific fractions can be easily compared.

- **Four digits**   *Problem solving*

Use the four digits 3, 4, 5 and 6 each once to complete this number statement.

$$\frac{\Box}{\Box} < \frac{\Box}{\Box}$$

How many different ways can you find of completing it? Use a calculator to help you.

Try again using the digits 1, 3, 5 and 7.

TIP: A fraction wall may help.

- **Limits of fractions**   *Problem solving*

  (1) Students could first explore how a fraction changes in size as the denominator increases by 1.

TIP: This could be done using a spreadsheet.

	A	B	C
1	numerator	denominator	Numerator ÷ denominator
2	2	2	1
3	2	3	0.666666666666
4	2	4	
5	2	5	
6	2	6	
7	2	7	

  (2) Students could also explore the effect of changing the fractions by adding 1 to both the numerator and the denominator. What happens if the numerator is greater than the denominator?

	A	B	C
1	numerator	denominator	Numerator ÷ denominator
2	1	2	0.5
3	2	3	0.666666666666
4	3	4	
5	4	5	
6	5	6	
7	6	7	

	A	B	C
1	numerator	denominator	Numerator ÷ denominator
2	5	2	2.5
3	6	3	
4	7	4	
5	8	5	
6	9	6	
7	10	7	

Volumes of cuboids

Learning objectives

Learning objectives covered in this chapter: 7Ma3, 7Ma4

- Derive and use the formula for the volume of a cuboid; calculate volumes of cuboids.
- Calculate the surface area of cubes and cuboids from their nets.

Key terms

- cube
- cuboid
- volume
- face
- net
- surface area

Prior knowledge assumptions

- Students should be familiar with facts about cubes.
- They should know how to find the area of a square and a rectangle.

The work covered in this chapter is developed at Stage 8 when students will find the volume of other prisms and find the surface area of a range of 3D shapes.

Guidance on the hook

Centimetre cubes   *Problem solving*

Purpose: This hook introduces students to the concept of volume. It also introduces students to the formula for the volume of a cuboid.

Use of the hook: Construct three 8 by 3 by 1 cuboids from 72 connectable cubes. Illustrate how these separate layers can be stacked on top of each other to form an 8 by 3 by 3 cuboid.

Discuss features of this cuboid, such as the shapes of its faces and its length, width and height. Discuss as a class how they can use the values of the length, width and height to find the total number of cubes (72).

Then split the class into small groups to see if they can find other cuboids that can be made from exactly 72 cubes. After a period of time bring the class back together and explore how many different cuboids can be found.

> BEWARE: Students may need to think about whether an 8 by 3 by 3 cuboid is different from a 3 by 3 by 8 cuboid.

Adaptation: Students could use wooden or plastic cubes to help them to find possible cuboids that can be made using exactly 72 cubes. To make it easier for some students, the number of cubes could be reduced to 36.

Extension: Ask students to find the largest cube that can be made from some of the 72 cubes.

Starter ideas

Mental maths starter

How many faces does a cuboid have?	A cuboid is formed by joining together two cubes. How many square faces does the cuboid have?	How many square faces does a cube have?	How many vertices does a cube have?
Work out 7^2	Write down the square root of 16	Work out 9^2	Write down the square root of 36
A rectangle has length 7 cm and width 4 cm. Find the area.	A square has sides measuring 6 cm. Find the area.	A rectangle has length 9 cm and width 6 cm. Find the area.	A rectangle has length 8 cm and width 7 cm. Find the area.
A cube is made from centimetre cubes. There are 9 cubes on the bottom layer. How many cubes are needed altogether?	A cuboid is made using centimetre cubes. There are 16 cubes on the bottom layer and 4 layers. How many cubes are used altogether?	A cuboid is made from centimetre cubes. There are 12 cubes on the bottom layer and 5 layers. How many cubes are needed altogether?	A cuboid is made using centimetre cubes. There are 18 cubes on the bottom layer and 3 layers. How many cubes are used altogether?
Work out $3 \times 4 \times 6$	Work out $5 \times 6 \times 4$	Work out $7 \times 3 \times 4$	Work out $6 \times 8 \times 2$

- **Start point check: Area sort**

  Split students into small groups (twos or threes). Give each group a set of rectangle cards (see photocopiable resources).

  Students should place the rectangles into groups, so that all the rectangles in a group have the same area.

  Students could also try to find at least one more rectangle of their own that could join each group.

> TIP: Give each group a sheet of A3 paper and some glue. Ask each group of students to present their work on the paper.

- **Interactive class discussion: Net of a cube?**

  Show students some diagrams showing six squares. Ask students to decide if the diagram shows the net of a cube. For example:

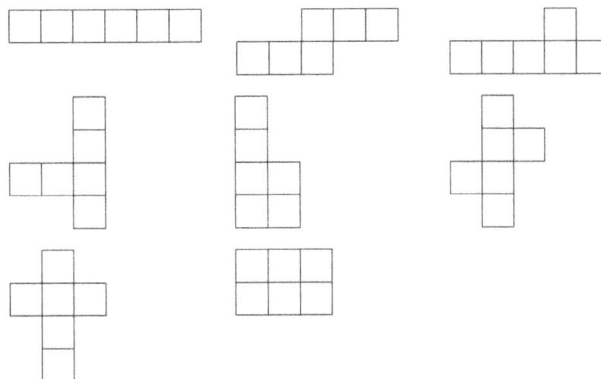

  Ask students for their own suggestions for a possible net of a cube.

> TIP: Students could draw each possible net on squared paper and cut it out to see if it folds up to make a cube or not.

Discussion ideas

Probing questions	Teacher prompts
Explain why the number of cubes in this cuboid is given by the product 4 × 2 × 3:	Encourage students to think about how many cubes are on each layer and how many layers there are. Would it matter if the product was written as 3 × 2 × 4?
Why is volume measured in cubic units such as cm^3, m^3 or mm^3?	Establish that volume is a property of three dimensional objects and that we have to take into account the length and width and height of the object.
A cuboid measures 10 cm by 6 cm by 4 cm. How many centimetres cubes could fit inside it? How many cubes of side length 2 cm could fit inside? How many cubes of side length 3 cm could fit inside?	Discuss how many 2 cm cubes would be on each layer and how many layers there would be. Point out that the number of 2 cm cubes is not half of the number of centimetre cubes. When the 3 cm cubes are placed into the cuboid, students should appreciate that there will be some empty space.
Show me a cuboid that has a volume of 40 cm^3. And another... How many different cuboids can be found?	Discuss whether a cuboid with dimensions 2 by 2 by 10 is different from one with dimensions 2 by 10 by 2. Encourage students to suggest cuboids where not all of the dimensions are integers. TIP: As each cuboid is suggested, get other students in the class to say whether the volume is 40 cm^3 or not.
Show me a cuboid which has a volume that is numerically larger than the surface area. Show me a cuboid which has a volume that is numerically smaller than the surface area.	If students struggle to come up with examples, encourage them to focus on cubes.
Convince me that this statement is not true: If I build two cuboids from 24 centimetre cubes, the surface areas of the two cuboids must be the same.	Seek several possible sizes for the cuboids. Determine the surface area of each.
Ryan has 1000 centimetre cubes. How many cubes with volume 1 m^3 can he fill?	A likely wrong answer will be 10. Encourage students to consider how big 1 m^3 is. How many centimeter cubes will be needed for one layer? Establish that 1 000 000 centimetre cubes are needed to fill a volume of 1 m^3.

Probing questions	Teacher prompts
Find a cube with a volume of 125 cm^3. Can a cube have a volume of 100 cm^3?	Students should appreciate that the sides of a cube do not have to be whole numbers. Introduce students to the cube root button on their calculator; alternatively point out that $4.6^3 = 97.336$ and $4.7^3 = 103.823$ so there will be a cube with a side length somewhere between 4.6 cm and 4.7 cm that has a volume of exactly 100 cm^3.

Common errors/misconceptions

Misconception	Strategies to address
Some students may multiply together the lengths of more than 3 sides when finding the volume.	Reinforce that volume is measured in cubic units and is found by multiplying together three lengths. Encourage students to identify the length, width and height of each cuboid.
When finding the surface area of a cuboid, some students may not add together the area of all 6 faces (they could for example only add together the area of the front, the top and one side).	Encourage students to draw the nets of the cuboids so that the six faces are explicit. If students struggle to draw the nets themselves, diagrams of the nets of some of the cuboids in the Student's Book are given in the photocopiable resources online.
Students often believe that doubling the lengths of all sides of a cuboid will double the volume.	Explore the effect of doubling the dimensions of a cuboid. For example, consider a cuboid with dimensions 1 cm by 2 cm by 3 cm and another with dimensions 2 cm by 4 cm by 6 cm. Discuss how the volumes of the two cuboids are related.
Students often confuse the terms volume and capacity.	Emphasise that volume relates to the amount of space an object takes up. Capacity relates to the amount of liquid that a container can hold. Consider a cube of side length 4 cm. Discuss that the volume is 64 cm^3 whether the cube is solid or not. Note however that the cube would not have a capacity if it was solid.

Developing conceptual understanding

7Ma3 Derive and use the formula for the volume of a cuboid; calculate volumes of cuboids.

- FIX: Give students opportunities to build models of cuboids using centimetre cubes in order to develop an understanding of volume in practical situations. It is best for students to begin by counting the number of cubes in a single layer and then multiplying by the number of layers. Once they are confident with this approach and have an intuitive understanding of the formula for volume, students could then get some practice at applying the formula.

- Students could also create their own net and then build their own cuboid with a given volume (for example, 30 cm^3).   *Problem solving*

STRETCH: If students have mastered how to find the volume of a cuboid, they could begin to look at finding the volume of composite objects formed by joining two or more cuboids together.

7Ma4 Calculate the surface area of cubes and cuboids from their nets.

- FIX: Use 3D models of cubes and cuboids to illustrate the concept of surface area.

- FIX: Give students the nets of the cuboids to help them find the surface area. The nets of many of the cuboids in the Student's Book are given in the photocopiable resources online.

STRETCH: Students who have mastered the idea of surface area of a cuboid, could extend the work by considering the surface area of objects formed by combining two cuboids.

BEWARE: Students may just try adding together the surface areas of the two separate cuboids. Make sure they are clear that some surface area is covered up when two cuboids are connected.

End of chapter mental maths exercise

1. A cuboid is made using centimeter cubes. There are 14 cubes on the bottom layer and 5 layers. How many cubes are used altogether?
2. Work out 6^2.
3. A rectangle has an area of 28 cm^2. The length of the rectangle is 7 cm. Write down the width.
4. Work out $3 \times 7 \times 5$.
5. A cuboid has sides measuring 5 cm, 2 cm and 8 cm. Find the volume of the cuboid.
6. A cube has sides measuring 10 cm. Find the surface area of the cube.

Technology recommendations

- **Maximum volume**   *Problem solving*

A piece of paper measures 24 cm by 24 cm.

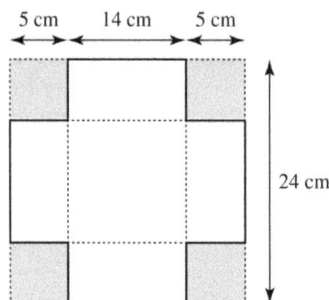

A square is removed from each corner. The remainder of the piece of paper is folded up to make an open top box.

Ask students to find the volume of the box formed when the square removed has sides of length 1cm, 2 cm, ..., 12 cm.

Ask students to use a spreadsheet package to draw a graph showing the volume of the resulting cuboids plotted against the side of the square removed.

When is the volume at its maximum?

TIP: Students could design a spreadsheet to record the results:	

	A	B	C	D	E
1	Size of square	L	W	H	volume
2	1	=24 – 2*A2	=B2	= A2	=B2*C2*D2
3	2				
4	3				

© HarperCollins*Publishers* 2018

- Students could try to design a spreadsheet for finding the surface area of different cuboids. For example:

	A	B	C	D	E	F	G	H	I	J
1	L	W	H	top	bottom	side	side	front	back	total
2	4	5	6	= A2*B2						
3	3	7	2							

Investigation/research tasks

- **Investigation: surface area and volume**   *Problem solving*

  Mick has 48 centimetre cubes. How many different cuboids can be make that use all of his cubes? Find the surface area of each of the cuboids. Which has the smallest surface area? Which has the largest surface area?

- **Problem solving activity: surface area**   *Problem solving*

  Ask students to find a cuboid with integer side lengths that has a surface area close to 100 cm^2. How close to this surface area can students get? Can anyone get a surface area of exactly 100 cm^2?

- **Investigation: models from cubes**   *Problem solving*

  Jethro makes a sequence of models by connecting together cubes:

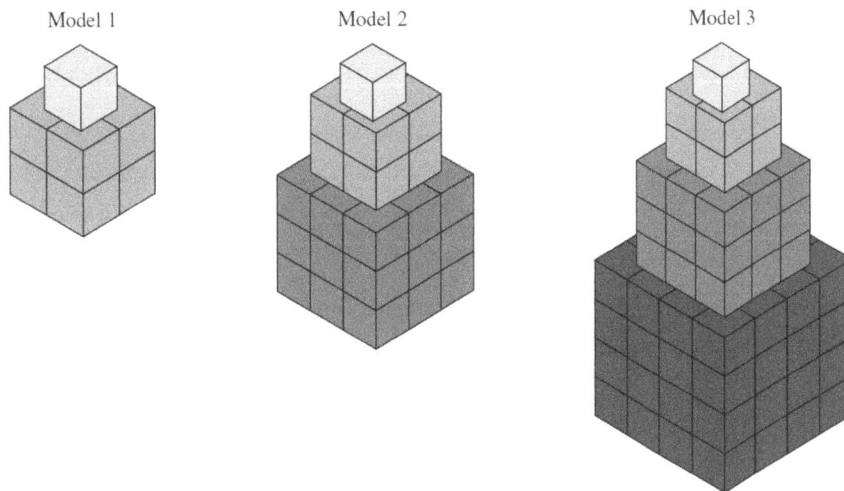

Model 1   Model 2   Model 3

How many cubes are needed for each model?

Predict how many cubes are needed for Model 4? Explain your answer.

What do you notice about the total number of cubes in each model?

Graphs in real-life contexts

Learning objectives

Learning objectives covered in this chapter: 7Mt1

- Draw and interpret graphs in real-life contexts involving more than one stage, for example, travel graphs.

Key terms

- interpreting
- travel graph

Prior knowledge assumptions

- Students should be able to read scales.
- They should be able to read and plot coordinates on a graph.
- They should be able to draw and interpret line graphs.
- Students should have an understanding of the 24-hour clock.

This will be helpful when you learn more about finding distance, speed and acceleration from travel graphs and speed/time graphs

Guidance on the hook

Interpreting a real-life graph   *Problem solving*

Purpose: this hook introduces students to real-life graphs and their interpretation.

Use of the hook: Start by asking students some questions about the graph. What is plotted on the vertical axis? What is plotted on the horizontal axis? What does one square on each axis represent? Discuss why the vertical axis starts at 50 cm. Ask students what the depth of water was at certain times, such as at 12:00.

Ask students to work in pairs to discuss the questions posed in the textbook. After a few minutes, discuss the questions as a whole class.

BEWARE: Because the vertical axis does not start at 0, care is needed when interpreting the diagram. For instance, the point at 12:00 has a vertical height that is nearly double the height at 08:00, but the depth of water is not nearly double at that time.

Adaptation: You could give some statements relating to the graph and ask students to decide if they are true or false. For example,

There is more water in the barrel at 10 p.m. than at 10 a.m.

Between 10:00 and 12:00, the water level increases.

Extension: Students could write down some sentences of their own describing the story that the graph is telling.

TIP: It might be helpful to have a large copy of the diagram that all the class can see (for example using a projector or interactive whiteboard).

Starter ideas

Mental maths starter

How many minutes are there in $1\frac{1}{4}$ hours?	How many minutes are there in $2\frac{1}{2}$ hours?	How many minutes are there in $\frac{3}{4}$ hour?	How many minutes are there in $2\frac{1}{4}$ hours?
Write 3:15 a.m. in the 24-hour clock.	Write 2:40 p.m. in the 24-hour clock.	Write 7:30 p.m. in the 24-hour clock.	Write 10 past midnight in the 24-hour clock.
A film lasts for 1 hour 45 minutes. It starts at 7:05 p.m. Write down the time when it finishes.	A concert lasts for 1 hour 30 minutes. It starts at 8:45 p.m. Write down the time when it finishes.	A lesson lasts for 70 minutes. It starts at 11:15 a.m. Write down the time when it finishes.	A shop is open for 5 hours 30 minutes. It opens at 9:45 a.m. At what time does it close?
Write 18:25 in the 12-hour clock.	Write 01:16 in the 12-hour clock.	Write 15:55 in the 12-hour clock.	Write 17:40 in the 12-hour clock.
How long is it between 11:15 a.m. and 12:40 p.m.?	How long is it between 3:50 p.m. and 6:25 p.m.?	How long is it between 10:30 and 15:05?	How long is it between 09:55 and 13:35?

- **Start point check: Three in a line**

  Split the students into small groups (either pairs or threes). Give each set of students a set of coordinate cards (see photocopiable resources online).

  Ask each group to draw a coordinates grid with x- and y-axes numbered from –3 to 3.

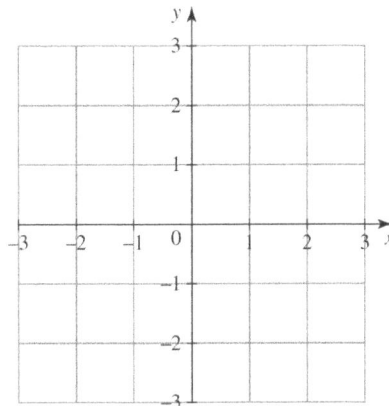

  Students take it in turns to choose one of the coordinate cards. They mark the point on the grid. The winner is the first person to plot 3 points in a horizontal or vertical line.

  TIP: Each student should use a different colour to mark on points.

- **Start point check: Target board**

  Show students the target board and ask them to select from the time that matches questions such as:

  o quarter past midnight in the 24 hour clock
  o 7:35 p.m. in the 24-hour clock
  o 16:20 changed to the 12-hour clock
  o 2:05 p.m. changed to the 24-hour clock
  o 3 hours 25 mins after 7:55 a.m.
  o 45 minutes before 20:20

12:15 a.m.	4:20 p.m.	19:35	09:15
00:15	07:35	12:05	17:35
02:05	8:25 a.m.	14:20	11:20 a.m.
6:20 p.m.	14:05	3:30 p.m.	12:15 a.m.

TIP: You could ask students to pose some of their own questions relating to the target board.

Discussion ideas

Probing questions	**Teacher prompts**
Here is my journey to a friend's house. 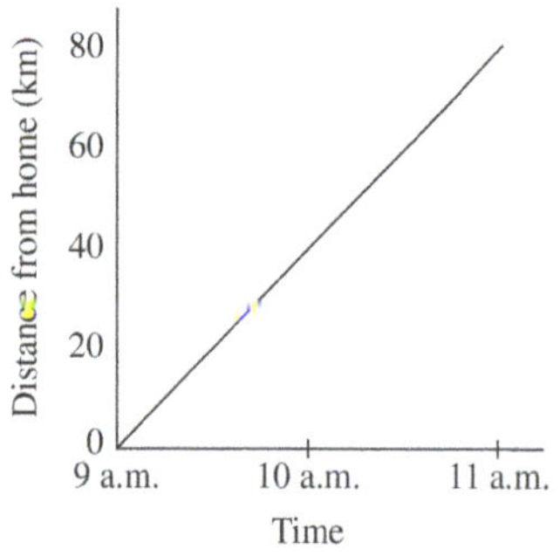 At what time do I leave my house? How can you tell? How far is my friend's house from my house? How can you tell? How long does my journey take? How can you tell? Describe my speed throughout the journey.	Ask follow-up questions such as: How would the graph be different if I travelled faster for the first part of the journey than in the second half? How would the graph change if I stopped for 15 minutes halfway to my friend's house?
Ask students to give a thorough description of a journey that matches this travel graph: 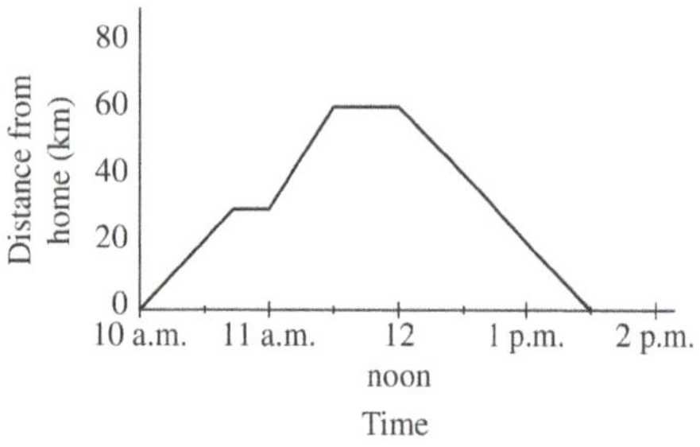 	Encourage students to include information such as: • time leaving home/time arriving home • total amount of time away from home • time reaching destination and how far it is from home • what happened on the outward journey/how the return journey was different.
This diagram shows the depth of water in a tank: 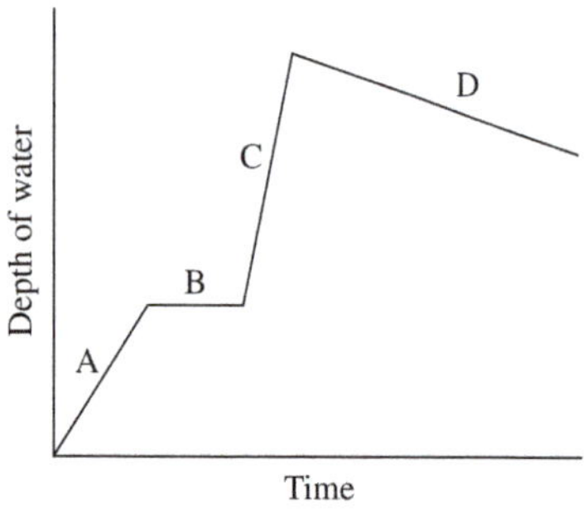 What was happening at A, B, C and D? The graph is steeper at C than at A. What does this mean?	Encourage students to see that water must be poured into the tank at A and C. They should also appreciate that the water depth is remaining constant at B and water must be taken out of the tank at D.

Probing questions	Teacher prompts
Here is a travel graph to show a train journey between two stations: A slower train does the same journey. Show me what this travel graph would look like. A train does the journey in reverse. Show me what the travel graph for this journey would look like.	If necessary, prompt students to appreciate that a slower train would cover the same distance in a longer time. Encourage students to appreciate that a train covering the journey in reverse will start 30 km away.

Common errors/misconceptions

Misconception	Strategies to address
Students sometimes interpret a travel graph with a positive gradient as representing a journey uphill and a negative gradient as a journey downhill	Ensure that you discuss with the whole class the interpretation of some travel graphs and that students have lots of practice giving their own interpretations
Students sometimes do not look carefully at the horizontal and vertical scales and so read from them incorrectly	Encourage students to work out what each division on the scale represents. TIP: They could check this by counting up to make sure the next numbered value is consistent.
Students sometimes think that graphs must always start at zero	Ensure students are given a range of graphs to interpret in different contexts, such as: or Interpret what the intercepts represent.

Developing conceptual understanding

7Mt1 Draw and interpret graphs in real-life contexts involving more than one stage, for example, travel graphs.

- Ask students to create a travel graph for a journey that they are familiar with (such as their journey to school or to a friend's house).

> TIP: They should think carefully about how long the journey takes and the distances involved.

> TIP: Encourage students to pair up with a partner – the first student should ask the second to interpret their graph.

- FIX: To develop skills at interpreting graphs, students could work in small groups to play the *pairs game* (see photocopiable resources online).

- FIX: When interpreting a scale, encourage students to look carefully and decide how much each small square is equivalent to. If students find it difficult give them some scales to practice reading from, for example:

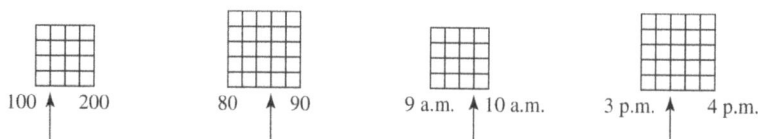

100 ↟ 200   80 ↟ 90   9 a.m. ↟ 10 a.m.   3 p.m. ↟ 4 p.m.

- FIX: To help students understand travel graphs, you could ask students to sketch a travel graph to show your movements across the classroom, for example you could mimic journeys that match these graphs.

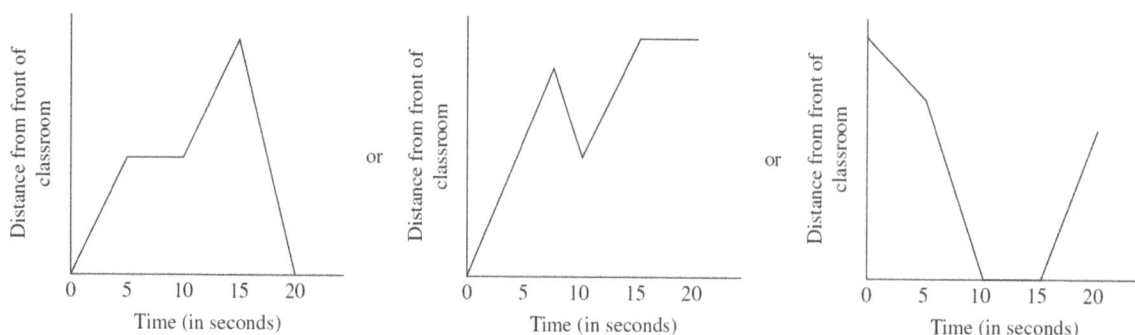

STRETCH: If students have secured a good grasp of this objective, they could begin to think about drawing a speed–time graph for a journey.

End of chapter mental maths exercise

1. How many seconds are there in $4\frac{1}{2}$ minutes?	4. Aman eats at 7:25 p.m. Write this time in the 24-hour clock.
2. Write 16:37 in the 12-hour clock.	5. How long is it between 10:25 a.m. and 2:10 p.m.?
3. An exam lasts for 2 hour 30 minutes. It starts at 1:45 p.m. Write down the time when it finishes.	

Technology recommendations

- There are some interactive websites relating to travel graphs, for example:

  http://www.transum.org/Maths/Activity/Travel_Graphs/Default.asp?Level=1

  http://www.colmanweb.co.uk/Assets/SWF/Skate_boarders.swf

  http://www.colmanweb.co.uk/Assets/SWF/Swimming.swf

  https://www.geogebra.org/m/S4Yc2fda

- Ask students to draw a poster to illustrate a journey (for example a train journey or flight). Students could use the internet to research distances and journey times.

> TIP: Ask students to write some sentences to describe their journey.

Investigation/research tasks

- **Exploring real-life graphs in other contexts**   *Problem solving*

  Students could draw a graph to illustrate one of the following things:
  - happiness levels during the course of a week/year
  - hunger levels during the course of a day
  - activity levels during the course of a day.

  Ask students to write some sentences to describe what their graph shows.

- **Investigation: filling containers**   *Problem solving*

  Students could explore how quickly the water level rises when water is poured into different shaped vases:

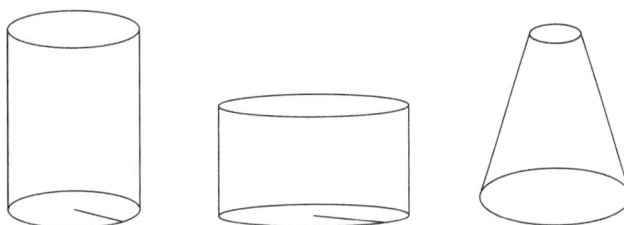

  Ask students to sketch a graph showing the depth of water against time for each container.

> TIP: The activity on the following website is related to this investigation.
> http://nrich.maths.org/7419

- **Train journey**   *Problem solving*

  A train travels from Alexandria to Cairo. It travels at a constant speed, leaving Alexandria at 7 p.m. and arriving at Cairo 2 hours 10 minutes later.

  A second train travels from Cairo to Alexandria. It also travels at a constant speed. It leaves at 7:10 p.m. and arrives at Alexandria 2 hours and 20 minutes later.

  The distance from Alexandria to Cairo is 200 km.

  By drawing a travel graph, find when and where the trains pass each other.

Statistics

Learning objectives

Learning objectives covered in this chapter: 7Dc3, 7Di1, 7Di2

- Construct and use frequency tables to gather discrete data, grouped where appropriate in equal class intervals.
- Draw conclusions based on the shape of graphs and simple statistics.
- Compare two simple distributions using the range and the mode, median or mean.

Key terms

- frequency table
- class
- discrete data (and continuous data by contrast)
- grouped frequency table
- grouped
- class interval
- conclusion
- consistent

Prior knowledge assumptions

- Students can find the mode (or modal class for grouped data), median and range for a list of data or from a frequency table
- Students can calculate the mean, including from a simple frequency table.
- Students have used and constructed frequency tables as data collection sheets.
- Students can solve a problem by extracting and interpreting data given in tables, graphs, charts and diagrams
- Students can draw and interpret bar-line graphs and bar chart, frequency diagrams for grouped discrete data, pictograms and simple pie charts

This will be helpful when you learn more about comparing two large sets of data

Guidance on the hook

Purpose: This task is designed to look critically at graphs (and other statistics) to check that they are not being misled.

Use of the hook: Show students the 3D bar chart presented in the Student's Book.

Explain that it shows the results of the market research asking people which snack they prefer.

Ask the students what the bar chart shows.

Ask the students if they can produce the frequency table that the chart was drawn from.

Then ask them if they have any issues with the chart?

Possible answers:

- not a big enough sample of people asked
- the Great Snack bar looks a lot bigger than it should do because it is 3D (although they are ahead, the 3D shape emphasises this)

BEWARE: Students might comment on the bars not touching, which is a common misconception

How else could Great Snack present this data to emphasise their own product and performance?

Adaptation: Students could collect graphs and charts from magazines and newspapers to analyse them and decide whether they are misleading.

Extension: Ask the students to draw their own misleading graph.

Possible options:
- not starting a scale at 0 (to exaggerate differences)
- not stating the sample size and using a very small number (for example, for a pie chart)
- using different symbols for a pictogram that are of different sizes (larger for your own product)
- using a scale that does not go up linearly.

Starter ideas

Mental maths starter

Calculate the mean of 7, 9 and 17	Calculate the mean of 2, 11, 15 and 20	Calculate the mean of 14, 16 and 21	Calculate the mean of 101, 103 and 111
4 numbers have a mean of 7. What is their sum?	5 numbers have a mean of 9. What is their sum?	6 numbers have a mean of 7.5. What is their sum?	3 numbers have a mean of 2.6. What is their sum?
The lowest value in a data set is 78 and the highest is 241. Calculate the range	The lowest value in a data set is 23 and the highest is 182. Calculate the range	The lowest value in a data set is 148 and the highest is 632. Calculate the range	The lowest value in a data set is 2.3 and the highest is 24.1. Calculate the range
What number is halfway between 7 and 12?	What number is halfway between 4 and 11?	What number is halfway between 19 and 30?	What number is halfway between 65 and 102?
A set of data covers a range of 34 with a lowest value of 5. Suggest 4 equal class intervals to cover the data set.	A set of data covers a range of 63 with a lowest value of 2. Suggest 4 equal class intervals to cover the data set.	A set of data covers a range of 58 with a lowest value of 12. Suggest 5 equal class intervals to cover the data set.	A set of data covers a range of 76 with a lowest value of 23. Suggest 5 equal class intervals to cover the data set.
A pie chart represents 24 pieces of data. How many degrees is each piece of data worth?	A pie chart represents 18 pieces of data. How many degrees is each piece of data worth?	A pie chart represents 40 pieces of data. How many degrees is each piece of data worth?	A pie chart represents 72 pieces of data. How many degrees is each piece of data worth?

Start point check: Class survey/show of hands:

Complete a quick class survey about, for example, the number of hours of television they watched last week.

List the data initially and then ask students to calculate the mode, median, mean and range.

Then complete a survey of, for example, shoe sizes, but immediately record the data in a frequency table.

As the students to calculate the mode, median, mean and range once more.

You could then ask students to produce and interpret a pictogram/bar chart/pie chart from this data.

Investigation: Which of these tables is the best one for grouping this data?

Data:

47	58	21	39	41	51	43	29	31	27	19	28
37	44	48	27	38	62	54	49	37	32	59	34

Data	Frequency
0–7	
8–15	
16–23	
24–31	
32–39	
40–47	
48–55	
56–63	

Data	Frequency
0–11	
11–23	
24–35	
36–47	
48–59	
60–71	

Data	Frequency
0–19	
20–39	
40–59	
60–79	

TIP: The data and the possible tables are provided in the photocopiable resources online.

Give the students 5 minutes to look at the data and to try to complete the tables.

Then discuss as a class which is the best table. Encourage the students to reflect on which was the easiest to fill in as well as which gives us the most useful information.

Discussion ideas

Probing questions	Teacher prompts
Is it better to have as few classes as possible when grouping your data?	Prompt students to explain that fewer classes makes constructing the table easier and any charts simpler. However, they need to recognise that some accuracy is lost in this way which can be a problem.
True or False? You have to start your class intervals from 0 when grouping data	This is not true but many students will think it is – encourage them to avoid having lots of empty classes or classes that are too big to cover this range. The starter task investigation can help explore this.
How can you tell which set of data has higher values overall?	Encourage students to suggest calculating the average – and prompt them to suggest mode, median and mean. This relates to the earlier work of Chapter 22.
How can you tell which set of data is more consistent?	Encourage students to suggest finding the range to see which set of data is closer together. You could get students to represent the data as points on number lines to help them visualise spread and consistency.

Probing questions	Teacher prompts
True or False? The range can be misleading because just one piece of data can make it seem a lot higher	Discuss the concept of an outlier with students if appropriate. You can also hint at other ways of finding a measure of spread that are more sophisticated than the range (for example, interquartile range). Students working at greater depth could come up with their own measures and suggestions. For example, they may suggest taking off the lowest and highest piece of data first as in some sports scoring systems.

Common errors/misconceptions

Misconception	Strategies to address
Overlapping class intervals when grouping data so that it is unclear where to place the data	Ask students where to position an overlapping piece of data to help them realise the problem. For example: given response boxes $0–10, $10–$20 and $20–$30, where would you place an answer of $10?
Starting grouped data from 0, even if the first data point is significantly above 0	Allow students to work through an example like this to see that they either end up with lots of empty classes (categories) or that their data is all bunched together in one or two larger categories (or classes). A good example is students' height, where the initial categories are likely to be empty and, if too widely spaced, a few later categories will be highly populated. Encourage them to find the highest and lowest values first to help them break up the range into equal class intervals.
Thinking that class intervals must always be equal	Although we are using equal class intervals in Stage 7, it is important for later learning that students realise that it is possible to use different class intervals but just more complicated when trying to produce these. Share an example of age, where the structure of society may affect the categories for example, 0–5, 6–18, 19–40, 41–65, 66–100.
Believing that having a higher mean is necessarily 'better' than a lower one	Try using an example where a low value is a good thing, for example, times in running races to help students see that this cannot always be true.
Believing that having a higher range is necessarily 'better' than a lower one	Encourage students to think of the range as a way of judging the consistency of the data. In some situations we want consistency, for example, in sporting performance or manufacturing Ask students to think of situations where consistency is not so necessary.
Continued errors from average work: • Forgetting to order the data before finding the median • Giving 2 values for the median when there are an even number of pieces of data as there are 2 'middle' numbers • Believing that the range is a type of average	See Chapter 22 for further support in this area

Misconception	Strategies to address
• Forgetting to use brackets when calculating the mean and hence making an error with the calculator For example, to find the mean of 4, 5 and 6 a student may incorrectly type 4 + 5 + 6 ÷ 3 and hence get a result of 11, instead of the correct (4 + 5 + 6) ÷ 3 = 5 • Using the number of rows in a frequency table as the total frequency, rather than the sum of the individual frequencies (especially when calculating the mean) • Calculating the range from a frequency table by finding the difference between the lowest and highest frequency rather than the lowest and highest piece of data	
Continued errors from drawing and interpreting graphs and charts work: • not realising that a pie chart only gives proportions of data, rather than absolute values • drawing bar charts with bars touching when they should be separated for discrete data • forgetting to use the key in a pictogram	See Chapter 23 for further support in this area.

Developing conceptual understanding

7Dc3 Construct and use frequency tables to gather discrete data, grouped where appropriate in equal class intervals.

• FIX: It can be helpful to use a number line to mark the lowest and highest data points in a data set before breaking the range up into equal class intervals.

These can be marked on the number line first before being written into a frequency tablet to help students develop the concepts.

TIP: It is recommended that you use one data set and split it into different class intervals so that students can see the costs and benefits of using more or fewer intervals.

• FIX: As in the Student's Book, you can scaffold the process of creating class intervals for students by giving them the first one and asking them to produce the rest from there.

For example:

Number of hours of studying	Tally	Frequency
0 – 4		
5 –		

7Di1 Draw conclusions based on the shape of graphs and simple statistics.

• When drawing conclusions, all students should be able to read key information from a chart and solve a simple problem.

STRETCH: Students working at greater depth can begin to combine these skills with the use of fractions, decimals and percentages. For example, they can find a total from a bar chart or pictogram and convert it to a percentage to draw or test a conclusion.

7Di2 Compare two simple distributions using the range and the mode, median or mean.

- FIX: You could try plotting the individual data points on a number line for two data sets being compared to help students see that the data that is more clustered/consistent has a lower range or spread.

STRETCH: Students working at greater depth could consider the mode and median as well as the range and mean when comparing data sets. For example, when looking at clothing sizes and their sales, the mode and median can be more useful.

End of chapter mental maths exercise

1. Calculate the mean of 23, 45 and 31	5. A set of data covers a range of 126 with a lowest value of 48.
2. 7 numbers have a mean of 4.2. What is their sum?	Suggest 6 equal class intervals to cover the data set.
3. The lowest value in a data set is 4.5 and the highest is 17.1. Calculate the range	6. A pie chart represents 54 pieces of data. How many degrees is each piece of data worth?
4. What number is halfway between 48 and 61?	

Technology recommendations

- Use dynamic statistics software to produce a table of data and then charts using this data. Enter a frequency table of data.

  Then construct a chart from this data.

  Then edit the table and observe the effect on the chart. The charts will alter as the data is updated and edited so the students can see the effect of changing the data on the chart.

  Extension: Use a spreadsheet to calculate statistics such as averages and range for a raw set of data. Then grouping the data and producing as a frequency table and calculating the same statistics to compare. This can give students a sense of the advantages and disadvantages of grouping data, namely ease versus accuracy.

Investigation/research tasks

- **Shoe Size Investigation**

  Measure the shoe size of students in your class.

  Produce a frequency table.

  Calculate the mean, mode, median and range from your table.

  Here are the results from another class of students:

Mean	Mode	Median	Range
144 cm	148 cm	147 cm	39 cm

  Compare your data with this class.

This task is designed to be done relatively independently. Therefore, students should make their own decisions about how to best collect the data and how to record it. They should also design their own frequency table.

Once the students have found the averages and range from the table, you could stop the class and compare their findings.

> TIP: It is useful to discuss why there are differences between the answers of different groups. Students may focus on errors in measuring/recording etc. but it is worth reminding them of the impact of sampling data too.

The students can then compare their results to the data given above and draw conclusions.

At the end, encourage students to reflect on their data collection process and how they might do things differently next time.

- **Estimation Investigation**

  Some students were asked to estimate the number of pages in a book. The correct answer was 55.

  The gender of each student and whether they were right or left handed was also recorded.

  Here is the data (see data sheet in photocopiable resources online)

  Analyse this data to investigate the hypothesis that

  'Males are better at estimating than females'

  You can either leave students to explore this data themselves or structure the investigation more yourself.

  You might want to ask them to produce a frequency table for males and for females. They may also choose to try to group their data to make it easier to work with as a first step.

  > TIP: Students can highlight all the males/females to make it easier to separate the data.

  You could bring students back together once their tables are complete to ask them what they will do next. They may choose to calculate averages and/or to draw charts.

  Once they have drawn their conclusions, bring the group back together to discuss their findings. How reliable are their results?

  STRETCH: Students working at greater depth could also look at the role of left and right-handedness and see if there is a link to estimation.

- Use the internet to investigate the work of William Playfair, who introduced the bar chart, line graph and later the pie chart in the late 18th century.

Transformations

Learning objectives

Learning objectives covered in this chapter: 7Gp2

- Transform 2D points and shapes by:
  - reflection in a given line
  - rotation about a given point
  - translation.
- Know that shapes remain congruent after these transformations.

Key terms

- reflection
- rotation
- translation
- transformation
- original
- image
- congruent
- mirror line
- angle of rotation
- centre of rotation
- direction; clockwise; anticlockwise
- opposite; inverse

Prior knowledge assumptions

- Students know the definition of a vertex or vertices.
- Students can reflect a shape in a given mirror line and predict where the image of such a reflection will be.
- Students can translate a shape a given number of units left, right, up or down and predict where the image of such a translation will be.
- Students can rotate a shape 90° about one of its vertices and predict where the image of such a rotation will be.

Guidance on the hook   *Problem solving*

Purpose: This task enables students to revisit the process of reflection and remember that the object and image are the same distance from the mirror line.

Use of the hook: Give each student a piece of paper, they will also need a pencil, ruler and protractor.

Encourage them to use the language of reflection to describe the position of points.

Ask students to fold the paper again on the original line and pierce the paper again to get another two points and measure again.

Ask for their conclusions.

Adaptation: You could ask students to fold the paper and pierce the points at the corners of a capital E through the two layers. They can then open the paper and see what they notice.

Extension: Ask students to consider if they were given the points A and B could they find the fold line. Would they need more than 1 set of points?

Starter ideas

Mental maths starter

Imagine a letter E. Rotate the E 90° clockwise about its top left corner. Draw the resulting image.	Imagine a letter Y. Rotate the Y 90° clockwise about its vertex. Draw the resulting image.	Imagine a letter A. Rotate the G 90° anticlockwise about its top vertex. Draw the resulting image.	Imagine a letter M. Rotate the M 90° anticlockwise about its top left corner. Draw the resulting image.
Imagine a letter L. Reflect the shape in the vertical line of the L. Draw the resulting image.	Imagine a letter H. Reflect the shape in the horizontal bar of the H. Draw the resulting image.	Imagine a letter P. Reflect the shape in the vertical line of the P. Draw the resulting image.	Imagine a letter A. Reflect the shape in the horizontal bar of the A. Draw the resulting image.
How many vertices does a parallelogram have?	How many vertices does a scalene triangle have?	How many vertices does a hexagon have?	How many vertices does a pentagon have?

Start point check

Give the students a piece of squared paper.

Ask them to draw an original shape, or object, made up of straight lines and then draw a vertical mirror line (you may want to get them to copy this from the board).

Students must then

a) reflect their shape in the line

b) rotate their shape 90° clockwise about one of its vertices

c) translate their shape 2 units right and 3 units up.

Students can then put their work on their desks and stand up to view other people's solutions.

Give them 5 minutes to look at other's work, ask them questions and make any adjustments to their own work.

Meanwhile circulate yourself to check what their prior knowledge is.

Game

Students will need a grid drawn on squared paper and a pair of simple congruent shapes, labelled A and B, made up of 3 or 4 squares of the squared paper. L shapes are good for this. Start with a small grid – 6 × 6 squares.

Students work in pairs. A and B are placed onto the grid. A can be moved but B must not be moved. The object is to be the first to get shape A onto shape B. Students take it in turn to move shape A either one or two squares. They must choose one direction to move, up, down, left or right. Each player can only make a particular move once in the game so there are 8 possible moves that each player can make. They will need to keep a note of the moves that have been made so that moves are not repeated. Each must try to stop the other moving A completely onto B. If they move any part of their shape A off the squared paper they lose the game. If the game finishes without A landing on B then the game is a draw.

Variations

The moves can be written on pieces of paper which are placed face down and chosen by the students in turn. Moves could be single stage or two stage, for example, the paper could say 'move 2 squares left and 1 square down'. The size of grid can be increased – but stay within the maximum range of the moves.

Discussion ideas

Probing questions	Teacher prompts
True or False? When the mirror line touches the original shape, the reflected image will touch or overlap the original shape.	Students can try this out practically or using dynamic geometry software. They should discover that when there is one point of connection between the original and the mirror line, the image touches also at exactly that point. However, prompt them to look at what happens when the mirror line crosses through the original, and the image fully overlaps the original.
Does rotating an object through 180° about any point always turn the image upside down?	Again, students can try this practically or using dynamic geometry software. They can try doing the rotation about points in the shape, on the edge of the shape or outside the shape.
Can you tell whether a transformation that has happened was a reflection, rotation or translation?	Prompt students to talk about the orientation of the image. Is it the same exactly as the original? (Translation) Does the image fit exactly over the original with some rotation (without needing to be turned over)? (Rotation) Does the image need to be flipped over to fit over the original? (Reflection)
What is the opposite transformation to a translation of a units up and b units right?	Prompt students to literally reverse the process to realise that they move a units down and b units left. Students working at greater depth may be able to express this as $-a$ units up and $-b$ units right.
Always, Sometimes, Never? It is possible to tell by looking at two shapes if one is a reflection of the other?	This is an opportunity to explore what happens with the image of a reflection. What about squares being reflected? Can we tell they are reflected unless their vertices are labelled. What about other regular shapes?
What kind of transformation would lead to an image not being congruent to the original shape?	Students may think of some form of enlargement or stretch. It is useful for them to realise that there are other possible transformations that we can do to a shape, even though these are not being studied in Stage 7.

Common errors/misconceptions

Misconception	Strategies to address
Keeping the orientation of a shape when reflecting it in a diagonal line (as if it were a translation)	Try getting the student to turn the page so the mirror line appears vertical to help them see why their image is incorrect (and to visualise the correct image). Then rotate the page back afterwards to look at the orientation of the shape.
Struggling when the mirror line passes through a shape and the image overlaps the original shape	Using 2 different colours can help here to separate the original and the image. Encourage students to treat the two sections of the shape on each side of the line differently to help them break it up.
Believing that the centre of rotation must be contained within the shape when rotating	Use dynamic geometry software, or a cut-out shape and the white board, or an interactive display, to set up a rotation and allow the centre of rotation to be moved to explore the impact and show that it can sit outside the shape.
Counting the squares between the original and image when translating, rather than the squares between two corresponding points	Either: apply the translation they have described to the shape using a geometry package to get students to see there is an error and try to work out what the problem is themselves. Or: draw a shape on the board and translate it incorrectly by counting squares between object and image and ask students to explain to the class why it is incorrect and how the error has been made. This can also be done using an interactive display. Why has the shape not moved enough?
Thinking that shapes are only congruent if they are oriented the same	This is an issue of a limited definition of congruent in the student's mind – try using a cut-out copy of the original shape in card and trying to overlay it onto possible congruent images can help here. The students can flip it, turn it and move it to find congruent shapes.

Developing conceptual understanding

7Gp2 Transform 2D points and shapes by:

- reflection in a given line
- rotation about a given point
- translation.

Know that shapes remain congruent after these transformations.

- FIX: Use tracing paper to help students to see where the image of a reflection will go. They can draw around the original shape and then fold the tracing paper along the mirror line. The drawn shape will now appear in its new position.

- FIX: Turning the page a reflection question is drawn on so that the mirror line appears vertically to a students' eyes can help them to visualise where the image will be.

- FIX: Again, tracing paper can provide a useful guide when rotating a shape. Students can draw around the original shape and then use their pencil point to fix the tracing paper at the centre. They can then rotate the tracing paper through the correct angle, using their protractor if necessary. The drawn shape will now appear in its new position.

- FIX: Lastly tracing paper can help to show the process of translation as a set of small individual movements combined to eliminate errors in counting the squares between shapes.

> TIP: It is very helpful to use dynamic geometry software as explained below to help students to visualise reflections, rotations and translations.

> TIP: It is really useful to show students images of shapes that are not congruent as well as those that are so that they can see what the limits of the definition are.

STRETCH: These students may also be able to plot the graph of a diagonal mirror line when given its equation explicitly in terms of y for example, $y = x$ based on earlier work from Chapter 19 and hence use this to carry out more complex reflections.

End of chapter mental maths exercise

1. Imagine a letter R.
   Rotate the R through 90° anticlockwise about its bottom left corner.
   Draw the resulting image.
2. Imagine a letter F.
   Reflect the shape in the top, horizontal, line of the F.
   Draw the resulting image.
3. I have moved a shape 3 squares left and 2 squares down.
   Which two moves that will take my image back to the original shape?
4. Are all equilateral triangles of side 6 cm congruent?
5. Are all squares congruent?

Technology recommendations

- Use a dynamic geometry software package to reflect, rotate and translate shapes.

  For example, here is a rotation being shown:

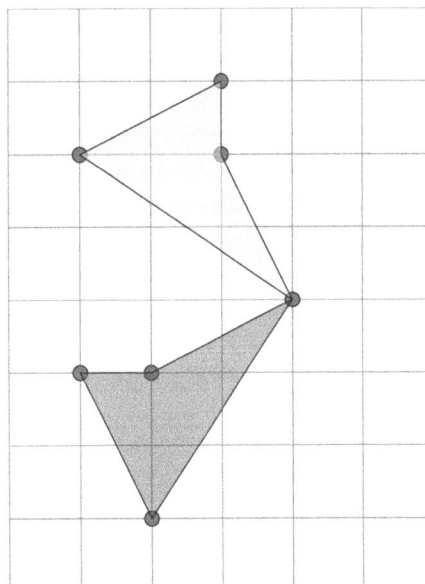

  You can then manipulate the original shapes by dragging their vertices to see how the image changes to match. You can also move the centre of rotation to see the effect.

  You can also use software to show reflections and the effect of moving the mirror line.

- Interactive displays can also be used to help students' understanding of transformations. For example, draw an object, the mirror line and the image. Hide the image using simple tools such as white pen. Ask a student to draw the image on the screen and then reveal the correct answer.

- Ask students to use the internet to investigate how many practical uses of rotation they can find online – wheels, gear wheels, wind turbines - and ask them how many everyday things would not be possible without using rotations. You could extend this to reflection – things that are made in pairs with one a reflection of the other. Examples could include shirt sleeves and earrings.

Investigation/research tasks

- **Transformation hunt**

   Which transformations can you see here?

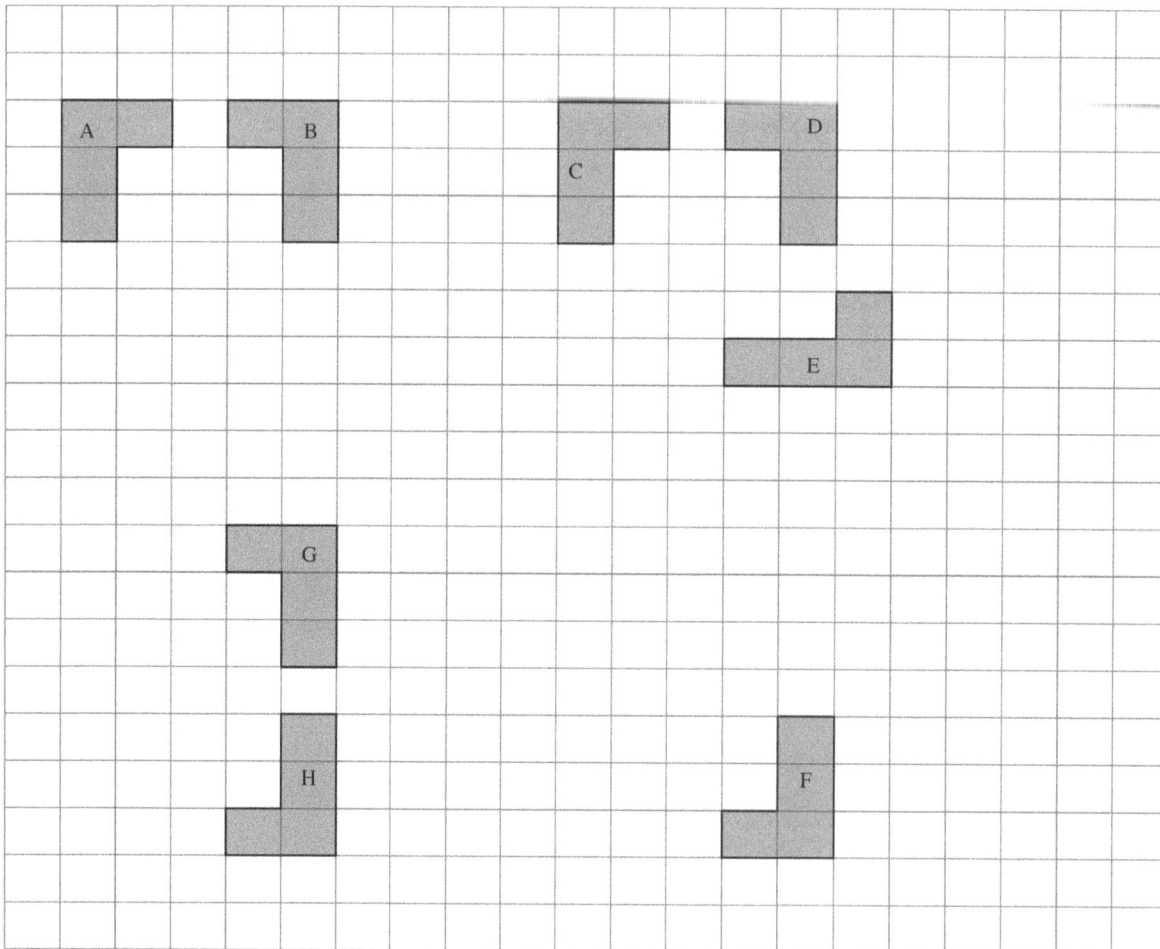

   Ask students to write down pairs of shapes that are reflections of each other and see how many they can find. Then do the same with rotations (they don't need to state the centre or angle for the rotation, just that it is a rotation) and finally list the translations.

   > TIP: If students have completed the task, ask them: 'how do you know you have got them all?'

- **Cutting quadrilaterals**   *Problem solving*

   Is this statement always true, sometimes true or never true?

   If you cut a quadrilateral in half along a diagonal, you will have two congruent shapes.

   Investigate!

   > TIP: You may need to explain what is meant by a diagonal.

   > TIP: You could give students card and scissors to make quadrilaterals that they can then cut into two pieces to compare.

BEWARE: Students may do this initially for a simple shape such as a square or rectangle and conclude that the statement is true. However, you can prompt students to try all the different types of quadrilateral to check whether the statement is always true.

Draw students' attention to shapes where the choice of diagonal matters for example, a kite as well as shapes where both diagonals result in non-congruent shapes for example, a (non-isosceles) trapezium.

- Use the internet to research the art of MC Escher, looking for examples of reflections, rotations and translations.

- For example:

Symmetry drawing number 99

How does the artist use transformations to produce these patterns?

Can you find examples of reflection, rotation and translation hidden inside some of the pictures?

Geometrical reasoning and 3D shapes

Learning objectives

Learning objectives covered in this chapter: 7Gs8, 7Gs7

- Recognise and describe common solids and some of their properties, for example, the number of faces, edges and vertices.
- Solve simple geometrical problems by using side and angle properties to identify equal lengths or calculate unknown angles, and explain reasoning.

Key terms

- 3-dimensional (shape); 3D shape; solid
- 2-dimensional (shape); 2D shape
- surface
- edge
- vertex; vertices
- polyhedron
- curved surface
- face
- prism
- cross-section
- pyramid
- tetrahedron
- sphere
- cone
- cylinder
- hemisphere

Prior knowledge assumptions

- Students know the names and properties of 2D shapes such as isosceles triangles, parallelograms and regular pentagons.
- Students know the names of common 3D shapes such as pyramids and cuboids.
- Students know the meaning of the terms faces, edges and vertices.
- Students can use the notation and labelling conventions for points, lines, angles and shapes.
- Students can estimate the size of acute, obtuse and reflex angles to the nearest 10° and so use this to check whether an answer is reasonable.
- Students can calculate the sum of angles at a point, on a straight line and in a triangle, and prove that vertically opposite angles are equal; they can derive and use the property that the angle sum of a quadrilateral is 360°.

Guidance on the hook   *Problem solving*

Purpose: This task is an investigation into Euler's Theorem to help students revisit the ideas of faces, edges and vertices in a problem-solving context.

Use of the hook: Show students the shapes in the book and ask them to count the number of faces, edges and vertices of each.

TIP: If possible, show the students models of the shapes alongside the drawings to help them count the vertices, edges and faces.

Ask students to copy and complete the table shown with their results from the three shapes.

Can the students suggest any other 3D shapes that could be analysed? Add these results to the table.

BEWARE: Avoid shapes that are not polyhedra!

Ask students what they notice about the sum of the vertices and faces compared to the number of edges?

They should spot that there is a difference of 2 i.e. that $V + F - E = 2$.

Tell students that this is Euler's formula for polyhedral.

Ask them to think of another shape to check whether it works.

> TIP: You might want to check whether it works for a non-polyhedron too to help students realise the limitations.

Adaptation: You could make this a theory test rather than trying to discover the theory by sharing it at the start and asking students to see if it is true or false.

Extension: Students could explore bigger polyhedral and investigate whether the theorem works. For example, they could look at an icosahedron.

They could also think about shapes with unusual features for example, a cuboid with a hole in it:

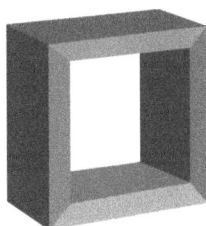

Starter ideas

Mental maths starter

Name two shapes with 6 faces.	Name two shapes with 5 faces.	Name two shapes with 6 vertices.	Name two shapes with 8 faces (challenge!)
Sketch a cylinder.	Sketch a cone.	Sketch a tetrahedron.	Sketch a square-based pyramid.
How many edges does a triangular prism have?	How many vertices does a hexagonal prism have?	How many faces does a pentagonal prism have?	How many vertices does a tetrahedron have?
There are two angles on a straight line. One is 57°. What is the other?	There are two angles around a point. One is 274°. What is the other?	There are three angles on a straight line. Two of them are 38° and 58°. What is the other?	There are three angles around a point. One is 142°, another is 94°. What is the third?
One of the angles in a parallelogram is 43°. What are the other three angles?	One of the angles in an isosceles triangle is 40°. What could the other two angles be?*	One of the angles in a rhombus is 112°. What are the other three angles?	Two of the angles in a kite are 110° and 50°. What could the other two angles?*

*There are multiple solutions here that could be interesting to explore afterwards.

English language leading into vocab feature: Describe it

Use the shape key terms cards (see photocopiable resources online).

Give one students a random selection of six cards.

The student then has to describe the key term to the rest of the class without saying the word itself or any variant of it.

The other students try to guess the word on the card from the description.

Time how long the student takes to describe all six words.

Then give another student a turn and see who can do it the quickest!

Repeat.

TIP: Draw It!

The same game can be used where the student with the cards draws a diagram to represent the key term rather than using words.

Start point check: Game: I'm thinking of a shape ... 20 questions

The teacher thinks of a shape.

Students take it in turns to ask the teacher questions to help work out the identity of the shape. The questions they ask can only have yes/no answers.

For example:
- Is your shape a 3D shape?
- Does your shape have more than six faces?
- Does your shape have any rectangular faces?

If a student asks a question that cannot be answered with yes or no, or they repeat an earlier question, then they lose their turn and one question has been used up.

The teacher keeps track of the number of questions asked using a tally.

The students have to work out the shape in fewer than 20 questions!

TIP: It is useful to play a round and then encourage students to think of questions that help to eliminate shapes so the game is efficient.

Start point check: Angle mind map

Ask students to work in pairs to produce a mind map of everything they know about angles. This could include:

- what an angle is
- how they are measured
- how we name an angle
- types of angle and sizes of these
- angle rules for example, straight line, around a point, vertically opposite
- angles in shapes for example, triangles, quadrilaterals, ...
- shapes with special angle features for example, isosceles triangles, parallelograms, etc.

Share these maps at the end to see of there any extra features that can be added.

Discussion ideas

Probing questions	Teacher prompts
Is a cone a pyramid? (Similarly, is a cylinder a prism?)	Encourage students to revisit the definition of a pyramid to construct their argument. For example, a polyhedron with a polygon base and all other faces triangles that rise to a vertex. Since the base of a cone is a circle, which is not a polygon, it cannot be a pyramid. However, also prompt them to explore a cone as the limit of pyramids as the bases get more and more edges. Ask students to imagine an icosagonal pyramid (one with a base of 20-sided polygon) and to see that it would look very like a cone.
Convince me that a cuboid is a prism.	Again, prompt students to use the mathematical definition to prove this. i.e. a polyhedron with a fixed polygonal cross-section and all other faces rectangular. A cuboid has a fixed rectangular cross-section and all other faces are rectangular, so yes, it is a prism. You may want to get students to re-write and refine their solutions to improve the mathematical technical language.
What's the same and what's different about: • a tetrahedron and a triangular prism • a cylinder and a cone • a cuboid and a cube • an heptagonal pyramid and a hexagonal prism. (Other similar questions also possible.)	Prompt students to describe the features that are the same and those that are different. For example: • Both have some triangular faces, both polyhedral but one is a pyramid and one is a prism so one has rectangular faces and the other does not. You might want to prompt students to sketch each shape first or find a model of them to help compare.
True or False? The number of vertices in a polyhedron > the number of edges. (Also consider the number of vertices in a 3D shape > the number of faces.)	Students can test this out on different shapes initially to develop a sense of whether it is true or false. It is in fact false, because every vertex joins to at least three edges to produce a shape. Each edge connects 2 vertices so, even if you share the edges out between the vertices, there is still more than 1 edge per vertex.
What's the difference between a face and a surface?	Get students to think about curved shapes (those that are not polyhedral) to respond to this. Technically a face should be a flat surface and so a sphere has no faces but one curved surface. Faces are a subset of surfaces.
Can an isosceles triangle be right-angled? What about an equilateral triangle?	Encourage sketching to find the case of 90° 45°, 45°. Prompt students to show that the angles in an equilateral triangle are all 60° and hence cannot also be 90°.
Convince me that if I know one angle of an isosceles triangle (and it isn't 90°), there are 2 possible solutions for the other 2 angles.	Try getting students to start with an example for example, 70° and exploring what the other angles could be before generalising.
How many angles of a kite do I need to be given to know them all?	You may need to prompt students to consider different cases here to answer the question.

Common errors/misconceptions

Misconception	Strategies to address
Using imprecise language to describe a shape For example, they may say "a tetrahedron is made of triangles" rather than saying "a tetrahedron has four triangular faces".	Take the student's explanation literally to show why it cannot be correct. For example, show the net of a shape made of seven triangles and ask 'is this a tetrahedron? why not?' Model accurate and technical mathematical language throughout. Prompt students to amend and refine their language when they are explaining verbally or in writing.
Struggling to see definitions of some shapes as inclusive For example, to see that the family of prisms includes cuboids (which in turn includes cubes).	Recap the definition of a prism and go through each point to see if a cuboid meets it. Use shape sorting activities to help understand that a pyramid is actually a family of shapes.
Giving a definition of a shape that is not sufficient to define it For example, saying that "a cube is a 3D shape with 6 faces" is insufficient as this could also describe a cuboid or a pentagonal pyramid.	Try drawing an example of a shape that meets their definition but is not the desired shape to prompt the student to improve their definition. So in this example, in response to "a cube is a 3D shape with 6 faces", you could draw a pentagonal pyramid and say, "like this" to get them to add in more detail.
Thinking that a cone is a pyramid (and a cylinder is a prism) because they have similar properties	Reinforce the idea that prisms and pyramids must be made of polygonal faces and so the circles of a cone and cylinder are not acceptable.
Struggling to identify equal angles from symmetry when a shape is oriented differently For example, some students might look at this triangle 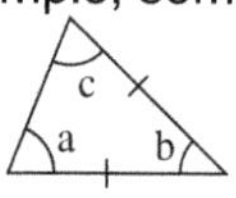 and think that the equal angles are a and b, rather than a and c which it should be.	Encourage students to turn their page to show the diagram with the base angles that are equal at the bottom of the page to help them spot their error. Emphasise that diagrams are not always drawn to scale and so can be misleading.
Finding it hard to focus on one element of a diagram to apply an angle rule For example, students may find it hard to 'see' vertically opposite angles if there is a third line going through. They may also struggle to see angles on a straight line embedded in a shape diagram.	Use colour to highlight the bit of a diagram that is being used at each moment. You could also give students a view-finder made from card that they can use to exclude the rest of a diagram and focus on a specific piece.
Being led by a misleading diagram and assuming that the picture is accurate rather than deducing properties themselves from the information given. This is particularly true when they believe they can see a right angle in the diagram.	Remind students that diagrams are not drawn accurately and encourage them to prove every new angle that they find.

Developing conceptual understanding

7Gs8 Recognise and describe common solids and some of their properties, for example, the number of faces, edges and vertices.

* FIX: It is useful to provide students with models of 3D shapes that they can handle and explore practically. Old packaging as well as more formal 3D shape resources work well.

> TIP: You could also make some shapes from nets like those provided in the photocopiable resources online.

* FIX: Students benefit from trying to classify and categorise a range of shapes into families. This can help them understand the definitions better and see how different shapes fit in more than one category.

* Include lots of opportunity to sketch shapes from their names and features as well the more usual reverse work. This will help students to become confident in the structure of the shapes.

STRETCH: Students working at greater depth can begin to consider 3D shapes with more faces as well as what happens when we cut up these shapes. For example, they could explore truncated pyramids or bisected prisms. They can describe the planes of symmetry of a 3D shape also.

7Gs7 Solve simple geometrical problems by using side and angle properties to identify equal lengths or calculate unknown angles, and explain reasoning.

* FIX: For geometrical reasoning work, it is helpful to highlight the section of the diagram being worked on so that students can spot angle rules they could use. You could also give students a viewfinder to help isolate a specific bit of the diagram.

> TIP: Encourage students to find any missing angle they can when searching for a specific one as there are often multiple steps needed to reach the final angle.

STRETCH: Students working at greater depth could construct their own angle problems by producing a diagram and labelling it with sufficient information to deduce the missing angles.

End of chapter mental maths exercise

1. Name two shapes with 10 faces (challenge!)	5. Imagine a tetrahedron. I cut the shape in half by cutting down through the top vertex (apex) and through the base. Sketch one of the pieces produced.
2. Sketch a pentagonal prism.	
3. How many edges does a pentagonal pyramid have?	6. There are three angles around a point. One is 91°, another is 114°. What is the third?
4. Imagine a hexagonal prism. I cut the prism in half by cutting through the cross-section and down the length of the prism. Sketch one of the pieces produced.	7. Sketch 2 different kites containing a right angle.
	8. A quadrilateral contains these angles: x, $2x$, $3x$ and $4x$. Calculate the value of the first angle x.

Technology recommendations

- Use dynamic geometry software to build 2D shapes with given angles and explore what possibilities there are for their other angles.

  For instance, students could draw a kite with two given angles and look at whether there is any choice in the other two.

  Example: *Problem solving*

  a) Use dynamic geometry software to produce a kite that contains an angle of 30° and an angle of 70°. Is this the only one that is possible? Explain your answer.

  b) Now use the software to produce a kite that contains an angle of 110°.

     Is this the only one that is possible?

     If so, explain why.

     If not, how many possibilities are there? Explain your answer.

- Use the internet to research stems (prefixes) of words linking to shape.

  Students can find other related words and explain the meaning of the prefix itself.

  For example:
  - hemi/semi/demi
  - poly
  - tetra.

Investigation/research tasks

- **Tetrahedra**   *Problem solving*

  Here are four different types of triangle that can be faces of a tetrahedron:

  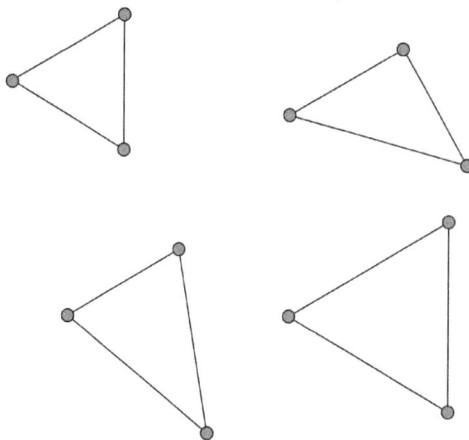

  There is a large equilateral, a small equilateral, an isosceles and a right-angled isosceles triangle.

  How many different tetrahedra can you make out of any combination of these faces?

  You have an unlimited supply of each type.

  How do you know you have got them all?

  Solutions:

  There are 10 different tetrahedra that can be made:
  - 4 large equilateral triangles
  - 4 small equilateral triangles
  - 3 isosceles and 1 small equilateral

- o 3 right-angled and 1 large equilateral
- o 2 right-angled and 2 isosceles (make 2 different types)
- o 2 isosceles and 2 large equilateral
- o 2 right-angled and 2 small equilateral
- o 2 isosceles, 1 right-angled, 1 large equilateral
- o 2 right-angled, 1 isosceles, 1 small equilateral.

Give each student a copy of the triangle sheet from the photocopiable resources section online.

> TIP: You could get students to cut out multiple copies of these triangles to piece them together to help them see which can form a complete shape.

- **Angle hunt:**   *Problem solving*

Here are two equilateral triangles.

Find the value of angle x.

You should show your reasoning at each stage.

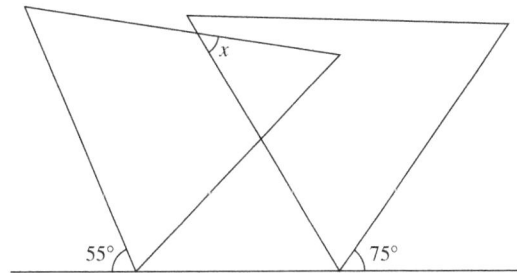

Try this again with different starting angles.

Repeat once more with different angles again.

Now you have three results, can you predict what the value of x will be if you know the two angles at the bottom?

Students should use their angle facts to derive that angle x is 50° in the example shown.

They can then spot from their other results that $x = 180 - $ (*sum of given angles*).

You might want to prompt them to prove this algebraically.

For example:

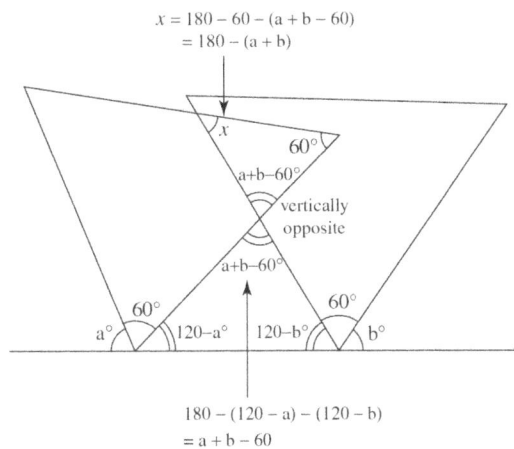

- **Shape categorisation**

  As a class come up with a list of 3D shapes (or use the 3D shape cards from the photocopiable resources online)

  Then give students a feature to sort their shapes by. For example: number of faces or number of edges or shape type.

  In pairs students then organise their shapes into categories.

  You may need to prompt them to produce a suitable table to capture their results.

  For example, for number of (sur)faces, students might produce this table (some extension answers shown too):

Number of Surfaces	1	2	3	4	5	6	7
Shapes	Sphere	Hemi-sphere Cone	Cylinder	Tetra-hedron	Square-based pyramid Triangular Prism Pentahedron!	Pentagonal Pyramid Cube Cuboid Other prisms with quadrilateral cross-section e.g. parallelepiped Truncated Square-based pyramid! Hexahedron!	Hexagonal Pyramid Pentagonal Prism Heptahedron

  You could also explore Venn diagrams or Carroll diagrams that can be completed with these shapes.

  Can the students make up a criterion for others to sort by and produce a solution card?

Construction

Learning objectives

Learning objectives covered in this chapter: 7Gs10

- Use a ruler, set square and protractor to:
  - measure and draw straight lines to the nearest millimetre; measure and draw acute, obtuse and reflex angles to the nearest degree
  - draw parallel and perpendicular lines; construct a triangle given two sides and the included angle (SAS) or two angles and the included side (ASA)
  - construct squares and rectangles and regular polygons, given a side and the internal angle.

Key terms

- measure
- construct
- sketch
- reflex
- protractor
- parallel
- perpendicular
- set square

Prior knowledge assumptions

- Students can use a ruler to measure and draw a line accurate to the nearest centimetre and millimetre.
- Students can recognise and estimate acute, obtuse and reflex angles.
- Students have experience of using a protractor to measure and draw angles.
- Students can recognise and describe parallel and perpendicular lines.
- Students know the properties of 2D shapes including triangles and quadrilaterals.
- Students recognise, name and can describe regular polygons.

Guidance on the hook

Purpose: This task helps students re(familiarise) themselves with the use of compasses for constructing circles and think about the structure of designs.

Use of the hook: Show students the image of the seed of life from the Student's Book. Discuss the shapes that make up this design (seven circles) and how they intersect. Does this shape have reflection symmetry? What about rotational symmetry? Of what order?
Ask students to try to construct a copy of the image, either using their own approach or by following the bullet point instructions in the book.
All students will need a piece of plain paper and a pair of compasses.

BEWARE: Students need to keep their compasses open to the same size for all seven circles!

Once complete, ask students why it is important to keep their compasses open to the same size throughout. What happens if you do not do this?

Then ask students to use the internet to search for other similar designs to construct.
Possible designs include: flower of life, egg of life, curves of pursuit

Adaptation: Students could complete this task on a large scale using string and chalk on the playground or other similar surface.

Extension: Students could produce their own design by constructing using circles. They could then provide a set of written instructions for this and swap with other students to test their instructions out.

Starter ideas

Mental maths starter

Sketch a regular pentagon	Sketch a regular hexagon	Sketch a regular octagon	Sketch a decagon
Sketch an angle of approximately 30°	Sketch an angle of approximately 160°	Sketch an angle of approximately 330°	Sketch an angle of approximately 210°
A regular hexagon has angles of 120°. What is the sum of the angles in a hexagon?	A regular decagon has angles of 144°. What is the sum of the angles in a decagon?	A regular nonagon has angles of 140°. What is the sum of the angles in a nonagon?	A regular pentagon has angles of 108°. What is the sum of the angles in a pentagon?
(Draw an angle of approx. 220° on the board.) What type of angle is this? Estimate its size in degrees.	(Draw an angle of approx. 100° on the board.) What type of angle is this? Estimate its size in degrees.	(Draw an angle of approx. 300° on the board.) What type of angle is this? Estimate its size in degrees.	(Draw an angle of approx. 135° on the board.) What type of angle is this? Estimate its size in degrees.
A triangle has base of length 11 cm and a right side of length 4 cm. The angle between them is approximately 120°. Sketch the triangle.	A triangle has base of length 5 cm and a right side of length 10 cm. The angle between them is approximately 70°. Sketch the triangle.	A triangle has base of length 12 cm and a right side of length 4 cm. The angle between them is approximately 65°. Sketch the triangle.	A triangle has base of length 4 cm and a right side of length 7 cm. The angle between them is approximately 20°. Sketch the triangle.

Start point check: Measuring

Give students some shapes on a sheet of paper.

Ask them to measure the angles in each shape and measure the lengths of the lines.
They can then compare their answers with three other students to see if they agree. If they disagree, they should work out who is correct together.

Then, using the same shapes, ask the students to find a pair of parallel lines (or sides). Similarly, ask them to find a pair of perpendicular lines.
Discuss together which shapes have parallel lines or perpendicular lines for example, trapezia and rectangles respectively.

Construction challenge   *Problem solving*

Construct a triangle where all the angles are

* multiples of three
* multiples of five
* prime numbers
* square numbers!

Challenge: can you do a quadrilateral of each type too?

TIP: For the last one, students will need to think first about the square numbers that they know that are less than 180° – it is useful to produce a list of these first.

This is a good chance for students to revisit earlier work on number properties and practise their construction skills.

Solutions:

- Multiples of 3 – there are many solutions including 60, 60 and 60 degrees or 123, 9 and 48 degrees. Look out for students realising that they just need to think of three numbers that add up to 60 and then multiply them all by 3.

- Multiples of 5 – there are many solutions including 60, 60 and 60 degrees or 125, 35 and 20 degrees. Look out for students realising that they just need to think of three numbers that add up to 36 and then multiply them all by 5.

- Prime numbers – there are only a few solutions. Since all prime numbers except 2 are odd, any two of these will sum to an even number leaving a non-prime final angle. So 2 must be one the three angles and hence we need two other primes that sum to 178. For example, 2, 11 and 167 degrees. Alternatively, 2, 29 and 149 degrees.

    BEWARE: constructing an angle of 2° is very challenging.

- Square numbers – there is only one solution: a triangle with angles of 100, 16 and 64 degrees.

Discussion ideas

Probing questions	Teacher prompts
Convince me that these lines are perpendicular. (Show students two lines that do not meet but would meet at right angles.)	Students often think this is not true because the lines are not actually intersecting. Prompt them to see that, since the lines would intersect at right angles, we define them as perpendicular.
True or False? Only straight lines can be parallel.	Get students to consider curves that are a fixed distance apart – dynamic geometry software can help here.
True or False? To construct a triangle, you need to know the three angles.	Use students' experience to realise that they can draw a triangle using its lengths and one angle only if they need to. Also ask them whether they can find the third angle if they know the other two – this is a good way of checking their accuracy after a construction.
If you are given two sides and one angle of a triangle, how many different triangles is it possible to construct? Does it matter which angle you are given?	This is best explored as a practical investigation to discover that, when the angle given is the included angle, the triangle is unique but when it is not, the triangle is not unique.
What if you were given the three angles?	Prompt students to realise that lots of (similar) triangles have the same angles but different sides and so you would not know how big to make the triangle.

Common errors/misconceptions

Misconception	Strategies to address
Reading the angle on a protractor using the wrong scale (often by not starting from 0)	Ask students to estimate the size of their angle just by looking (See Chapter 9 for further guidance on this). Then ask them if that matches what they are measuring to help them see that they have made an error. Encourage students to actively find the 0° mark that corresponds to their first line before reading round from that to find the value of the angle.
Misaligning a protractor so that the end of the line marking the angle is not at the centre	Show students that the angle being read changes as you move the protractor away from the centre. Ensure students check the alignment before measuring/drawing
Misaligning a ruler or set square so that the line does not start at 0	Directly show students a line and measure it from the end of the ruler, rather than 0 – ask them 'is this right?'. Ensure students check the alignment before measuring/drawing.
Confusing sketching and constructing	Show students a sketch and an accurate construction of the same shape. Ask them what is the same and different. Focus on the command words Sketch and Construct and their meanings of roughly draw and accurately draw.
Struggling to draw/measure a reflex angle using a standard protractor	Try getting students to draw the 180° line on to help the find the 'leftover' angle they need to measure and add on.

Developing conceptual understanding

7Gs10 Use a ruler, set square and protractor to:

- measure and draw straight lines to the nearest millimetre; measure and draw acute, obtuse and reflex angles to the nearest degree

- draw parallel and perpendicular lines; construct a triangle given two sides and the included angle (SAS) or two angles and the included side (ASA)

- construct squares and rectangles and regular polygons, given a side and the internal angle.

- Students may need some considerable practice in using the equipment to draw and measure accurately.

- FIX You can model the process using large scale equipment on a normal blackboard or whiteboard or electronically using a visualiser or webcam.

> TIP: You can also use dynamic software packages to show the processes, but many students find it easier to follow the steps when the teacher is using the same equipment as them.

- Encourage students to use and write information in mathematical notation such as $AB = 7.2$ cm or $\angle PQR = 35°$

- Students should develop competence and confidence in measuring and drawing individual angles and lines first, before then combining into more complex diagrams as they move to greater depth.

STRETCH: Students working at greater depth can begin to analyse the types of shapes they can construct and consider whether they are unique.

End of chapter mental maths exercise

1. Sketch a regular heptagon.	4. (Draw an angle of approx. 280° on the board.) What type of angle is this? Estimate its size in degrees.
2. Sketch an angle of approximately 225°.	
3. A regular octagon has angles of 135°. What is the sum of the angles in an octagon?	5. A triangle has base of length 8 cm and a right side of length 3 cm. The angle between them is approximately 150°. Sketch the triangle.

Technology recommendations

- Use a visualiser or webcam to model the use of the equipment so that students can see and follow along.

  You could work step by step with the students completing the same steps alongside you. Alternatively you can demonstrate the whole process and then give students a few minutes to replicate it.

  TIP: You could also record your demonstration and then rerun it for students to help them.

- Use dynamic geometry software to explore the properties of the shapes being constructed and discover if there is more than one way to produce a shape with these features.

  You can also explore dynamic diagrams of perpendicular and parallel lines.

- Using logo programming to create programs to construct given shapes and designs.

  You could start by constructing simple shapes such as squares and rectangles before exploring equilateral triangles and hexagons and so on.

BEWARE: To construct regular polygons in Logo students need to know and use the exterior angle of the shape.

Investigation/research tasks

- **A4 investigation**   *Problem solving*

  How many different shapes can be made by folding a piece of A4 paper exactly once?

  Sketch your shapes.

  For example:

  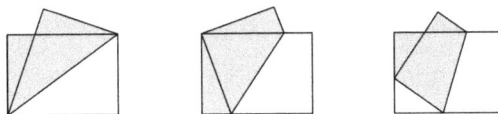

  TIP: Students can experiment with this practically using A4 paper to help them come up with some initial ideas.

BEWARE: Initially they may try to fold the paper so that the two pieces overlap exactly but you can prompt them to consider other folds.

You may need to discuss what counts as 'different' in this task. If you include all the different trapezia formed by folding along the line joining two points on opposite sides, there will be an infinite number.

However, you could group these together and see how many different <u>types</u> of shape are possible.

Encourage students to think about the different ways they can position the two points that will form the fold on the perimeter of the rectangle.

Essentially they can either be placed:

- at opposite corners (producing two triangles)

- on opposite sides (producing either two rectangles or a square and a rectangle if the points are the same distance along the side or two trapezia if they are different distances along)

  on adjacent sides (producing one triangle and one pentagon).

- **Tessellation:**

  Construct a tessellating pattern using regular polygons.

  You could start by using dynamic geometry software to produce your design.

  Can you produce your design using compasses too?

  Students could start by producing a simple design using equilateral triangles, for example.

  They could also explore more complex shapes to construct, such as regular hexagons as shown here in this honeycomb.

  Using dynamic geometry software will help them find shapes that actually tessellate before then trying to construct them with compasses.

- **How many triangles?**   *Problem solving*

  Draw a triangle with one side of length 6 cm and another of length 8 cm.

  How many such triangles are possible?

  What is the shortest possible length of the third side?

  And the longest?

  Investigate.

  Students should realise that they have not been given an angle and so they can choose the angle between the two sides.

  They could use dynamic geometry software to produce two lines of fixed length and then vary the angle to see the triangles they can produce.

  This gives them an infinite number of possible triangles.

  They should then consider the limits of their triangles.

TIP: Prompt students to think about how the sum of the two shorter sides > longest side to help them with this.

This means the longest side cannot be greater than 6 + 8 = 14 cm.

The shortest side, x, has to be at least 2 so that $6 + x > 8$ cm.